ULTIMATE FOOTBALL
QUIZ

FIFA OFFICIAL LICENSED PUBLICATION

Published in 2020 by Welbeck

An imprint of Welbeck Non-Fiction Limited,
part of Welbeck Publishing Group.

20 Mortimer Street London W1T 3JW

A CIP catalogue record for this book is available from the British
Library

ISBN 978 1 78739 396 7

Printed in Great Britain

10 9 8 7 6 5 4 3 2 1

ULTIMATE FOOTBALL
QUIZ

FIFA OFFICIAL LICENSED PUBLICATION

OVER 100 QUIZZES
FROM THE WORLD OF FOOTBALL

MAX WADSWORTH

WELBECK

CONTENTS

INTRODUCTION

When writing this quiz book, I tried to stick to some basic rules, which I will sum up here so that you can understand how I put this book together:

1. I didn't make the questions too easy, as I'm assuming that my audience will be pretty knowledgeable. I know that if I looked at a quiz book and got all the answers correct on the first page, then I wouldn't read on!
2. Equally, I didn't make the questions too difficult. If I could not get any of them right at first glance, then again I'm sure that I would reject it.
3. As much as possible I tried to avoid boring questions, for obvious reasons!
4. Because of rule number three, I tried to avoid lifestyle questions – they are repetitive and dull.
5. Importantly, I tried to avoid questions that might go out of date quickly. The questions in this book should be date-proof until at least the next FIFA World Cup. If you are looking to use the questions in this book to create your own football quiz, you can rest assured that they should still be correct for years to come.
6. The questions in this book have been spread evenly over a number of years, from the very first FIFA World Cup in 1930 to the present day. No matter who is reading this book, or what age they may be, there should be at least several quizzes that will appeal to them.

In the short time since I compiled this book, the outbreak of Covid-19 has caused the suspension of football in most countries throughout the world, and the 2020 UEFA European Championship has been delayed by a year. I suppose that, as a result, some of my questions will take a little longer to go out of date, which can only be a good thing!

On a personal health note, I suffered a heart attack and underwent triple heart bypass surgery whilst compiling this book. I would like to thank my wife Lucy, my children George and Molly, and my sister Mary for getting me through this difficult period.

I hope that you enjoy the book. If you find a tiny error or a repeat question, please don't hesitate to write in to the publisher to let them know, and it will be updated on all future reprints.

Max Wadsworth
March 2020

FIFA WORLD CUP™ QUIZZES

The FIFA World Cup is the most prestigious football tournament in the world. Just to compete in it is the pinnacle of most professional footballers' careers; those talented few who have won it have had their names inscribed in history. As of the year 2020, there have been 21 editions of the men's tournament and eight of the women's tournament, with 11 different nations able to claim to be champions of one or the other. Many people will be able to remember those victorious teams, but can you remember who scored the winning goals? These quizzes will test your knowledge of all of the most memorable moments of each and every tournament.

1930 FIFA WORLD CUP
URUGUAY™

1. How many countries competed at these finals?

2. The Argentine co-manager Juan Jose Tramutola set which unbroken record at these finals?

3. In which city were all the matches played?

4. What were France and USA the first to achieve at these finals?

5. What was the USA's Bert Patenaude the first to achieve against Paraguay at these finals?

6. What was unusual about the match ball in the final?

7. What was the score in the final?

8. Which was the only European country to reach the semi-final at these finals?

9. Which game between a European and a South American nation was witnessed by a reported 300 people at these finals – the smallest crowd in FIFA World Cup history?

10. Which FIFA president presented the trophy at these finals?

11. What did Mexico's Manuel Rosas do at these finals for the first time in FIFA World Cup history against Chile?

12. The final was a repeat of which major men's football final held two years previously?

13. What was the name of the stadium that hosted the final?

14. What refereeing mistake was made in the France versus Argentina game at these finals?

15. At these finals which French goalkeeper with the same first name as a famous Northern Irish snooker player saved the first-ever FIFA World Cup penalty?

16. In terms of days of the week, what was the difference between the 1930 final and the other FIFA World Cup finals that have taken place since?

17. What nationality was John Langenus, who refereed the final?

18. Which player who went on to coach his country scored a hat-trick in Uruguay's semi-final win over Yugoslavia at these finals?

19. Which player, who shares his surname with an American golfer called Billy, was the only black player in the Uruguay team that played in the final?

20. One of the scorers in the final had accidentally amputated his forearm when he was 13. Can you name him? He shares his surname with a famous Cuban politician.

21. What record did Uruguay's coach Alberto Suppici set at these finals which is still held today?

22. At these finals what happened to Peru's Placido Galindo for the first time in FIFA World Cup history against Romania?

23. Why did Argentine student Manuel Ferreira miss their second match against Mexico at these finals?

24. Who at these finals scored the first-ever FIFA World Cup penalty? He shares his first name with Germany's goalkeeper.

25. What notable record did Uruguay's Pablo Dorado achieve at these finals?

26. Who was the FIFA World Cup's first-ever winning captain?

27. What emphatic scoreline was shared by Argentina and Uruguay in winning their semi-final matches at these finals?

28. Which was the only European country that failed to win a match at these finals?

29. Which South American nation entered these finals having never won a match in their brief history?

30. What injury misfortune did USA's Ralph Tracy suffer against Argentina in the semi-final at these finals?

1934 FIFA WORLD CUP
ITALY™

1. What was significant about the Italy versus Spain match at these finals?

2. Oldrich Nejedly finished as the top scorer at these finals. Against which country did he score a hat-trick?

3. Of the 16 countries that participated at these finals, how many were from Europe – 10, 11 or 12?

4. Which famous Spanish goalkeeper who went on to coach the national side participated at these finals?

5. Despite getting to the final Czechoslovakia were behind in their first match at these finals, but against which team?

6. Which city housed a stadium at these finals that was named after Italian dictator Benito Mussolini?

7. What did hosts Italy have to do prior to these finals which no other hosts have had to do since?

8. Which team did Italy have to beat in a quarter-final replay at these finals?

9. Three days before the finals began the USA beat which near neighbour to qualify?

10. Chronologically what was unusual about all eight last 16 matches at these finals?

11. The Italian side that played the USA at these finals included five players that were born in which continent?

12. Who at these finals became the first man to play in two FIFA World Cup finals?

13. What was significant about the Austria versus France match at these finals?

14. Why did holders Uruguay decline to participate at these finals?

15. Imre Markos was sent off playing for which country against Austria at these finals?

16. Italy's Angelo Schiavio scored a hat-trick against which country in the round of 16 at these finals?

17. Which player, who shares his first name with the first man to conquer Mount Everest, scored four goals for Germany at these finals, including a hat-trick against Belgium?

18. What was the most eastern city used at these finals – so east it is very close to Slovenia?

19. One of the favourites at these finals was 'Das Wunderteam', a nickname ascribed to which country?

20. Rome hosted the final for the first time, but in which year did it host it for a second time?

21. Which country finished third at these finals, beating Austria 3-2 in the third place play-off?

22. What was unusual about the two captains in the final?

23. How old was Argentina's coach Felipe Pascucci when he was in charge at these finals – 26, 27 or 28?

24. What was the score in the final?

25. Who at these finals became the first-ever African side to take part in a FIFA World Cup?

26. Italy became the second host country to win the FIFA World Cup at these finals. Who became the third?

27. How many European countries qualified for the final eight at these finals?

28. Who was Italy's coach at these finals? He also coached them to success four years later and is the only coach to have won the FIFA World Cup twice as a manager.

29. Which Italian club's blue jerseys were borrowed by Austria to avoid a clash of colours in their semi-final against Germany at these finals?

30. The Stadio Nazionale del PNF hosted the final. What is the name of the stadium that replaced it in 1957?

1938 FIFA WORLD CUP
FRANCE™

1. What is the name of the stadium, still used by the city's major team, that was built for these finals in Marseille?

2. Austria and Germany both qualified for these finals, but why did only Germany compete?

3. Which Hungarian player scored in every round at these finals?

4. In which year did Norway next appear at the finals following this one?

5. Who scored five goals for Italy at these finals, including two in the final?

6. Which stadium hosted France's two matches at these finals, as well as the final?

7. Which Asian country participated in their first, and so far only, finals?

8. What nationality was Georges Capdeville, who refereed the final?

9. How many of the seven round of 16 matches at these finals went into extra time – three, four or five?

10. The final finished 4-2 to Italy. Name the two subsequent years the FIFA World Cup final has finished 4-2.

11. At these finals Polish striker Ernest Wilimowski became the first man to achieve what against Brazil?

12. Italy and Brazil met in the semi-final at these finals. Name the subsequent years they've met in a FIFA World Cup final.

13. Brazil and Czechoslovakia met in the quarter-final at these finals. How many years later would they meet each other in a FIFA World Cup final?

14. What was the score after 90 minutes in the Brazil versus Poland match at these finals?

15. How many players were sent off in the Brazil versus Czechoslovakia match at these finals, known as the Battle of Bordeaux?

16. Which Caribbean island participated in their first, and so far only, finals?

17. Which town only 50km from the Italian border was used as a venue at these finals?

18. The Netherlands conceded three goals in each of their first two FIFA World Cup matches. Which nation did they lose 3-0 to at these finals?

19. Which Brazilian was top scorer at these finals with seven goals?

20. How many players scored hat-tricks in Sweden's quarter-final win over Cuba at these finals?

21. France became the first hosts to fail to win the trophy at these finals – true or false?

22. What did Italy's Gino Colaussi achieve for the first time in a FIFA World Cup final?

23. Which near neighbour did France beat in their first match at these finals?

24. How many years were winners Italy world champions for?

25. Which country at these finals lost 6-5 in its very first FIFA World Cup match?

26. In which year did the Netherlands next appear at the finals following this one?

27. The second version of which stadium was used at these finals – its subsequent third version also being used at the 1998 FIFA World Cup?

28. Sweden and Brazil met in the third place play-off at these finals. How many years later would they meet each other in a FIFA World Cup final?

29. Why did Sweden not have to play a match before reaching the quarter-finals at these finals?

30. Which nation were the top scorers at these finals with 15 goals, including five in the semi-final against Sweden?

1950 FIFA WORLD CUP
BRAZIL ™

1. Which player appeared in the first of his five FIFA World Cup tournaments at these finals?

2. The oldest ever referee officiated at these finals. He was 53 years and 236 days old. Can you name him? He shares his surname with someone who likes books.

3. Which Brazilian player made the first of his three top two FIFA World Cup finishes at these finals (1950, 1958 & 1962)?

4. What was the official attendance in the decisive match between Uruguay and Brazil at these finals – 189,854, 199,854 or 209,854?

5. Name either of the two Spaniards who scored four goals at these finals.

6. Which nation finished third at these finals?

7. Which two nations were banned from these finals due to their participation in the Second World War?

8. FIFA originally planned this FIFA World Cup to take place in 1949 – true or false?

9. Uruguay won despite winning the fewest number of matches at a FIFA World Cup. How many matches did they win at these finals?

10. Which nation was the top scorer at these finals with 22 goals?

11. Which stadium hosted the decisive match of the final group stage at these finals?

12. Which was the only Eastern European nation to take part at these finals?

13. Which three nations originally qualified for these finals but later withdrew?

14. How many nations participated at these finals?

15. For which country did Oscar Miguez score five goals at these finals?

16. Which was the only nation making its FIFA World Cup debut at these finals?

17. Which two outcomes in their decisive match against Uruguay did Brazil need in order to win the tournament?

18. Which nation's only match at these finals was an 8-0 defeat?

19. Which was the only nation to lose all three matches at these finals?

20. What is the decisive match between Uruguay and Brazil at these finals often known as?

21. How many nations were in Group 4 at these finals?

22. How many matches went into extra time at these finals?

23. Which city beginning with the letter R was the most northerly venue used for matches at these finals?

24. How many goals were scored in total at these finals – 88, 98 or 108?

25. These finals would be the United States's last FIFA World Cup appearance until which year?

26. Which two European nations did Brazil beat 7-1 and 6-1 respectively in the final round at these finals?

27. Which manager was in charge of his first FIFA World Cup at these finals and went on to manage the same country in three more finals after this?

28. The average attendance at these finals was a new record figure of 61,000 per game. In which year would this record attendance figure be finally broken?

29. Which city with the initials P.A. was the most southerly venue at these finals?

30. Who became the first former FIFA World Cup player to also become a FIFA World Cup coach at these finals?

1954 FIFA WORLD CUP
SWITZERLAND™

© FIFA TM

1. Austria and Switzerland shared 12 goals in their quarter-final at these finals. What was the score?

2. Which nation lost 4-1 in their first match at these finals, won 7-0 in their second and lost 7-2 in their third?

3. Name two of the three nations making their FIFA World Cup debut at these finals.

4. This has been the only FIFA World Cup to date where all nations lost at least one match – true or false?

5. A total of 21 players scored at least how many goals each at these finals?

6. Who scored four goals in Hungary's 8-3 win over West Germany in the group stage at these finals?

7. How many goals were scored in total at these finals – 120, 130 or 140?

8. Which two European nations' first FIFA World Cup meeting was at these finals and they would go on to meet on a further six occasions at the tournament?

9. Which nation did Turkey eliminate by the drawing of lots in the qualifiers for these finals?

10. Which Rhineland club provided five of West Germany's winning squad at these finals?

11. Which was the most westerly city used for matches at these finals?

12. Which nation conceded a record 16 goals in two games at these finals?

13. Which nations played out a 4-4 draw at these finals?

14. Which side beat Scotland 7-0 and later eliminated England at these finals?

15. Name three of the four players who scored at least six goals at these finals.

16. Which two goalscoring records did West Germany set at these finals?

17. At these finals West Germany became the first team to win the FIFA World Cup having lost a match. Can you name the other three nations to have lost a match but still won the tournament?

18. Which match became known as the 'Battle of Berne' at these finals, in which three players were sent off?

19. Which town beginning with the letter L hosted only one match at these finals?

20. How many hat-tricks were scored at these finals – a FIFA World Cup record?

21. Which future Manchester United and Scotland manager played for Scotland at these finals?

22. In terms of continents, what was unique about West Germany's win at these finals?

23. How many goals per game did Hungary score at these finals – 3.4, 4.4 or 5.4?

24. Bora Milutinovic, who coached five different nations at the FIFA World Cup, had a brother Milos who scored Yugoslavia's 1-0 winner against which European nation at these finals?

25. How many players scored at least four goals at these finals – 11, 12 or 13?

26. Extra time was played in the group stage matches at these finals – true or false?

27. Who scored twice in the final?

28. Sandor Kocsis scored two consecutive hat-tricks at these finals. Who is the only other man to have scored successive FIFA World Cup hat-tricks?

29. Which was the most northerly stadium used for matches at these finals?

30. Which nation would be making their last FIFA World Cup appearance for 48 years at these finals?

1958 FIFA WORLD CUP
SWEDEN™

1. Who at these finals became the youngest ever player in a FIFA World Cup final at the age of 17 years and 249 days?

2. Which nation did France's Just Fontaine score the 2-1 winner against at these finals?

3. Who scored Brazil's first two goals in the final?

4. Which future England manager played at these finals?

5. Who scored in his first FIFA World Cup for Germany at these finals and would go on to score in the next three tournaments?

6. Name two of the three nations, all of them European, that were making their FIFA World Cup debuts at these finals.

7. How many of the British Home Nations appeared at these finals – the only occasion this has happened?

8. Who scored in all three of Argentina's matches at these finals?

9. What was the name of the stadium that hosted the final?

10. Which player, who shares his first name with a future Germany manager called Ribbeck, was sent off for Germany against Sweden in the semi-final, becoming the first-ever German to be sent off in an international game?

11. Sweden played all of their matches in Stockholm at these finals with the exception of the semi-final. In which city did they play their semi-final?

12. How many venues were used for these finals – 11, 12 or 13?

13. Which Northern Ireland goalkeeper who played for Manchester United was voted in the team of the tournament by journalists at these finals?

14. Who won the first of two FIFA World Cups as a player at these finals and also went on to win it as a manager?

15. These finals marked the first and only occasion that a FIFA World Cup hosted in Europe was not won by a European team – true or false?

16. Which now defunct nation did Northern Ireland beat in a play-off to reach the quarter-final at this tournament?

17. Which country was the only one that avoided defeat to Brazil at these finals?

18. At these finals Brazil became the first nation to win the FIFA World Cup on a different land mass. Who became the second, and in which year?

19. Which town beginning with the letter S was the most northerly used for matches at these finals?

20. What FIFA World Cup record did Brazil set in the final?

21. How many goals were scored in the six matches in Group 2 at these finals – 27, 29 or 31?

22. Mexico drew 1-1 with Wales at these finals to avoid defeat in a FIFA World Cup match for the first time. How many matches had they lost prior to this?

23. Brazil has been involved in all of the three biggest winning margins in FIFA World Cup final history. Can you name the years they've been involved in those big wins?

24. Geographically what was significant about Hungary's matches against Wales and Mexico at these finals?

25. Which two countries were involved in the first-ever goalless draw in FIFA World Cup history at these finals?

26. What injury did Frenchman Robert Jonquet suffer in the semi-final against Brazil at these finals?

27. Which was the only nation not to concede a goal in the group stage at these finals?

28. Which was the most southerly stadium used for matches at these finals?

29. 1958 is the only occasion that the hosts have finished FIFA World Cup runners-up – true or false?

30. Which nation did France's Just Fontaine score four goals against at these finals, and at which stage?

1962 FIFA WORLD CUP
CHILE™

1. In which city was the final held?

2. Brazil won the FIFA World Cup twice in succession at these finals. How many times has this been achieved by a nation since then?

3. Which nation failed to qualify for the knockout stage at these finals despite beating Colombia in their opening match?

4. Which all-time great was a member of Spain's squad at these finals but did not play because of injury?

5. Which two managers were managing their countries for a fourth FIFA World Cup at these finals?

6. Which other South American nation put in a bid to host these finals?

7. Which two nations were making their debuts at these finals?

8. Name either of the two players, one from each team, that were sent off in the Brazil versus Chile semi-final at these finals.

9. Against which team did Pele get injured, meaning he had to miss the rest of these finals?

10. Who scored twice for Brazil in both the quarter-final and semi-final at these finals?

11. Who scored Chile's winners against the Soviet Union in the quarter-final and against Yugoslavia in the third place match at these finals?

12. How many stadiums were used at these finals?

13. Who replaced Pele in the Brazil team after he was injured at these finals?

14. What was unusual about Marcus Coll's goal for Colombia against the Soviet Union at these finals?

15. This was the second FIFA World Cup that Brazil would go unbeaten. How many finals have they gone unbeaten in since?

16. Who scored for Czechoslovakia after only 15 seconds in their match against Mexico at these finals?

17. Who scored in England's opening two matches at these finals?

18. Which two teams played in the 'Battle of Santiago' at these finals, in which two players were sent off and police intervention was required on four occasions?

19. Who scored four goals for Yugoslavia at these finals?

20. Who was Brazil's winning manager at these finals?

21. Gerry Hutchens was the only member of England's squad who was not playing his club football in England at the time of these finals. Which Italian club was he playing for?

22. Which was the only nation to lose all three group stage matches at these finals?

23. Which Chilean was the joint top scorer at these finals with four goals?

24. What natural disaster hampered preparations for these finals in 1960?

25. Which South American nation had the worst defensive record at these finals, conceding 11 goals in the group stage?

26. Who was Brazil's winning captain at these finals? He shares his surname with Spain's most capped player called Sergio.

27. Which country was the only one that avoided defeat to Brazil at these finals?

28. Who scored four goals for the Soviet Union in the group stage at these finals?

29. Florian Albert scored a hat-trick for which nation against Bulgaria at these finals?

30. Which nation at these finals finally recorded their first-ever FIFA World Cup win at the 14th attempt with victory over Czechoslovakia?

© FIFA TM

1966 FIFA WORLD CUP
ENGLAND™

1. Who scored West Germany's late 2-2 equaliser in the final? He shares his first name with a famous Austrian composer.

2. England won as hosts at these finals. How many hosts have won the FIFA World Cup in total?

3. The final was the first England versus West Germany FIFA World Cup encounter to go into extra time. Can you name the other two years in which their meetings have gone into extra time?

4. What part did Karol Galba of Czechoslovakia play in the final?

5. What was the name of the commentator whose words during the last goal in the final were: "And here comes Hurst. He's got… some people are on the pitch, they think it's all over. It is now!"?

6. This was the first FIFA World Cup held in the English-speaking world – true or false?

7. Which Chilean made his FIFA World Cup debut at these finals and would also be playing for his country at the 1982 edition?

8. At the age of 19 years and 191 days North Korea's Lee Chang-Myung created what FIFA World Cup record against the Soviet Union at these finals?

9. England's team for the final included three players whose first name began with the letter G. Can you name them?

10. Their defeat to Hungary at these finals ended a run of how many FIFA World Cup matches unbeaten for Brazil – unlucky for some?

11. Which legendary coach was in charge for the first of his four successive FIFA World Cup tournaments at these finals?

12. Which was the most northerly stadium used at these finals?

13. 31 nations from which continent boycotted these finals?

14. Which was the only team England did not beat at these finals?

15. What was the name of the dog that found the FIFA World Cup trophy after it had been stolen?

16. What was the name of the mascot at these finals, and what animal was it?

17. Portugal finished third on their FIFA World Cup debut at these finals. Which other nation has achieved this feat, and in which year?

18. What was the name of the other stadium used in London at these finals besides Wembley Stadium?

19. Exactly the same number of goals were scored at these finals as were scored in 1962. How many goals was that – 79, 89 or 99?

20. On what date was the final, the latest date that any FIFA World Cup has concluded?

21. Which Brazilian, who shares his three-lettered name with a former Arsenal midfielder, was named in their squad for these finals at the age of 16 years and 339 days?

22. What subsequent new record did England set in their opening 0-0 draw at these finals?

23. Name the two Argentines who were sent off at these finals.

24. Who scored three of England's goals in the group stage at these finals?

25. In reaching the quarter-final at these finals what new record did North Korea set?

26. Apart from Portugal, which other nation made their debut at these finals?

27. Brazil became the second defending champion to be eliminated in the first round at these finals. Can you name the other five defending champions this has happened to, and in which year?

28. Which stadium was the most westerly used for matches at these finals?

29. Which nation scored the most goals at these finals, with 17?

30. Who was West Germany's leading scorer at these finals with six goals?

1970 FIFA WORLD CUP
MEXICO™

1. What disciplinary measure was introduced for the first time at these finals?

2. What was the name of the trophy that Brazil got to keep after winning this FIFA World Cup?

3. Who scored his only goal for England in the quarter-final against West Germany at these finals?

4. Name two of the three nations making their debuts at these finals.

5. Geographically, what first was this FIFA World Cup?

6. Apart from Pele, who also scored in a fourth FIFA World Cup in a row at these finals?

7. Who was Italy's captain in the final?

8. Which Middle Eastern country, which now plays in the European zone, qualified for the finals for the first time?

9. What was the name of the mascot at these finals?

10. Which nation were the top scorers at these finals with 19 goals?

11. What was the name of the stadium used in the city of Leon at these finals? It shares its name with the home of the 1992 European Cup winners.

12. Which nation failed to qualify for these finals for the only time in its history?

13. Who scored four goals in three group stage games for Peru at these finals?

14. Mexico faced the Soviet Union in the opening match at these finals. This was the last time since which year that the hosts began the tournament?

15. How many goals were scored in extra time in the Italy versus West Germany semi-final at these finals?

16. Which player representing the Soviet Union at these finals became the first-ever substitute to be used in a FIFA World Cup match?

17. Which German scored his only international goal in the semi-final against Italy at these finals?

18. Who was England's goalkeeper in their quarter-final match against West Germany at these finals?

19. Which two nations had to be separated by the drawing of lots in Group 1 at these finals?

20. How many players were sent off at these finals?

21. Who was Brazil's winning captain at these finals?

22. In beating El Salvador, which nation won its first-ever FIFA World Cup match at these finals?

23. How many outfield players touched the ball in the lead up to Brazil's final goal in the final?

24. Who scored two hat-tricks in the group stage at these finals?

25. Which nation conceded the only own goal at these finals? It was scored by Javier Guzman.

26. Two of West Germany's squad at these finals were playing their club football in which country at the time?

27. Which two nations competed in the match for third place at these finals, and what was the score?

28. Who scored for Brazil as they beat England 1-0 at these finals?

29. At these finals Morocco were the first African FIFA World Cup representatives since which nation in 1934?

30. Which South American nation returned to the FIFA World Cup for the first time in 40 years at these finals?

1974 FIFA WORLD CUP
WEST GERMANY™

1. This FIFA World Cup was the last one where no extra time was played in any of the matches – true or false?

2. How many different scorers were there in Yugoslavia's 9-0 win over Zaire at these finals?

3. Which nation were the top scorers at these finals with 16 goals?

4. Which European was the top scorer at these finals with seven goals?

5. Which Caribbean island made its FIFA World Cup debut at these finals?

6. Which future FIFA World Cup-winning nation failed to qualify for these finals but would qualify for every subsequent one?

7. Which unwanted disciplinary first did Chile's Carlos Caszely set at these finals?

8. Who scored the Netherlands' goal in the final – the fastest ever goal in a FIFA World Cup final?

9. Argentina failed to win their opening two matches at these finals. When would be the next year they would repeat this?

10. Which two European nations returned to the FIFA World Cup at these finals for the first time since 1938?

11. What were the names of the mascots at these finals?

12. Which nation was the surprise package at these finals, beating Argentina and Italy, as well as scoring seven past Haiti?

13. Which was the most northerly city used at these finals?

14. Which nation at these finals became the first-ever country to be eliminated from a FIFA World Cup without having lost a match?

15. Which Polish goalkeeper saved two penalties in normal time at these finals?

16. Name both of the two nations that lost all three matches at these finals.

17. Which European nation made its only FIFA World Cup appearance at these finals?

18. Which nation at these finals failed to qualify for the second stage for its fifth FIFA World Cup out of its previous six participations?

19. This FIFA World Cup was only the second occasion that a team had won the FIFA World Cup after losing a match. Can you name the first team that did this?

20. Which nation made its FIFA World Cup debut at these finals but would not appear at a FIFA World Cup again until it returned to Germany in 2006?

21. Which player, who shares a similar first name with a fashion designer with the surname Lauren, was Sweden's top scorer at these finals with four goals?

22. This tournament was the start of five meetings in five successive FIFA World Cups between which two nations?

23. Which nation did the Netherlands beat to reach the final?

24. Gunter Netzer became the first FIFA World Cup winner to play his club football outside his home country at these finals. Which Spanish club was he playing for at the time?

25. Which was the first team from sub-Saharan Africa to play at a FIFA World Cup at these finals?

26. What was the name of the English referee that officiated at the final?

27. Who scored five goals for Poland in the first group stage at these finals, including a hat-trick against Haiti?

28. Which was the only nation to win all three first round group stage matches at these finals?

29. Which match at these finals was the first in FIFA World Cup history in which a penalty shoot-out could potentially have been held?

30. Who scored a hat-trick in Yugoslavia's 9-0 win over Zaire at these finals?

Argentina '78 © ™ FIFA

1978 FIFA WORLD CUP
ARGENTINA™

1. Who were the only team to beat eventual champions Argentina at these finals?

2. At these finals Argentina would become the last host nation to win the FIFA World Cup until which country, and in which year?

3. Who at these finals became the first player to score at least five goals in two different FIFA World Cups?

4. Who scored four penalties in normal time at these finals?

5. Which two nations were the joint highest scorers at these finals?

6. Dieter and which other player with the surname Muller were in West Germany's squad at these finals?

7. Which Asian nation made its debut at these finals?

8. The logo at these finals was based on which person's signature gesture?

9. Which Mexican made his FIFA World Cup debut at these finals and would also be playing for his country at the 1994 edition?

10. Which former FIFA World Cup-winning nation failed to qualify for the finals for the first time since 1958?

11. Which FIFA World Cup landmark goal was Rob Rensenbrink's strike for the Netherlands against Scotland at these finals?

12. Who scored twice as Austria beat West Germany in the second phase at these finals?

13. Which nation finished above Brazil in the first stage group at these finals?

14. By what goal margin did Argentina need to beat Peru in their final group match to reach the final?

15. What was the name of the mascot at these finals, based on a national symbol in Argentina?

16. Which English club provided four players in Scotland's squad at these finals?

17. This was the first FIFA World Cup to include 24 teams – true or false?

18. Who was the only member of Argentina's squad at these finals that was not playing his club football in Argentina at the time, and which Spanish club was he playing for?

19. What was the surname of the twins who played in the final?

20. Which European nation lost all of its three first stage group matches at these finals?

21. Who scored in a 2-1 win over France at these finals – the first of nine FIFA World Cup goals he would go on to score?

22. Which European nation returned after a 20-year absence at these finals?

23. Which Scotsman was expelled from these finals after he was found to have taken a banned stimulant?

24. Which nation did Argentina beat 6-0 in the final second phase at these finals?

25. Who at these finals was sent off for the Netherlands against West Germany nine minutes after coming on as a substitute?

26. What was the name of the stadium that hosted the final?

27. Which was the most southerly city used for matches at these finals, located on the Atlantic coast?

28. Which nation became the first African country to win a FIFA World Cup match at these finals?

29. Which defender, born in Guadeloupe, captained France at these finals?

30. Which nation lost all of its three group stage matches for a third FIFA World Cup at these finals, having previously done so in 1930 and in 1950?

1. England's second phase matches against West Germany and Spain at these finals both finished with the same score. What was it?

2. Which CONCACAF nation was making its debut at these finals?

3. Which German made his FIFA World Cup debut at these finals and would also be playing for his country at the 1998 edition?

4. Which man, who shares his first name with an actor who previously played James Bond, coached Peru at these finals, 44 years after playing for Brazil at the finals?

5. Who at these finals became the third player to score in two different FIFA World Cup finals?

6. Which England player made the first of his national record 17 FIFA World Cup appearances at these finals?

7. Which African nation played in their first FIFA World Cup at these finals but was eliminated in the group stage despite not losing a match?

8. Who made his first appearance as coach at these finals and would go on to coach at a record six tournaments?

9. What was significant about the France v West Germany semi-final at these finals?

10. Which nation was eliminated from the second phase at these finals despite not losing a match in the whole tournament?

11. Which nation was the top scorer at these finals with 16 goals?

12. Who at these finals became the youngest player to appear at a FIFA World Cup?

13. This was the first FIFA World Cup in which teams from all six continental confederations participated – true or false?

14. Goalkeeper Richard Wilson kept nine consecutive clean sheets in qualifying for these finals. Which island nation did he represent?

15. Who was the only member of England's squad at these finals who was playing his club football abroad?

16. Who scored five goals for West Germany at these finals?

17. Who scored a hat-trick for Poland against Belgium in the second phase at these finals?

18. For the first time since 1966 all four semi-finalists were European at these finals. Name them.

19. What happened for the first time in 20 years at the opening game between Belgium and Argentina at these finals?

20. Apart from the Nou Camp, which was the other stadium in Barcelona used at these finals?

21. Italy won the tournament while failing to win a record how many matches?

22. Which French player was left unconscious following a foul by German goalkeeper Harald Schumacher in the semi-final at these finals?

23. Who was sent off towards the end of Brazil's 3-1 win over Argentina in the second phase at these finals?

24. Who scored after only 27 seconds of his country's opening match at these finals?

25. Which match was dubbed as the 'Disgrace of Gijon' at these finals?

26. Who were the 40-year-old and 18-year-old in Italy's final winning team at these finals?

27. Which two nations qualified from the first phase at these finals despite scoring only twice in their three matches?

28. Which became the first team to score ten goals in a FIFA World Cup match when they beat El Salvador 10-1 at these finals?

29. Which was the most southerly city that hosted a match at these finals?

30. Which nation returned to these finals after a 24-year absence?

1986 FIFA WORLD CUP
MEXICO™

1. What audience phenomenon appeared for the first time at these finals? A clue – think about the hosts.

2. At these finals the Azteca Stadium became the first stadium to host two FIFA World Cup finals. Which became the second?

3. Which Asian nation made its debut at these finals?

4. Which four former FIFA World Cup winners did Argentina beat at these finals?

5. Jose Batista was sent off in the first minute against Scotland at these finals, but who were Scotland's opponents?

6. Which nation was due to host these finals but in the end could not do so due to financial problems?

7. What was the official attendance at the final – 84,600, 94,600 or 114,600?

8. Which Dane was the leading scorer in qualification for these finals with eight goals?

9. Which African nation finished top of their group at these finals?

10. Which former Real Madrid player and manager scored four goals at these finals?

11. Argentina versus Germany is the most played FIFA World Cup final – true or false?

12. All the venues at these finals were located in central Mexico, except for which city further north?

13. Which two European nations played at these finals but have not appeared at a FIFA World Cup since?

14. Who scored a hat-trick for the Soviet Union against Belgium at these finals, but still ended up on the losing side?

15. Which Asian nation appeared at these finals – its first FIFA World Cup appearance for 32 years?

16. Captain Karl-Heinz Rummenigge scored in the final. Can you name three of the other five captains to have scored in a FIFA World Cup final?

17. Which nation played in three matches at these finals that went into extra time?

18. Who scored on his international debut against Northern Ireland at these finals, and also scored against Poland?

19. Who scored in four of Brazil's five matches at these finals?

20. Which was the only quarter-final match not to be decided by penalties at these finals?

21. At these finals Mexico City became the first city to host two FIFA World Cup finals. Which are the other three cities that have achieved this since?

22. Which nation won its group at these finals and thereby became the first African country to reach the second round?

23. After these finals the Azteca Stadium had hosted a record number of FIFA World Cup matches. How many?

24. Which goal at these finals was voted as the FIFA World Cup's greatest goal on FIFA.com?

25. Which England player suffered an injury against Morocco which would keep him out for the remainder of the tournament, and which other would receive a red card?

26. Two members of Scotland's squad, Graeme Souness and Steve Archibald, were playing their club football outside the UK at the time of these finals. Which clubs were they playing for?

27. Name either of the two players who missed Brazil's penalties in their quarter-final shoot-out defeat to France at these finals.

28. What was the name of the mascot at these finals, and what was it? The name is shared with a former Manchester United Spanish central defender.

29. Which European nation made its debut at these finals?

30. Which was the only nation that failed to score at these finals?

1990 FIFA WORLD CUP
ITALY™

1. Which Italian made his FIFA World Cup debut at these finals and went on to play in three more, making 23 appearances in all?

2. Who at these finals became the youngest ever captain in a FIFA World Cup match, leading his country at the age of 21 years and 109 days?

3. Who were the two Argentines sent off in the final?

4. Which city was the southernmost Italian city used for games at these finals?

5. Which nation has been involved in the most ever FIFA World Cup penalty shoot-outs, starting against Yugoslavia at these finals?

6. Which goalkeeper did not concede a goal in his opening five matches at these finals?

7. Which nation was appearing in its first FIFA World Cup for 56 years at these finals?

8. This was the first FIFA World Cup that introduced three points for a win – true or false?

9. Four of England's squad, Gary Stevens, Terry Butcher, Chris Woods and Trevor Steven, were on which club's books at the time of these finals?

10. How many of the knockout stage matches at these finals went into extra time – a joint record for one final?

11. Which goalkeeper replaced the injured David Seaman during these finals?

12. Which German scored three goals for his country at these finals and would score at least three goals in the next two tournaments after?

13. These finals produced the fewest ever goals per game ratio in FIFA World Cup history – true or false?

14. Who was the 26-year-old captain of Italy at these finals, already playing in his third FIFA World Cup?

15. Which operatic recital became the soundtrack at these finals?

16. Name either of the two Cameroonians sent off against Argentina at these finals.

17. How many previous FIFA World Cup titles did the four semi-finalists at these finals have between them?

18. Argentina reached the final despite scoring the fewest goals of any nation to reach a FIFA World Cup final. How many goals did they score – five, six or seven?

19. Who scored Cameroon's goal as they beat holders Argentina in the opening match at these finals?

20. The drawing of lots was used for the last time at these finals. Which two nations were involved in the drawing of lots?

21. Apart from having two players sent off, what other unwanted FIFA World Cup record did Argentina set in the final?

22. Which two players were sent off in the West Germany against the Netherlands last 16 match at these finals?

23. Which Middle Eastern country made their debut at the finals?

24. Nine of Cameroon's squad at these finals played their club football in which country?

25. Which nation at these finals reached the semi-final despite winning only one match in regulation time?

26. Which two stadiums were completely new venues opened for these finals – one in the south of the country and one in the north?

27. Who scored the crucial penalty that took the Republic of Ireland past Romania in a shoot-out in the round of 16 at these finals?

28. Which European nation failed to qualify for these finals – the first time they had not participated at a FIFA World Cup for 20 years?

29. Who saved two penalties in two separate shoot-outs at these finals?

30. Whose goal, the only one of his international career, earned England a 1-0 win over Egypt at these finals?

1991
FIFA WOMEN'S WORLD CUP
CHINA™

1. Which two nations played in the very first FIFA Women's World Cup match?

2. Which Norwegian scored six goals at these finals and would go on to score nine FIFA Women's World Cup goals in her career?

3. Which nation did the United States's Carin Jennings score a hat-trick against at these finals?

4. Which Chinese scored at these finals and would go on to score in the next three FIFA Women's World Cup tournaments?

5. Who was the United States's winning captain at these finals?

6. Hui Fang Lin was sent off in the sixth minute against Nigeria at these finals. Which Asian nation was she playing for?

7. Which Chinese city hosted the final?

8. Which nation failed to qualify for the knockout stage despite winning their first match at these finals?

9. Nkiru Okosieme captained her country at the age of 19 years and 261 days at these finals. Which nation did she represent?

10. Who scored four goals for Sweden at these finals and would go on to coach the United States to the Olympic gold medal in 2008 and 2012?

11. Who was the United States's winning coach at these finals at the age of 40?

12. Who scored after 30 seconds in Sweden's match against Japan at these finals – the fastest goal in FIFA Women's World Cup history?

13. Which two nations failed to score at these finals?

14. Who was named player of the tournament at these finals?

15. Which country finished third at these finals and has also finished third in 2011 and 2019?

16. Carolina Morace scored a hat-trick for which nation against Chinese Taipei at these finals?

17. Which two nations that played each other at these finals would also meet for a record sixth time at a FIFA Women's World Cup in 2019?

18. Who was Norway's coach at these finals and would go on to appear in five FIFA Women's World Cups as a manager?

19. What age-related record did the United States's winning team set in the final?

20. Who scored seven goals for Germany at these finals?

21. Which nation won a match in extra time at these finals and would go on to play five matches in extra time, the most in FIFA Women's World Cup history?

22. What was the score in the United States versus Chinese Taipei quarter-final match at these finals?

23. How many cities were used at these finals – four, five or six?

24. What duration were the matches at these finals?

25. Which three nations qualified for the knockout stage despite losing their first match at these finals?

26. Wendi Henderson played at these finals but would have to wait another 16 years to play at her second FIFA Women's World Cup in 2007. What nation did she represent?

27. Which nation did not concede a goal in the group stage at these finals but conceded six goals in their two knockout stage matches?

28. Two points were awarded for a win at these finals – true or false?

29. Which nation did Sweden beat 8-0 at these finals?

30. Which German scored at these finals and would go on to score in the next three FIFA Women's World Cup tournaments?

*WorldCup*USA**94**
© FIFA TM

1994 FIFA WORLD CUP
UNITED STATES™

1. Which nation returned after a 56-year absence at these finals?

2. Name four of the six players who scored at least five goals at these finals.

3. Who scored against Russia at these finals to make him the competition's oldest ever scorer?

4. Who won the Golden Ball award at these finals?

5. Which Brazilian at these finals played in the first of a record three consecutive FIFA World Cup finals?

6. What was the average attendance at these finals (a FIFA World Cup record) – 68,991, 73,991 or 78,991?

7. Who was the United States's coach at these finals?

8. Who scored both of Italy's goals against Nigeria at these finals – one a late equaliser and the other an extra-time winner?

9. Which European nation made its debut at these finals?

10. Which nation was the top scorer at these finals with 15 goals?

11. Who scored the first of two hat-tricks in two successive FIFA World Cups at these finals?

12. Which television personality was the master of ceremonies in the opening ceremony at these finals?

13. Who was Switzerland's coach at these finals, their first FIFA World Cup for 28 years?

14. Which city was the most southerly used for matches at these finals?

15. Who scored the only own goal at these finals and which nation did he play for?

16. This was the first FIFA World Cup with 32 nations – true or false?

17. A newly unified Germany took part in a FIFA World Cup at these finals for the first time since which year?

18. Which pop star gave a musical performance at the opening ceremony at these finals and despite missing the goal broke the goalposts in accordance with the stunt plans?

19. What was unusual about the final standings in Group E at these finals?

20. Cameroon had two players 25 years apart in age in their team at these finals, one 42-year-old and one 17-year-old. Can you name them both?

21. What was significant about the USA versus Switzerland match at the Pontiac Silverdome at these finals?

22. Marco Etcheverry was sent off four minutes after coming on as a substitute against Germany for which nation at these finals?

23. Which nation failed to qualify for the knockout stage at these finals despite winning its opening match?

24. For which country did Florin Raducioiu score four goals at these finals?

25. Which two players whose singular name began with the letter 'B' scored two of Brazil's three goals in their quarter-final win over the Netherlands at these finals?

26. What was the name of Sweden's captain who was sent off in their semi-final against Brazil at these finals?

27. Which nation reached the last four at these finals despite never having won a FIFA World Cup match before and losing its first match 3-0?

28. Who won the FIFA World Cup Golden Glove award at these finals?

29. Which Saudi Arabian scored at these finals and would also go on to score in the 1998 and 2006 editions?

30. What was the name of the mascot at these finals, and what animal was it?

1995
FIFA WOMEN'S WORLD CUP
SWEDEN™

© TM FIFA

1. Which nation did Norway beat 7-0 at these finals?

2. Which Japanese played in the first of her six FIFA Women's World Cups at these finals?

3. Which nation failed to qualify for the knockout stage despite winning their first match at these finals?

4. Who was the top scorer at these finals with six goals?

5. Which nation was originally awarded hosting rights for these finals but had to relinquish those rights?

6. Nigeria against Canada and the United States against China both ended in what scoreline at these finals?

7. Which American goalkeeper was sent off against Denmark at these finals?

8. In which city did the final take place?

9. How many own goals were scored at these finals?

10. At these finals Sweden became the only hosts to lose their opening match in FIFA Women's World Cup history – true or false?

11. What was Norway's goal difference at these finals – +17, +19 or +22?

12. Which Norwegian won the Golden Ball award at these finals?

13. Which two nations contested the very first penalty shoot-out in FIFA Women's World Cup history at these finals?

14. Which were the only debutants to reach the knockout stage at these finals?

15. Which nation reached the quarter-finals at these finals despite scoring only two goals in the whole tournament?

16. Sonia Gegenhuber was sent off for which nation against Denmark at these finals?

17. Which stage did Sweden reach at these finals – the second successive occasion the hosts had reached this stage?

18. Which nation came back from two goals down to win 3-2 at these finals, and against which country did they achieve this?

19. Which future FIFA Women's World Cup runners-up did Germany beat 6-1 at these finals?

20. What new record did the Rasunda Stadium set at these finals?

21. Which two nations met twice at these finals – the only time two countries have met twice at a FIFA Women's World Cup?

22. How many goals were scored at these finals – exactly the same number as is 1991 – 99, 109 or 119?

23. At these finals Norway became the first nation to play in two successive FIFA Women's World Cup finals. Which other three nations have played in two or more successive finals?

24. Which German scored in the first of her four FIFA Women's World Cups at these finals?

25. Which city beginning with the letter H was the most southerly venue at these finals?

26. Which nation at these finals became the first to score two penalties in regulation time in a FIFA Women's World Cup match?

27. Which was the only nation to lose all three matches at these finals?

28. At these finals the United States became the only holders not to win their opening match of the tournament in FIFA Women's World Cup history – true or false?

29. Which two nations qualified for the knockout stage despite losing their first match at these finals?

30. Who scored a hat-trick for Norway against Nigeria at these finals?

1998 FIFA WORLD CUP
FRANCE™

1. Who scored the only goal England conceded in qualification for these finals, in a 1-0 win for Italy at Wembley Stadium?

2. Who is the only Scottish player to have been sent off at the FIFA World Cup, getting a red card against Morocco at these finals?

3. Against which nation at these finals did Ronaldo score his first-ever FIFA World Cup goal?

4. How many goals were scored at these finals (a new record) – 161, 171 or 181?

5. Which former UEFA European Championship-winning nation did not play at these finals but would appear in every one since?

6. What happened for the first time in FIFA World Cup history when Laurent Blanc scored in extra time against Paraguay at these finals?

7. Name three of the five European nations that participated at these finals but have not made a FIFA World Cup appearance since.

8. Which nation lost its third successive FIFA World Cup penalty shoot-out at these finals?

9. This was the first FIFA World Cup where fourth officials used electronic boards – true or false?

10. Which Cameroonian at these finals became the first man to be sent off in two FIFA World Cup matches?

11. Which nation failed to qualify for these finals despite being ranked third in the FIFA World Rankings at the time?

12. Who were the two Dutchman sent off at these finals? One was on AC Milan's books and the other was on PSV's books.

13. What was the name of the mascot at these finals, and what animal was it?

14. Which Cameroonian striker was the youngest player at these finals at the age of 17 years and three months?

15. Who sang the official song at these finals, entitled 'The Cup of Life', aka 'La Copa de la Vida'?

16. How many goals did France concede in their seven matches at these finals?

17. Which nation qualified from their group without winning a match at these finals?

18. Who scored the only goals of his international career in France's semi-final win over Croatia at these finals?

19. Who scored the Netherlands' 2-1 extra-time winner against Yugoslavia in the round of 16 at these finals?

20. Which nation drew against the Netherlands at these finals and would go on to draw their next four FIFA World Cup matches?

21. Which nation was the only group's top seed not to advance to the knockout stage at these finals?

22. Who was in Italy's squad for these finals but did not play? He would, however, go on to play in the next four FIFA World Cups, making 14 appearances.

23. Which stadium and city was the most northerly used for matches at these finals?

24. Who were the three Frenchman sent off at these finals?

25. Which African nation made its debut at these finals?

26. Name three of the five stadiums that were used both at these finals and at the 1938 FIFA World Cup.

27. Only one member of the Netherlands' squad at these finals was playing for Real Madrid at the time. Can you name him?

28. Which Scotsman was the oldest player at these finals at the age of 39 years and 11 months?

29. Which Asian nation was making its first FIFA World Cup appearance for 20 years at these finals?

30. Which club contributed to the most players at these finals, with 13?

1999
FIFA WOMEN'S WORLD CUP
UNITED STATES™

1. Which was the only city not located on either the west or east coasts to host matches at these finals?

2. Apart from the United States, which other nation was unbeaten at these finals?

3. Which African nation made its debut at these finals?

4. Which Chinese player won the Golden Ball award at these finals?

5. At these finals the United States became the first and so far only hosts to win the FIFA Women's World Cup – true or false?

6. Which Brazilian scored seven goals at these finals?

7. Which European nation lost all three matches at these finals?

8. Alicia Ferguson was sent off in the second minute for which nation against China at these finals?

9. Which nation had a -14 goal difference at these finals, scoring once and conceding 15 in the group stage?

10. At these finals Ifeanyi Chiejine became the youngest ever FIFA Women's World Cup player at the age of 16 years and 34 days. Which nation did she represent?

11. Which game at these finals saw seven of the eight goals in total being scored in the first half?

12. Group B at these finals was known as the 'Group of Death'. Which four nations were in the group?

13. Which nation's run of ten successive FIFA Women's World Cup wins ended at these finals?

14. Which singer performed at the closing ceremony at these finals?

15. Which were the only debutants to reach the knockout stage at these finals?

16. Which American played at these finals and would go on to play in the next four FIFA Women's World Cup tournaments?

17. Inka Grings scored a hat-trick for which nation against Mexico at these finals?

18. Which city hosted the final?

19. Which African nation had two players sent off at these finals?

20. Which nation were the top scorers at these finals with 19 goals?

21. These finals witnessed the first-ever goalless draw in FIFA Women's World Cup history. Can you name the two nations involved?

22. Which European nation made its debut at these finals?

23. How many red cards were issued at these finals – a FIFA Women's World Cup record?

24. What was the name of the stadium used at these finals located in East Rutherford, New Jersey?

25. Which two nations qualified for the knockout stage despite losing their first match at these finals?

26. Which two nations drew 3-3 in the group stage at these finals?

27. Sissi and which other player scored a hat-trick in Brazil's 7-1 win over Mexico at these finals?

28. Which nation went 3-0 behind in the quarter-finals against Brazil at these finals, then came back to 3-3 before losing 4-3 to a golden goal?

29. Who missed the only penalty in the final shoot-out?

30. Which two other major football events has the Rose Bowl staged?

2002 FIFA WORLD CUP
JAPAN AND SOUTH KOREA™

1. Which member of the Republic of Ireland squad played alongside his uncle Gary Kelly at these finals?

2. Who scored the solitary goal of the game in Germany's quarter-final and semi-final matches at these finals?

3. Which Asian nation made its debut at these finals?

4. Souleymane Mamam played in a FIFA World Cup qualifier in 2001 at the age of 13 years and 310 days for which African nation?

5. Which country had two men sent off against the Korea Republic at these finals?

6. Who scored a hat-trick on his FIFA World Cup debut at these finals, against Saudi Arabia?

7. This was the first FIFA World Cup that allowed three substitutions per game – true or false?

8. Who was sent off against the Korea Republic in the round of 16 at these finals?

9. Which player, who shares his first name with an Argentine striker who played for both Manchester clubs, scored eight goals for Guatemala in 2002 FIFA World Cup qualifying and would go on to score a record 39 goals in qualifiers for his country?

10. Who made the first of a record 17 FIFA World Cup appearances as captain at these finals?

11. Which South American country qualified for these finals for the first time?

12. How many games at these finals were decided by the golden goal rule?

13. Who was the Real Betis star whose missed spot kick in the quarter-final shoot-out saw Spain go out at these finals?

14. Which goalkeeper saved two penalties in regular play at these finals?

15. Who was sent off from the bench against Sweden at these finals?

16. Only one member of Spain's squad at these finals was playing their club football outside Spain at the time. He was on Lazio's books. Can you name him?

17. What were the names of the mascots at these finals?

18. By what scoreline did Australia beat American Samoa in 2002 FIFA World Cup qualification?

19. Which match at these finals saw a FIFA World Cup record 16 cautions?

20. Who scored Senegal's surprise winner against France at these finals?

21. Who scored a hat-trick of penalties in Switzerland's 2002 FIFA World Cup qualifying win over the Faroe Islands in October 2000?

22. What was Brazil's goal difference at these finals – a new FIFA World Cup record?

23. Which nation was involved in two penalty shoot-outs at these finals, winning one and losing one?

24. Who scored an injury-time equaliser for the Republic of Ireland against Germany at these finals?

25. Which nation came from three goals behind to draw 3-3 with Senegal at these finals?

26. Which coach's run of 12 FIFA World Cup matches unbeaten began at these finals?

27. Which was the most northerly city in Japan to host a match at these finals? It begins with the letter S.

28. Who was sent off in the England versus Brazil quarter-final at these finals?

29. What did Brazil achieve at these finals which no other nation had done previously at a FIFA World Cup?

30. Which side did England beat 3-0 in the round of 16 at these finals?

2003
FIFA WOMEN'S WORLD CUP
UNITED STATES™

1. Who scored four goals for Brazil at these finals?

2. Which Canadian scored at these finals and would go on to score in the next four FIFA Women's World Cup tournaments?

3. The Germany against Russia quarter-final match at these finals produced a FIFA Women's World Cup record number of goals for a knockout stage match. What was the score?

4. Which was the only nation that failed to score at these finals?

5. Which two nations qualified for the knockout stage despite losing their first match at these finals?

6. Dianne Alagich scored the only own goal at these finals, against Russia. Which nation did she represent?

7. Which nation was originally awarded the right to host these finals but did not due to a severe outbreak of SARS?

8. Who at these finals became the youngest scorer in FIFA Women's World Cup history when she netted for Russia against Germany at the age of 16 years and 107 days?

9. Who scored twice for the United States against North Korea at these finals? She was the only college player in their squad.

10. Mio Otani scored the only hat-trick at these finals, against Argentina. Which nation did she represent?

11. Which two cities/towns were used for matches at these finals as well as being used four years previously?

12. Group A at these finals included three teams from the previous edition's Group A. Which three?

13. Who was Germany's winning captain at these finals?

14. Which nation had a -14 goal difference at these finals, scoring once and conceding 15 in the group stage?

15. Which Asian nation made its debut at these finals?

16. Which American scored her first FIFA Women's World Cup goal at these finals and would go on to score 14 in all in her career?

17. How many different goalscorers did Germany have at these finals – 10, 11 or 12?

18. Who was the top scorer at these finals with seven goals?

19. At these finals Paulo Goncalves became the oldest coach in FIFA Women's World Cup history at the age of 66 years, 10 months and 13 days. Which nation did he manage?

20. Who scored Germany's golden goal winner in the final, ten minutes after coming on as a substitute?

21. Which nation was eliminated in the group stage at these finals despite scoring seven goals?

22. Which American at these finals became the first-ever person to represent her country as both a player and then as a coach?

23. Which nation did the United States beat in the third place play-off at these finals?

24. In which city did the final take place?

25. Who came on as a substitute in five of the United States's six matches at these finals?

26. Which European nation made its debut at these finals?

27. Natalia Gatti received the only red card at these finals, getting her marching orders against Japan. Which nation did she represent?

28. Which two nations failed to qualify for the knockout stage at these finals despite winning their first match?

29. Name two of the three nations to lose all three matches at these finals.

30. Who at these finals scored three minutes after coming on as a substitute in Germany's match against Russia in the quarter-final?

2006 FIFA WORLD CUP
GERMANY™

1. Who knocked out Australia with a late penalty in the last 16 at these finals?

2. Who scored a hat-trick of penalties in Brazil's 2006 FIFA World Cup qualifying win over Argentina in June 2004?

3. Which goalkeeper at the end of these finals had kept a FIFA World Cup-equalling record ten clean sheets in his career?

4. How many hat-tricks were scored at these finals?

5. Who was sent off after the match in the Argentina versus Germany quarter-final at these finals?

6. Which country was eliminated in the round of 16 at these finals despite not conceding a goal in actual play?

7. Which Argentine picked up his first booking at these finals and went on to receive a FIFA World Cup record seven cautions in his career?

8. Which nation were the top scorers at these finals with 14 goals?

9. Which player scored at these finals and has gone on to score in the last three FIFA World Cups since?

10. This FIFA World Cup saw a record number of yellow cards handed out. How many cautions were there – 345, 355 or 365?

11. Angola was drawn in the same group as which country at these finals, once their colonial occupiers?

12. Which nation ended Brazil's run of 11 successive FIFA World Cup wins at these finals?

13. Who at these finals became the oldest goalkeeper in FIFA World Cup history to save a penalty in a shoot-out?

14. Name two of the four African nations that were making their FIFA World Cup debuts at these finals.

15. Which future English Premier League star scored twice in the Czech Republic's win over the USA at these finals?

16. Which nation was eliminated from these finals without losing a match in regulation play for the third time in their FIFA World Cup history?

17. Which goalkeeper did not concede any penalties in Ukraine's shoot-out win over Switzerland at these finals?

18. Which now defunct nation made its one and only FIFA World Cup appearance at these finals?

19. Who missed a penalty for Ghana against the Czech Republic at these finals, and would do so again against Uruguay four years later?

20. Which nation participated in their first FIFA World Cup for 32 years at these finals?

21. Which nations played in the 'Battle of Nuremberg' at these finals, in which four red cards were issued?

22. What was significant about the first goal at these finals scored by Germany's Philipp Lahm and the last goal of the tournament scored by Italy's Marco Materazzi?

23. Which nation knocked out Mexico in extra time in the last 16 at these finals?

24. Which was the only nation that did not score at these finals?

25. Which two nations were making their FIFA World Cup debuts as independent nations at these finals?

26. Name four of the five nations that were unbeaten in regulation play at these finals.

27. Who was England's goalkeeper at these finals?

28. This FIFA World Cup saw a record number of red cards handed out. How many sendings off were there – 26, 28 or 30?

29. Who at these finals scored Italy's two extra-time goals against Germany in the semi-final?

30. Which goalkeeper saved three penalties in a penalty shoot-out at these finals?

2007
FIFA WOMEN'S WORLD CUP
CHINA™

1. Which African nation conceded 15 goals in their three group stage matches at these finals?

2. Which nation was eliminated in the group stage despite scoring seven goals at these finals?

3. Who scored six goals for Norway at these finals, including a hat-trick against Ghana?

4. Who scored for the United States after 53 seconds against Nigeria at these finals?

5. Anne Dot Eggers Nielsen scored against China at these finals, 12 years after scoring her previous FIFA Women's World Cup goal. Which nation did she represent?

6. Which Australian scored three of her four goals as a substitute at these finals?

7. How many goals did Germany concede at these finals?

8. Eva Gonzalez scored for both teams in the same match at these finals. Which nation did she represent and which team did she do this against?

9. Which nation won all three group stage matches at these finals and would go on to win their three group matches in the next two FIFA Women's World Cups?

10. Who saved a Marta penalty in the final?

11. Who was sent off for Argentina against England – the only red card at these finals?

12. Which was the only nation Germany failed to beat at these finals?

13. Which Chinese city beginning with the letter T was the most northerly used at these finals?

14. Who captained her country at these finals and went on to lead her side in the next three FIFA Women's World Cups after that?

15. Who won the Golden Ball and the Golden Shoe Awards at these finals?

16. How many matches went into extra time at these finals?

17. Which nation in beating Ghana at these finals recorded its first-ever FIFA Women's World Cup win at the tenth attempt?

18. Which English woman scored four goals at these finals – two against Japan and two against Argentina?

19. In which city did the final take place?

20. Which nation reached its fourth FIFA Women's World Cup semi-final at these finals but has not reached the last four since?

21. Which German appeared in her third FIFA Women's World Cup final at these finals?

22. Apart from Germany, which other nation did not concede a goal in the group stage at these finals?

23. Which nation did Brazil beat 4-0 in the semi-final at these finals to inflict their biggest ever FIFA Women's World Cup defeat?

24. Which American won her record 24th and last FIFA Women's World Cup match at these finals?

25. 2007 was the only year in FIFA Women's World Cup history that the final was played between nations from Europe and South America – true or false?

26. Which nation reached its first-ever FIFA Women's World Cup quarter-final at these finals?

27. Melissa Tancredi scored after 37 seconds against Australia at these finals. Which nation did she represent?

28. Which nation did Germany beat 11-0 at these finals – a FIFA Women's World Cup record win at the time?

29. Which was the only nation that failed to score at these finals?

30. Who was Germany's winning coach at these finals?

2010 FIFA WORLD CUP
SOUTH AFRICA ™

1. Who scored five goals at these finals and would go on to score five goals in 2014 as well?

2. How many goals did Spain concede in their four knockout stage matches at these finals?

3. Which nation picked up nine cautions in a match at these finals, a joint FIFA World Cup record?

4. Name the three former FIFA World Cup winners that Germany beat at these finals.

5. Which nation was the only undefeated team at these finals?

6. Who scored England's consolation goal in their 4-1 defeat to Germany at these finals?

7. How many goals did Spain score at these finals – the fewest number of goals scored by the champions at a FIFA World Cup?

8. Which nation was making its FIFA World Cup debut as an independent country at these finals?

9. In terms of continents, what FIFA World Cup first did Spain achieve at these finals?

10. Which group stage match at these finals produced the biggest ever upset in terms of FIFA World Cup Rankings difference? The winner was ranked 83 and the loser was ranked 9.

11. Who scored five of Spain's first six goals at these finals?

12. Which nation were the top scorers at these finals with 16 goals?

13. Which European nation, ranked 10th in the world at the time, failed to qualify for these finals for the first and only time since its debut in 1998?

14. Three brothers, Johnny, Jerry and Wilson, all played for which nation at these finals?

15. Which two stadiums were used in Johannesburg at these finals?

16. Which two brothers were on opposing teams in a match at these finals?

17. Two of Spain's winning squad at these finals were playing for Liverpool at the time. Can you name them both?

18. Which continent's nations all progressed to the round of 16 at these finals?

19. Who at these finals became the oldest FIFA World Cup coach ever, aged 71 years and 317 days?

20. Which was the most northerly city used at these finals? It begins with the letter P and it means 'Place of Safety'.

21. Who was the only player to score a hat-trick at these finals, doing so against the Korea Republic?

22. Which two nations failed to score at these finals?

23. Which African nation had no players from clubs in their own league at these finals?

24. At these finals Italy became the third defending champions to be eliminated in the group stage. Who are the other two and in which years were they eliminated?

25. Who was sent off in the final?

26. 117 players from which country's league were in the nations' squads at these finals?

27. What was the name of the mascot at these finals, and what animal was it?

28. Which Paraguayan played in his fourth FIFA World Cup at these finals?

29. Who became the oldest ever FIFA World Cup-winning coach at these finals?

30. Which nation was making its first FIFA World Cup appearance for 44 years at these finals?

2011
FIFA WOMEN'S WORLD CUP
GERMANY™

1. Which two nations were eliminated from these finals despite not losing a match in regulation time?

2. Genoveva Anonma scored twice in a 3-2 defeat to Australia at these finals. Which African nation did she represent?

3. Which French woman at these finals became the oldest captain in FIFA Women's World Cup history at the age of 37 years and 334 days?

4. Which Japanese at these finals became the first player to be sent off in a FIFA Women's World Cup final?

5. Which South American nation was making its debut at these finals?

6. How many penalty shoot-outs were there at these finals – a FIFA Women's World Cup record?

7. Which Japanese scored the only hat-trick at these finals, against Mexico?

8. Which nation did eventual champions Japan lose to in the group stage at these finals?

9. Which two nations lost every match in the group stage at these finals?

10. Which Japanese goalkeeper saved three spot kicks in the final penalty shoot-out against the United States at these finals?

11. Berangere Sapowicz was sent off against Germany at these finals. Which nation did she represent?

12. How many goals did eventual champions Japan score at these finals – a record low – 11, 12 or 13?

13. Which was the only nation that did not concede a goal in the group stage at these finals?

14. Which two nations played out the only goalless draw at these finals?

15. The fewest goals in FIFA Women's World Cup history were scored at these finals. How many were scored – 82, 84 or 86?

16. Which city beginning with the letter A was the most southerly used for matches at these finals?

17. How many matches at these finals went into extra time – a FIFA Women's World Cup record?

18. Which nation failed to qualify for the knockout stage at these finals despite winning its first match?

19. Who was Japan's winning coach at these finals?

20. Who was sent off for Sweden against France in the third place match at these finals?

21. Who was the only American to score a penalty in the final shoot-out against Japan at these finals?

22. At these finals Germany became the first, and so far only, holders not to reach the semi-finals – true or false?

23. Which African nation was eliminated from the group stage at these finals despite conceding only two goals?

24. How many players received yellow cards in the United States versus Brazil match at these finals – a FIFA Women's World Cup record – 8, 9 or 10?

25. Which nation were the top scorers at these finals with 13 goals?

26. Which nation qualified for the knockout stage at these finals despite losing its first match?

27. At these finals Cecilia Santiago became the youngest goalkeeper in FIFA Women's World Cup history at the age of 16 years and 251 days. Which nation did she represent?

28. Which two nations failed to score at these finals?

29. Which nation lost for the first time in 16 FIFA Women's World Cup matches at these finals?

30. Which African nation was making its debut at these finals?

2014 FIFA WORLD CUP
BRAZIL ™

1. Who played at these finals almost 16 years to the day after he had previously appeared in a FIFA World Cup match – the longest ever period between appearances?

2. Which player by the end of these finals had played in a record 14 FIFA World Cup knockout stage matches?

3. The goalscorer in the final shares the same first name with the scorer of two goals in the 1978 FIFA World Cup final. What are the two full names of both scorers?

4. The opening goal at these finals was an own goal by which Brazilian defender?

5. Who scored in the 121st minute against Germany at these finals?

6. Which nation won its fourth penalty shoot-out at these finals, equalling a FIFA World Cup record?

7. Who got through the last 16 in a penalty shoot-out at these finals but were eliminated in identical manner in the next round against the Netherlands?

8. Who was sent off after just 37 seconds of Bahrain's 2014 FIFA World Cup qualifier against Iran?

9. Which player was Luis Suarez involved in a biting incident with at these finals?

10. Which nation were the top scorers at these finals with 18 goals?

11. Which unfancied team kept Argentina at bay for ninety minutes at these finals before Lionel Messi scored an injury-time winner?

12. Which nation was the only debutant at these finals?

13. Which defender scored Germany's quarter-final winner against France at these finals?

14. What two new innovations did match officials use at these finals for the first time?

15. Who scored two goals in 69 seconds against Brazil at these finals?

16. Who scored a hat-trick as Germany beat Portugal 4-0 in their opening match at these finals?

17. Which nation was the only country to use all of its 23 players during these finals?

18. Who scored a hat-trick of penalties in Gabon's win over Niger in 2014 FIFA World Cup qualification in June 2013?

19. Countries from which region of the world did not participate at a FIFA World Cup for the first time in 32 years at these finals?

20. Which three members of Germany's squad were playing for Arsenal at the time of these finals?

21. Who scored for Brazil in both the round of 16 and the quarter-final at these finals?

22. Which city, located near the Amazon forest, was used for matches at these finals?

23. At what temperature were cooling breaks allowed to take place at the referee's discretion after the 30th minute of each half at these finals?

24. Which African side took Germany to extra time in the round of 16 at these finals?

25. What was the name of the mascot at these finals, and what animal was it?

26. Who won the Golden Ball award at these finals?

27. Who scored a hat-trick for Switzerland at these finals?

28. Who scored both of Colombia's goals in their round of 16 win over Uruguay at these finals?

29. Who missed the only penalty in regulation play at these finals, against Switzerland?

30. How many matches went into extra time at these finals, a FIFA World Cup record-equalling number?

2015
FIFA WOMEN'S WORLD CUP
CANADA™

1. Which three European nations were making their debuts at these finals?

2. This FIFA Women's World Cup had the most different goalscorers ever. How many though – 70, 80 or 90?

3. Who at these finals became the oldest ever player in a FIFA Women's World Cup final at the age of 40 years and 11 days?

4. Goalkeeper Shirley Berruz conceded a FIFA Women's World Cup record 17 goals at these finals. Which nation did she represent?

5. No South American nations reached the quarter-finals at these finals. When was the last year that this had happened?

6. Which German was appearing in her fifth FIFA Women's World Cup as a player and head coach combined at these finals – two as a player and three as a coach?

7. Which Norwegian scored at these finals against the Ivory Coast and England, 16 years after she scored her first FIFA Women's World Cup goal against Canada in 1999?

8. Near which English seaside town was the United States's winning coach Jill Ellis born?

9. Which two African nations were making their debuts at these finals?

10. Which nation was taken to extra time twice at these finals and has been taken to extra time on a record five occasions in total?

11. Fabienne Humm scored the fastest goal in FIFA Women's World Cup history against Ecuador at these finals. Which nation did she represent?

12. Can you name the two players who scored hat-tricks for Germany in their match against the Ivory Coast at these finals?

13. Who scored three minutes after coming on as a substitute in Sweden's match against Nigeria at these finals?

14. Who scored after 34 seconds of France's match against Mexico at these finals?

15. How many goals were scored at these finals – a new FIFA Women's World Cup record – 146, 148 or 150?

16. In which city did the final take place?

17. Which were the only two nations to win all three group stage matches at these finals?

18. Angie Ponce scored two own goals and a penalty against Switzerland at these finals. Which nation did she represent?

19. Five nations qualified for the knockout stage after losing their opening match at these finals. Can you name three of them?

20. Which nation drew all of their group stage matches at these finals?

21. At these finals, hosts Canada became the third host nation in a row to be eliminated at which stage of the tournament?

22. Which nation were the top scorers at these finals with 20 goals – the third time in the last four tournaments they'd held that accolade?

23. Who at these finals became the oldest scorer in FIFA Women's World Cup history at the age of 37 years and 98 days?

24. Catalia Perez was the only player sent off in the knockout stage at these finals. Which nation did she represent?

25. Which goalkeeper kept five successive clean sheets for the United States at these finals?

26. Which two nations drew 3-3 in the group stage at these finals?

27. Which nation at these finals scored a FIFA Women's World Cup record three penalties against Ecuador?

28. How many hat-tricks were scored at these finals – a FIFA Women's World Cup record?

29. At these finals Vanessa Arauz became the youngest coach in FIFA Women's World Cup history at the age of 26 years, 4 months and 3 days. Which nation was she coach of?

30. Which Asian nation was making their debut at these finals?

2018 FIFA WORLD CUP
RUSSIA™

1. Which nation made its debut at these finals, becoming the least populated country to participate in a FIFA World Cup?

2. Which two nations were involved in two penalty shoot-outs at these finals?

3. Which nation had 11 different scorers at these finals, including an own goal by an opponent?

4. Who scored 89 seconds after coming on as a substitute against Saudi Arabia at these finals?

5. Who captained his country at a fifth FIFA World Cup at these finals?

6. What was the surname of the Moroccan brothers that replaced each other as substitutes against Iran at these finals?

7. Which club provided a total of 16 players at these finals?

8. Who was sent off in Switzerland's round of 16 match against Sweden at these finals?

9. Which three games produced the most goals in a match at these finals (seven)?

10. Which African coach at these finals played for his country at the 2002 FIFA World Cup?

11. Which former FIFA World Cup runners-up were absent from these finals for only the second time in the last 32 years?

12. Which Egyptian at these finals became the oldest ever player to appear in a FIFA World Cup match?

13. Which city, a Formula One venue, was the most southerly venue used for matches at these finals?

14. Who scored the fastest goal at these finals, after 57 seconds against Croatia?

15. Who was the youngest player at these finals at the age of 19 years and 163 days?

16. Which nation was the only one to score two own goals at these finals?

17. Who scored after 8.1 seconds of Belgium's 2018 FIFA World Cup qualifier against Gibraltar in October 2016?

18. Which was the only nation at these finals to exclusively field squad players from its own domestic league?

19. Which two players scored hat-tricks at these finals?

20. Who won the Golden Ball award at these finals?

21. Who at these finals became the second oldest coach in FIFA World Cup history at the age of 71 years and 104 days?

22. What was the name of the official song at these finals?

23. What was significant about Aleksandr Erokhin coming on as a substitute for Daler Kuzyaev in the 97th minute of Russia's round of 16 match against Spain at these finals?

24. How many penalties were awarded at these finals – a new FIFA World Cup record?

25. What was the name of the mascot at these finals, and what animal was it?

26. Who took charge of a nation only two days before their first match at these finals, and whom did he replace?

27. Who scored four goals and provided two assists at these finals?

28. Which Swiss was appearing in his fourth FIFA World Cup at these finals?

29. Which coach at these finals played for his country at the 1990 FIFA World Cup?

30. Which two nations lost all three matches at these finals?

2019
FIFA WOMEN'S WORLD CUP
FRANCE™

1. What FIFA Women's World Cup record did Cristiane break at these finals?

2. Name three of the five nations that lost every group match at these finals.

3. Who was sent off for South Africa against Spain at these finals?

4. Who scored a hat-trick for Italy against Jamaica at these finals?

5. Which was the only match that went to a penalty shoot-out at these finals?

6. Who was the United States's winning coach?

7. Who was the only player to score in five separate games at these finals?

8. How many own goals were scored at these finals – a new FIFA Women's World Cup record – eight, nine or ten?

9. Which Norwegian scored a penalty after 4 minutes and 33 seconds at these finals – the fastest ever FIFA Women's World Cup penalty?

10. There were only two goalless draws at these finals. Which matches were they?

11. How many of the United States's seven matches at these finals did they win?

12. Who in scoring penalties for Spain against South Africa at these finals became the first player to score two penalties in a FIFA Women's World Cup game?

13. Which nation came back from two goals down to win the match 3-2 at these finals, and against which country did they achieve this?

14. Who scored the fastest goal at these finals, after two minutes and seven seconds against Norway?

15. Which England player missed two penalties at these finals?

16. Who was the only woman to score two goals in two different matches at these finals?

17. Who scored the United States's second goal in the final?

18. The United States and which other country did not concede a goal in the group stage at these finals?

19. What was the score at half-time in the USA versus Thailand match – a match which ended 13-0 to the USA?

20. In which city was the final held?

21. The United States set a new FIFA Women's World Cup record for most goals scored at one tournament. How many goals did they score?

22. Name three of the five nations that won every group match at these finals.

23. The United States became only the second nation to successfully defend their title. Which is the only other country to have successfully defended their title?

24. Who played in her seventh FIFA Women's World Cup tournament at these finals – a new record?

25. Which nation did Australia's Sam Kerr score four goals against?

26. Who missed a penalty in Canada's round of 16 defeat to Sweden?

27. How many penalties were scored in regulation time at these finals – a new FIFA Women's World Cup record – 17, 18 or 19?

28. Which nation came back from three goals down to draw the match 3-3, and against which country did they achieve this?

29. Who was sent off for Australia against Norway at these finals?

30. Thailand equalled the FIFA Women's World Cup record for most goals conceded at one tournament. How many goals did they concede at these finals – 18, 19 or 20?

MAJOR INTERNATIONAL TEAMS

FIFA is made up of hundreds of nations, every single one of which has their own storied history and star players. However, every four years only a few dozen are able to fight their way through the FIFA World Cup qualifiers to appear at the FIFA World Cup finals. This section will check how much you know about the top nations, with questions about their most famous wins and losses, who their most capped players are, which captains took them all the way to glory, or, in one unfortunate case, who was sent home from a FIFA World Cup before a ball was even kicked.

ARGENTINA

1. In which year did Argentina win the FIFA World Cup on home soil?

2. Which country did Argentina beat to win the 2008 Olympic Games men's final?

3. Which goalkeeper saved two penalties in their 1998 FIFA World Cup shoot-out win over England?

4. Only one player has scored in a FIFA World Cup final whose surname is a colour. He was Argentinian. Can you name him?

5. In which year did Argentina play their only FIFA World Cup final in Europe?

6. Argentina has been involved in the most penalty shoot-outs in FIFA World Cup history. How many?

7. Who made 20 FIFA World Cup appearances for Argentina from 2006 to 2018?

8. Who had two spells as Argentina coach, from 1990-94 and from 2006-08?

9. What three letters appear on Argentina's national team badge?

10. Argentina and which other country will host the 2021 Copa America, postponed from 2020 due to the coronavirus pandemic?

11. Who coached Argentina at the 1986 and 1990 FIFA World Cups?

12. Argentina won the first-ever FIFA Confederations Cup in 1992. Whom did they beat in the final?

13. Which country did Argentina lose to on penalties in the 2015 Copa America final?

14. Which Argentine was sent off at the 1966 FIFA World Cup?

15. Which player has scored the most FIFA World Cup goals for Argentina?

16. What is the surname of the two brothers Diego and Gabriel who played for Argentina?

17. Diego Maradona played in four FIFA World Cup tournaments, but which one was the only one he failed to score in?

18. Who was the only player to score more than one goal in Argentina's 2018 FIFA World Cup campaign?

19. Who captained Argentina in the 1978 FIFA World Cup final?

20. Against which now defunct country did Lionel Messi score his first FIFA World Cup goal?

21. Who scored for Argentina against Greece at the age of 36 at the 2010 FIFA World Cup?

22. Claudio Caniggia scored a FIFA World Cup landmark goal against Nigeria in 1994. Do you know which landmark goal this was?

23. Who top scored at the 2004 Olympic Games men's football tournament, helping Argentina win the gold medal?

24. Who scored a hat-trick for Argentina against the Korea Republic at the 2010 FIFA World Cup?

25. What was the score when Argentina met Scotland at the 2019 FIFA Women's World Cup?

26. Which country did Argentina lose to at the 2006 and 2010 FIFA World Cups, both at the quarter-final stage?

27. Which Argentine was involved in David Beckham's red card at the 1998 FIFA World Cup?

28. Who scored Argentina's 3-2 winner in the 1986 FIFA World Cup final?

29. Who scored twice for Argentina in the 1978 FIFA World Cup final?

30. Gabriel Batistuta scored two FIFA World Cup hat-tricks for Argentina. Can you name one of the countries he scored a hat-trick against?

AUSTRALIA

1. Who played at four FIFA World Cups for Australia from 2006 to 2018?

2. Which country beat Australia 6-0 in the 1997 FIFA Confederations Cup final?

3. What is the Australian men's football team nickname?

4. Australia has only ever reached the knockout stage at a FIFA World Cup once before, in 2006. Which nation did they face in the knockout stage?

5. By what method have Australia's last three FIFA World Cup goals been scored?

6. Which Dutchman was Australia's coach at the 2018 FIFA World Cup?

7. In which year did Australia win the Asian Cup on home soil, beating the Korea Republic in the final?

8. Who has scored the most goals for Australia in FIFA Women's World Cup history?

9. Who was sent off for Australia against Ghana at the 2010 FIFA World Cup?

10. Which goalkeeper holds the record for the most caps for Australia?

11. Who scored both of Australia's goals at the 2018 FIFA World Cup?

12. Which player, who shares his surname with a former England international manager, scored a hat-trick in Australia's 5-0 win over Nepal in FIFA World Cup qualifying in October 2019?

13. Which player, who shares his surname with a famous West Indian cricketer, became the first Australian to be sent off in a FIFA World Cup match, v Chile in 1974?

14. In which year did Australia first participate in the FIFA World Cup?

15. Which country did Australia record their first-ever FIFA World Cup win against?

16. Who scored five goals for Australia at the 2019 FIFA Women's World Cup?

17. Which former English Premier League defender captained Australia on 61 occasions from 2006 to 2013?

18. In which year did Australia lose all of their three FIFA World Cup matches, conceding three goals in each match?

19. Who once scored 13 goals in Australia's FIFA World Cup qualifier against American Samoa in 2001?

20. In which year did Australia host the men's and women's Olympic Games football tournaments?

21. Australia has only ever beaten a European nation once at a FIFA World Cup, and that came in 2010. Which nation?

22. In which year did Australia change Confederations from Oceania to Asia?

23. Which South American tournament has Australia been invited to play in for the first time in 2021?

24. Which Scotsman was Australia's coach from 1990 to 1996?

25. Who made a joint national record nine FIFA World Cup appearances for Australia from 2006 to 2014, a record he shares with Tim Cahill?

26. What is the Australian women's football team nickname?

27. Which now defunct nation was Australia's first-ever FIFA World Cup opponents in 1974?

28. Which nation did Australia beat in the AFC-CONCACAF play-off to book a place at the 2018 FIFA World Cup?

29. Who scored two of Australia's three goals at the 2010 FIFA World Cup?

30. Which former England manager also coached Australia?

AUSTRIA

1. In which year did Austria last win a FIFA World Cup match?

2. In which city did Austria play their matches at UEFA Euro 2008?

3. Which Marc scored seven goals in Austria's UEFA Euro 2016 qualifying campaign?

4. Which former Barcelona striker scored four goals for Austria at the 1978 FIFA World Cup?

5. Which country did Austria beat in a match known in Austria as the 'Miracle of Cordoba' at the 1978 FIFA World Cup?

6. How many of Austria's UEFA Euro 2016 squad were playing their club football in Austria at the time?

7. What FIFA World Cup record was set when Austria played Switzerland at the 1954 finals?

8. Which player with the initials A.H. was the first player to win over 100 caps for Austria?

9. Which Swiss coached Austria from 2011 to 2017?

10. Which South American country did Austria beat in the 1954 FIFA World Cup third-place match?

11. In which year did Austria last play in the FIFA World Cup?

12. What was unusual about all three of Austria's goals at the 1998 FIFA World Cup?

13. Who was sent off for Austria against Hungary at UEFA Euro 2016?

14. Which island country did Austria beat 9-0 in 1977 to record their biggest international win to date?

15. Who scored six goals for Austria at the 1954 FIFA World Cup, including a hat-trick against Czechoslovakia?

16. In which neighbouring country did 15 of Austria's 23 UEFA Euro 2016 squad play their club football at the time?

17. Whose three FIFA World Cup goals for Austria all came in wins – against Spain in 1978 and against Chile and Algeria in 1982?

18. Who is Austria's record goalscorer, netting 44 goals for his country?

19. Which country has Austria played the most internationals against (over 100), once part of an empire?

20. Which David scored six goals in Austria's 2014 FIFA World Cup qualifying campaign?

21. Which Baltic country did Austria beat 6-0 in September 2019 to record their biggest win for six years?

22. Which Austrian at UEFA Euro 2008 became the oldest ever scorer at a European Championship, scoring against Poland at the age of 38 years and 257 days?

23. Which FIFA World Cup-winning country did Austria beat in their very first FIFA World Cup match in 1934?

24. Who scored six goals in Austria's UEFA Euro 2020 qualifying campaign?

25. Who scored Austria's only goal at UEFA Euro 2016?

26. How many goals did Austria score at the 1954 FIFA World Cup – 13, 15 or 17?

27. In which year did Austria last play a knockout stage match at a FIFA World Cup?

28. Which famous Austrian coach who has a stadium named after him coached the Netherlands to runners-up spot at the 1978 FIFA World Cup?

29. Prior to 2021 Austria had never won a UEFA European Championship finals match – true or false?

30. Who captained Austria at UEFA Euro 2016?

BELGIUM

1. Who has made the most FIFA World Cup appearances for Belgium?

2. In which year did Belgium reach their first major tournament final?

3. What unwanted record did hosts Belgium set at UEFA Euro 2000?

4. What was the surname of brothers Leo and Franky, who played together at the 1986 FIFA World Cup?

5. Which country did Belgium lose 2-0 to at both UEFA Euro 2000 and at UEFA Euro 2016?

6. Up to and including the 2018 FIFA World Cup who was the last man to score in three matches at a major tournament for Belgium, doing so at the 2002 FIFA World Cup?

7. Who scored Belgium's 1-0 winner against England in the group stage at the 2018 FIFA World Cup – his only appearance at the finals?

8. What did Belgium achieve for the first time in November 2015?

9. Which country eliminated Belgium from the 1986 and 2014 FIFA World Cups?

10. In which year was Belgium eliminated from the FIFA World Cup group stage despite not losing a match?

11. Belgium's nickname is shared with which English Premier League club?

12. Who scored six goals over five major tournaments for Belgium from 1980 to 1990?

13. What was the surname of the brothers who played together for Belgium at the 1998 FIFA World Cup and at UEFA Euro 2000?

14. Which English club accounted for three of Belgium's 2014 FIFA World Cup squad?

15. Name one of the three other European countries that played alongside Belgium at the 1930 FIFA World Cup.

16. Doug Livingstone was in charge when Belgium played at the 1954 FIFA World Cup. Which country was he from?

17. Which former coach scored 30 goals for Belgium as a player from 1960 to 1974?

18. Belgium has reached two FIFA World Cup semi-finals – in 2018 and in which other year?

19. Who was in goal for Belgium at the 1990 and 1994 FIFA World Cups?

20. Belgium won Olympic Games gold in the football tournament on home soil, but in which year was this?

21. Which country did Belgium beat at the 2018 FIFA World Cup after being two goals behind?

22. Who scored four goals in Belgium's first two matches at the 2018 FIFA World Cup but did not score again in the tournament?

23. Which Belgian was sent off against the Korea Republic at the 2014 FIFA World Cup?

24. Romelu Lukaku and Thomas Meunier both scored hat-tricks in Belgium's 9-0 win over which country in 2017?

25. Only one member of Belgium's 2018 FIFA World Cup squad played his club football in Belgium. Who was he, and which club did he play for?

26. Which nation did Belgium beat in a penalty shoot-out at the 1986 FIFA World Cup?

27. Which manager with the initials G.T. is the only coach to have been in charge of over 100 internationals for Belgium?

28. What was the score when Belgium faced England at the 1954 FIFA World Cup?

29. Belgium lost 3-2 at UEFA Euro 84 to which country after being two goals ahead at one stage?

30. Belgium has hosted two UEFA European Championships, in 2000 and in which other year?

BRAZIL

1. Brazil has won only one FIFA World Cup in Europe. In which country was this?

2. Which player with the same first name as a recent Brazilian Formula One driver was sent off in Brazil's FIFA World Cup quarter-final defeat to the Netherlands in 2010?

3. What was the score when Brazil met Poland at the 1938 FIFA World Cup – there were 11 goals scored?

4. In 2019 which Brazilian became the first to appear in seven FIFA Women's World Cup tournaments?

5. Which Brazilian won both the FIFA World Cup and UEFA Champions League in 2002?

6. Which two Brazilians won both the UEFA Champions League and Copa America in 2019?

7. Nine of Brazil's eleven goals at the 2014 FIFA World Cup were scored by players from which three clubs?

8. In Brazil the national team is often known as 'Canarinha'. What is a 'Canarinha' translated into English?

9. Which Brazilian played in four successive FIFA World Cups from 1954 to 1966?

10. Which country did Brazil beat in the 2019 Copa America final?

11. Which player, who shares his surname with a type of explosive, scored for Brazil against Austria at the 1978 FIFA World Cup?

12. Pele was the last Brazilian to score a hat-trick at the FIFA World Cup, but against which country did he achieve it?

13. Who scored a hat-trick for Brazil against Jamaica at the 2019 FIFA Women's World Cup?

14. Which Brazilian scored and was sent off in the 2019 Copa America final?

15. Which country did Brazil beat on penalties to win the 2016 Olympic Games men's football tournament?

16. Who scored a hat-trick in Brazil's 7-1 win over Haiti at the 2016 Copa America?

17. Which Brazilian scored eight FIFA World Cup goals from 1998 to 2002 – Romario, Rivaldo or Ronaldinho?

18. Which striker with the initials L.F. scored twice for Brazil in their 2009 FIFA Confederations Cup final win over the USA?

19. Who won the FIFA World Cup with Brazil twice as a player and once as a manager?

20. In which year did Brazil reach the FIFA Women's World Cup final?

21. Which Brazilian has scored a record 17 FIFA Women's World Cup goals?

22. Who has had 3 spells as Brazil manager and was in charge at the 1994 and 2006 FIFA World Cups?

23. Which Brazilian won the Golden Boot at the 1950 FIFA World Cup with eight goals?

24. Brazil has won every match at a FIFA World Cup tournament twice before, in 2002 and in which other year?

25. Brazil has played two FIFA World Cup finals against which country?

26. Which Brazilian made 11 FIFA World Cup appearances as a substitute from 1998 to 2002?

27. Who captained Brazil in the 1994 and 1998 FIFA World Cup finals?

28. Which Brazilian scored in every FIFA World Cup match in 1970?

29. Which was the only country that Ronaldo scored against in two separate FIFA World Cup matches?

30. When did Brazil first host the FIFA World Cup?

CAMEROON

1. How many FIFA World Cup goals did Roger Milla score for Cameroon – four, five or six?

2. Which former Liverpool defender is Cameroon's most capped player?

3. What did Cameroon achieve at the 1990 FIFA World Cup that no other African nation had done previously?

4. In which year did Cameroon win the Olympic Games men's football tournament?

5. In which year did Cameroon make their FIFA World Cup debut?

6. What is the colour of Cameroon's first-choice shirts?

7. Which striker with the initials V.A. scored Cameroon's late 2-1 winner against Egypt in the 2017 Africa Cup of Nations final?

8. Which former Lyon and Rangers boss was Cameroon's manager from 2009 to 2010?

9. What is Cameroon's nickname?

10. Which former Paris St Germain, Cagliari and Parma striker scored 33 goals for Cameroon from 1995 to 2004?

11. Which player scored their 1-0 winner against Argentina at the 1990 FIFA World Cup and has made the most FIFA World Cup appearances for Cameroon?

12. Which tournament was due to be hosted by Cameroon in January 2021?

13. Who is Cameroon's all-time record goalscorer?

14. Which Cameroonian striker joined Paris St Germain in 2018?

15. What is Cameroon's FIFA three letter code?

16. Which former Arsenal player was sent off in Cameroon's 4-0 defeat to Croatia at the 2014 FIFA World Cup?

17. Cameroon failed to win a game at the 2017 FIFA Confederations Cup. Which three nations did they play?

18. Who scored both of Cameroon's goals in their 2-1 win over New Zealand at the 2019 FIFA Women's World Cup?

19. Cameroon has won more FIFA World Cup matches than any other African nation – true or false?

20. In which city is Cameroon's home stadium?

21. Which player, who shares his first name with a former German international called Littbarski, finished as Cameroon's top scorer in 2006 FIFA World Cup qualification with six goals?

22. Which former Dutch international midfielder was Cameroon's manager from 2018 to 2019?

23. Which goalkeeper was in four Cameroon FIFA World Cup squads from 1990 to 2002?

24. Which is the only European nation that Cameroon has beaten at the FIFA World Cup?

25. Which Cameroonian sadly collapsed and later died during a FIFA Confederations Cup match against Colombia in 2003?

26. Only two members of Cameroon's 2014 FIFA World Cup squad, Loic Feudjou and Cedric Djeugoue, played for a Cameroonian club. Which club? It shares its name with a Tony who played in goal for Watford and Manchester City in the 1980s and 1990s.

27. Cameroon was unbeaten in their first five FIFA World Cup matches. Which nation inflicted their first-ever World Cup defeat in 1990?

28. Who scored a hat-trick in Cameroon's 6-0 win over Ecuador at the 2015 FIFA Women's World Cup?

29. Which player with the initials P.S. was sent off in Cameroon's 2-0 defeat to Germany at the 2002 FIFA World Cup?

30. Which European nation did Cameroon lose to in the 2003 Confederations Cup final?

CROATIA

1. In which year did Croatia first participate at the FIFA World Cup?

2. Which country did Croatia beat in the 2018 FIFA World Cup qualifying play-offs?

3. How many of Croatia's matches at the 2018 FIFA World Cup went into extra time?

4. Who played one match for Yugoslavia and ten matches for Croatia at the FIFA World Cup?

5. Which former international coached Croatia to the UEFA Euro 2008 quarter-finals?

6. Which country did Croatia beat 10-0 in 2016 to record their biggest ever win?

7. Which former Derby and West Ham defender was the first Croatian to be sent off in a major tournament, doing so against Germany at UEFA Euro 96?

8. Which player, who shares his first name with a famous Croatian tennis player, scored Croatia's first-ever goal at a major tournament, a 1-0 winner against Turkey at UEFA Euro 96?

9. Which Croatian won the Golden Boot at the 1998 FIFA World Cup?

10. Who is the only goalkeeper to have won over 100 caps for Croatia?

11. Who was sent off for Croatia against Mexico at the 2014 FIFA World Cup?

12. Which brothers played together for Croatia at the 2002 FIFA World Cup and at UEFA Euro 2004?

13. Which Croatian's two FIFA World Cup goals were scored 12 years apart – one in 2002 and one in 2014?

14. Luka Modric and which other player, who shares his first name with an eight-time Grand Slam tennis champion from the 1980s, were the only ones to start every Croatia game at the 2018 FIFA World Cup?

15. Which player with the initials R.P. played three matches for Yugoslavia and six matches for Croatia at the FIFA World Cup?

16. Which Croatian goalkeeper saved three of Denmark's penalties in their shoot-out at the 2018 FIFA World Cup?

17. Croatia's matches against which nation are known as the Adriatic derby?

18. Which country did Croatia lose to in a penalty shoot-out at UEFA Euro 2008?

19. Croatia has won both of its two previous FIFA World Cup quarter-finals. They beat Russia in 2018 but whom did they beat in 1998?

20. What two colours are on Croatia's first-choice chequered shirts?

21. Since 1998, which is the only year in which Croatia has not participated in the FIFA World Cup?

22. Which Croatian player was shown the yellow card on three occasions by referee Graham Poll at the 2006 FIFA World Cup?

23. Who scored four goals in Croatia's final five UEFA Euro 2020 qualifying matches?

24. Which country did Croatia beat in the 1998 FIFA World Cup third place match?

25. Who scored three times for Croatia in the knockout stage of the 2018 FIFA World Cup?

26. In which English city did Croatia play their first-ever match at a major tournament?

27. Which Croatian was coached by his father Zlatko from 2004 to 2006?

28. Which Brazilian-born striker scored 29 goals for Croatia from 2004 to 2014?

29. Which Croatian played in four UEFA European Championships from 2004 to 2016?

30. Which country did Croatia beat and hence eliminate in their final UEFA Euro 2008 qualifying match?

1. Which Czech finished top scorer at UEFA Euro 2004 with five goals?

2. Who was the only member of the Czech Republic's UEFA Euro 96 squad who was playing his club football in the English Premier League at the time? He was a goalkeeper.

3. Which country beat the Czech Republic in the UEFA Euro 2004 semi-finals?

4. A player with the initials Z.Z. scored 4 goals for Czechoslovakia at the 1958 FIFA World Cup. His first name was Zdenek. What was his surname?

5. Which country effectively eliminated the Czech Republic from UEFA Euros 2008 and 2016 by beating them in their final group matches on both occasions?

6. Which country did the Czech Republic lose 5-0 to in March 2019 – their heaviest ever defeat?

7. Which 6ft 7in striker scored for the Czech Republic in three major tournaments from 2004 to 2008?

8. Which player, who shares his first name with a Berger who played for Liverpool, top scored in the Czech Republic's UEFA Euro 2020 qualifying campaign with four goals?

9. In which year did the Czech Republic play its first international – 1992, 1993 or 1994?

10. In which city did Czechoslovakia beat West Germany in the UEFA Euro 76 final?

11. The Czech Republic played six matches in reaching the final at UEFA Euro 96. How many of those matches did they win in normal time?

12. Czechoslovakia/Czech Republic has lost all three matches in only one major tournament. Which one?

13. What unwanted record did Czech Anton Ondrus set against the Netherlands at UEFA Euro 76?

14. Which country beginning with the letter M did the Czech Republic beat in the UEFA Euro 2012 play-offs?

15. Who scored the Czech Republic's goal in the UEFA Euro 96 final?

16. Which Czech won the Ballon d'Or in 2003?

17. When was the last year the Czech Republic played at the FIFA World Cup?

18. Name either of the Czech Republic players sent off at the 2006 FIFA World Cup.

19. Which Czech international scored for Liverpool in the 2005 UEFA Champions League final?

20. Which former Czech Republic manager scored twice for Czechoslovakia at the 1990 FIFA World Cup?

21. Who top scored in the Czech Republic's 2018 FIFA World Cup qualifying campaign with four goals?

22. Which now defunct nation did Czechoslovakia beat in the 1962 FIFA World Cup semi-finals?

23. Who scored a hat-trick in Czechoslovakia's win over Costa Rica at the 1990 FIFA World Cup?

24. Which nation did the Czech Republic beat on penalties in the UEFA Euro 96 semi-finals?

25. Who has scored the most goals in the FIFA World Cup for Czechoslovakia/Czech Republic with seven goals?

26. Which midfielder nicknamed 'the little Mozart' scored 23 goals in 105 appearances for the Czech Republic from 2000 to 2016?

27. Which country did Czechoslovakia lose to in the 1934 FIFA World Cup final?

28. Which German club were Jan Koller and Tomas Rosicky playing for when they appeared at the 2006 FIFA World Cup?

29. Which Czech famously scored the last penalty in the UEFA Euro 76 final shoot-out with a softly chipped shot up the middle?

30. Who coached the Czech Republic to runners-up spot at UEFA Euro 96?

DENMARK

1. Which former Arsenal midfielder scored Denmark's opening goal in the UEFA Euro 92 final?

2. Which country did Denmark beat 1-0 in 1986 to record their first ever win at the FIFA World Cup?

3. Who scored a hat-trick in Denmark's 6-1 win over Uruguay at the 1986 FIFA World Cup?

4. In which year did Denmark lose all three UEFA European Championship matches and fail to score?

5. Which Dane was awarded the Ballon d'Or in 1977?

6. Which country did Denmark replace at UEFA Euro 92?

7. Which German coached Denmark for 11 years from 1979 to 1990?

8. Two Danish players Martin and Mathias, who have both scored in a FIFA World Cup match, share which surname?

9. What is the furthest round Denmark has reached at the FIFA World Cup?

10. Who scored a national record five FIFA World Cup goals for Denmark – four in 2002 and one in 2010?

11. Which player, whose surname is something you would find at the beach, scored 16 seconds after coming on as a substitute in Denmark's win over Nigeria at the 1998 FIFA World Cup?

12. Who scored three of Denmark's four goals at UEFA Euro 96?

13. Who captained Denmark at the 2018 FIFA World Cup?

14. In which year did Denmark win the FIFA Confederations Cup – 1991, 1993 or 1995?

15. Who made a national record eleven FIFA World Cup appearances for Denmark from 1998 to 2010?

16. Which country did Denmark beat 6-0 home and away in UEFA Euro 2020 qualifying?

17. Which Danish referee famously sent off David Beckham at the 1998 FIFA World Cup?

18. Danish internationals Helveg, Sorensen and Gravesen share which first name?

19. Which country eliminated Denmark from UEFA Euro 84 and from the 1986 FIFA World Cup?

20. How many of their five matches did Denmark win in normal time at UEFA Euro 92?

21. In which city did Denmark win the UEFA Euro 92 final?

22. Who scored in two of Denmark's three games at UEFA Euro 2012?

23. What is the name of Denmark's national stadium?

24. Which Dane's two FIFA World Cup goals were scored 12 years apart – one in 1986 and one in 1998?

25. In which year did Denmark first appear at the FIFA World Cup?

26. Who was Denmark's manager for 15 years from 2000 to 2015?

27. Which former Ajax and Charlton Athletic winger won 126 caps for Denmark from 2000 to 2013?

28. How many of Denmark's penalties were saved against Croatia in the 2018 FIFA World Cup shoot-out?

29. Which country did Denmark beat in the 2018 FIFA World Cup qualifying play-offs?

30. Who scored eleven goals in Denmark's 2018 FIFA World Cup qualification campaign?

ENGLAND

1. Who was the first man to reach 100 England caps?

2. Which player with the first name Alan was the first man to be sent off while playing for England?

3. England wingers John and Peter share which surname?

4. Who captained England 65 times from 1982 to 1991?

5. Which country did England play in their opening match at the 2019 FIFA Women's World Cup?

6. Who managed England for only one game, against Italy in 2000?

7. Against which country did England play their first match at the 1998 and 2018 FIFA World Cups?

8. Who in 1978 became the first black player to be capped by England?

9. Which country came from two goals behind to beat England 3-2 at UEFA Euro 2000?

10. Against which country did Peter Crouch score an England hat-trick in 2006?

11. Which country scored only 8.3 seconds after kick-off against England in 1993?

12. Who scored six goals for England at the 2019 FIFA Women's World Cup?

13. In which stadium was Sven-Goran Eriksson's first match in charge of England played?

14. Which England player between 1977 and 1980 has a surname that begins and ends with the letter T?

15. Who won his first four England caps under four different managers from 1995 to 1999?

16. Against which country did England play their 1,000th match in 2019?

17. Who was the first man to be capped by England whose surname began with the letter Z?

18. In which year did England finish third at the FIFA Women's World Cup?

19. Who were England's first-ever FIFA World Cup opponents?

20. Who was the first post-war England goalkeeper called Joe?

21. Who scored his only goal for England against Sweden at the 2002 FIFA World Cup?

22. Who is Aston Villa's most capped England player, winning 42 caps from 1995 to 2001?

23. Which country beat England 7-1 in 1954 to inflict their heaviest ever defeat?

24. Who was the first player to be capped by England while playing for Juventus?

25. Who was the only player to score in the penalty shoot-out against Portugal at the 2006 FIFA World Cup?

26. Who became England's youngest ever player when he made his debut in 2006?

27. Which player has made a record 21 FIFA Women's World Cup appearances for England?

28. Who in 1980 became the first man to win an England cap while playing for Real Madrid?

29. Who was the first England goalkeeper to save a penalty at the European Championship finals?

30. In which Italian city did England lose to West Germany in the 1990 FIFA World Cup semi-final?

FRANCE

1. Which Frenchman scored twice in the 1998 FIFA World Cup final?

2. Who scored four goals and one own goal for France at the 2019 FIFA Women's World Cup?

3. Which French football administrator gave his name to European Championship trophy?

4. Stade de France replaced which one as France's national stadium in the 1990s?

5. How many times have France hosted the UEFA European Championship finals?

6. Which French player scored the first-ever FIFA World Cup finals golden goal?

7. Who is the only French player to be the FIFA World Cup finals leading goalscorer?

8. What animal appears on the French team badge?

9. In which year did France first reach their first-ever FIFA World Cup semi-final?

10. Which country did France beat in the final to win the 2001 FIFA Confederations Cup?

11. Whom did Laurent Blanc kiss on his shaven head before games as a good luck charm?

12. Which country did France play in the 2006 FIFA World Cup final?

13. France's biggest ever defeat was 17–1 in 1908, but which country inflicted the beating?

14. Which Frenchman scored the first-ever goal in the FIFA World Cup?

15. Who scored France's golden goal to win the 2000 UEFA European Championship Final?

16. Which man has won the most international caps for France?

17. Which tournament was hosted by France in 1997 as a test for the 1998 FIFA World Cup?

18. What was the score in the 2018 FIFA World Cup final?

19. Which French magazine awarded the Ballon d'Or to Europe's best player from 1956?

20. Who coached France to third place in the 1986 FIFA World Cup?

21. Who is the only man to have captained France on more than 80 occasions?

22. Which international FIFA tournament did France win on home soil in 2003?

23. Who was the only teenager in France's 2018 FIFA World Cup squad?

24. In which town, just outside of Paris, is the Stade de France?

25. Which country eliminated France from the 2019 FIFA Women's World Cup?

26. Which French player won the 2018 FIFA World Cup Bronze Ball and Silver Boot?

27. When did France last fail to qualify for the UEFA European Championship finals?

28. Which man has scored the most goals for France in full internationals?

29. At what stage did France exit the 2010 FIFA World Cup?

30. France has hosted two FIFA World Cups – in 1998 and in which other year?

GERMANY
(INCORPORATING WEST GERMANY AND EAST GERMANY)

1 Which German won the FIFA World Cup as captain in 1974 and as manager in 1990?

2 Who is Germany's record scorer in the FIFA Women's World Cup with 14 goals?

3 Which German made a record 25 FIFA World Cup appearances in his career?

4 In which year did West Germany first win the European Championship?

5 What was the score when Germany beat Brazil in the FIFA World Cup semi-final in 2014?

6 Which German was sent off against Sweden at the 2018 FIFA World Cup?

7 Who was in goal when West Germany won the 1974 FIFA World Cup?

8 Which country did West Germany beat on penalties at the 1986 FIFA World Cup?

9 Which man scored 45 goals for West Germany from 1976 to 1986?

10 Which South American nation did Germany beat in the 2017 FIFA Confederations Cup final?

11 At which major tournament did West Germany play East Germany?

12 Who scored Germany's 1-0 extra-time winner in the 2014 FIFA World Cup final?

13 Which German scored ten FIFA World Cup goals from 1954 to 1958?

14 Which German had a penalty saved against Serbia at the 2010 FIFA World Cup?

15 Which is the only year that Germany has failed to win a match at a FIFA World Cup finals?

16 Who was the first post-war manager of Germany who didn't play for the national side?

17 Which German played 38 matches at major tournaments from 2004 to 2016?

18 Germany has won the FIFA Women's World Cup twice, in 2003 and in which other year?

19 Who scored both of Germany's goals in the Euro 96 final against the Czech Republic?

20 Mario Gomez scored four goals for Germany in a 7-1 win over which Asian country in 2009?

21 Against which country did Miroslav Klose score a FIFA World Cup hat-trick for Germany?

22 In which stadium did Germany beat Belgium in the Euro 80 final? The stadium was also used in the 2009 UEFA Champions League final.

23 Which African nation did Germany beat 10-0 at the 2015 FIFA Women's World Cup?

24 In which year did East Germany win the Olympic Games men's football gold medal?

25 Which German was suspended from the 2002 FIFA World Cup final?

26 Which country did West Germany lose to on penalties in the UEFA Euro 76 final?

27 Who scored for West Germany in both the 1974 and 1982 FIFA World Cup finals?

28 In which year did Germany first host the FIFA World Cup?

29 German international Oliver Neuville who born in which country, famous for chocolate?

30 Who scored Germany's winning penalty in their UEFA Euro 96 semi-final shoot-out win over England?

GHANA

1. Who is Ghana's most capped player and all-time record goalscorer?

2. In which year did Ghana first participate at the FIFA World Cup?

3. Which Ghanaian with the initials A.A. finished as the joint top scorer at the 2015 Africa Cup of Nations with three goals?

4. Which two European nations has Ghana beaten at the FIFA World Cup?

5. Which FIFA World Cup host nation did Ghana beat on penalties in the final of the 2011 All-Africa Games?

6. What is Ghana's nickname. It appears on their emblem?

7. How many of Ghana's 13 FIFA World Cup goals has Asamoah Gyan scored – four, five or six?

8. Which former Lyon and Sunderland defender was Ghana's captain at the 2010 FIFA World Cup?

9. Who won the Ghana Player of the Year Award in 2018 and 2019 – a reason to celebrate?

10. Which nation has Ghana faced in all of their three FIFA World Cup appearances?

11. What colour are the sleeves on Ghana's first-choice shirt?

12. In which year did Ghana win the bronze medal at the Olympic Games men's football tournament – 1988, 1992 or 1996?

13. If Ghana had beaten Uruguay in the 2010 FIFA World Cup quarter-finals they would have become the first African nation to reach a World Cup semi-final – true or false?

14. Name the two South American nations that have eliminated Ghana from the FIFA World Cup knockout stage.

15. Which nation beginning with the letter L did Ghana lose to in a penalty shoot-out in the 2014 African Nations Championship final?

16. In 2010 Ghana became only the third African nation to reach the FIFA World Cup quarter-finals. Name the other two?

17. Which Serb was Ghana's manager when they reached the FIFA World Cup quarter-finals in 2010?

18. What is the name of Andre Ayew's younger brother, who also plays for Ghana?

19. Which sub-confederation is Ghana part of?

20. Apart from Asamoah Gyan, who is the only other player to score for Ghana at two different FIFA World Cups?

21. Which former international with the initials C.A. was appointed Ghana's manager in January 2020?

22. Which nation beat Ghana 1-0 in the 2010 Africa Cup of Nations final?

23. In August 2013 Ghana's Football Association became the first association on the African continent to launch what type of media?

24. Which former Ghanaian international won the UEFA Champions League with Chelsea?

25. Which West African nation does Ghana have their fiercest rivalry with?

26. What is the name of the Ayew brothers' father, who played for Ghana in the 1980s and 1990s?

27. What was the score in Ghana's penalty shoot-out defeat in the 2015 Africa Cup of Nations final against the Ivory Coast?

28. Which former Ghanaian international played in England for Tottenham and Portsmouth?

29. Which 1998 FIFA World Cup winner was born in Ghana?

30. Which former Bayern Munich defender won the Ghana Player of the Year Award a record three times, in 1998, 1999 and 2001?

GREECE

1. Who is Greece's most capped player, winning his caps from 1999 to 2014?

2. Which nation did Greece lose to in a penalty shoot-out at the 2014 FIFA World Cup?

3. In which year did Greece make their FIFA World Cup debut?

4. Which player with the initials K.K. was sent off for Greece against Japan at the 2014 FIFA World Cup?

5. Name two of the three nations that Greece lost to in the UEFA Euro 2008 group stage.

6. Which Dutchman took over as Greece's manager in July 2019?

7. Who captained Greece to their UEFA Euro 2004 success?

8. Which near neighbour did Greece play their first international against, in April 1929?

9. Who were Greece's first-ever FIFA World Cup opponents, losing 4-0 to them?

10. Greece's nickname is 'Ethniki' in Greek. What does 'Ethniki' mean in English?

11. Which near neighbour did Greece beat in the 2014 FIFA World Cup qualifying play-offs?

12. Who scored Greece's 1-0 winner against France in the UEFA Euro 2004 quarter-final?

13. Which Greek finished as UEFA's top scorer in 2010 FIFA World Cup qualification with ten goals?

14. In which year did Greece make their only FIFA Confederations Cup appearance?

15. Which Portuguese was Greece's manager from 2010 to 2014?

16. Which former Fulham and Benfica striker scored six goals in Greece's 2018 FIFA World Cup qualifying campaign?

17. Which former UEFA European Championship host country did Greece beat in the 2010 FIFA World Cup qualifying play-offs?

18. Who scored Greece's first-ever FIFA World Cup goal, against Nigeria in 2010?

19. Who was sent off on his Greece debut, against Saudi Arabia in May 2018?

20. In which year did Greece host the Olympic Games football tournaments?

21. Which former Portsmouth midfielder was Greece's second player to reach 100 caps, doing so in 2009?

22. Which Italian was Greece's manager for only four games in 2014?

23. Which player, who shares his first name with a famous Greek composer, scored on his full Greece debut, against Bosnia & Herzegovina in October 2019?

24. Which near neighbour did Greece lose to in the 2018 FIFA World Cup qualifying play-offs?

25. Who was Greece's manager when they won UEFA Euro 2004?

26. In which year did Greece make their UEFA European Championship debut – 1972, 1980 or 1988?

27. Which defender who prefers to have his first name on the back of his shirt was sent off for Greece against Poland at UEFA Euro 2012?

28. Greece has only won two FIFA World Cup matches in their history. Can you name both of the African nations they've beaten?

29. Which player with the initials N.A. is Greece's all-time record goalscorer, netting 29 goals from 1977 to 1988?

30. Who scored Greece's golden goal winner against the Czech Republic in the UEFA Euro 2004 semi-final?

HUNGARY

1. Which Hungarian was the top scorer at the 1954 FIFA World Cup with 11 goals?

2. How many times has Hungary won the gold medal at the Olympic Games men's football tournament – one, two or three?

3. Who scored twice in Hungary's 3-3 draw with Portugal at UEFA Euro 2016?

4. In 2013 Hungary suffered their biggest ever defeat (8-1) – against which fellow European country?

5. When was the last year Hungary competed at the FIFA World Cup?

6. Which nation did Hungary beat in the third place match at UEFA Euro 64?

7. How many international goals did Ferenc Puskas score in his 85 caps for Hungary?

8. In their 1954 FIFA World Cup final against West Germany what was the score after the opening nine minutes?

9. Which stadium in Hungary will be used during UEFA Euro 2020?

10. Which Hungarian in 2016 became the oldest ever player in UEFA European Championship history at the age of 40 years and 74 days?

11. What is Hungary's nickname?

12. Hungary were top scorers in the 1954 FIFA World Cup and in which other year?

13. Who scored seven FIFA World Cup goals for Hungary over two FIFA World Cups (1958 and 1962)?

14. Sandor Kocsis scored four goals for Hungary against which nation at the 1954 FIFA World Cup?

15. In which major tournament did Lajos Ku score Hungary's only goal?

16. How many goals did Tibor Nyilasi score in Hungary's 8-1 win in a UEFA European Championship qualifier against Luxembourg in 1975 – four, five or six?

17. Which Asian nation did Hungary beat 9-0 at the 1954 FIFA World Cup?

18. Which striker who has spent the majority of his club career in Germany scored four goals in Hungary's 2018 UEFA Nations League campaign?

19. What position did Hungary finish in their group at UEFA Euro 2016?

20. How many goals did Hungary score at the 1954 FIFA World Cup – a record – 25, 26 or 27?

21. Hungary has met an African nation only once before at the FIFA World Cup. Which nation?

22. Prior to 2016 in which year did Hungary previously play in the UEFA European Championship?

23. Which country has Hungary played the most internationals against (over 100), once part of an empire?

24. What was the score when Hungary met West Germany in the group stage at the 1954 FIFA World Cup?

25. Which Hungarian whose surname is a 'touch with the lips' scored the fastest ever hat-trick in FIFA World Cup history against El Salvador in 1982?

26. Which player with the initials D.H. scored 13 minutes into his Hungary debut against Azerbaijan in June 2019?

27. Which Scandinavian nation did Hungary beat in the UEFA Euro 2016 qualifying play-offs?

28. How many Hungarians were sent off in their 1978 FIFA World Cup match against Argentina?

29. Who scored in all four games for Hungary at the 1966 FIFA World Cup. He shares the same first name as the legendary Puskas?

30. Two Germans have coached Hungary before. Lothar Matthaus is one. Can you name the other? His surname is a large, white bird with long legs.

ITALY

1. Which country beat Italy in the UEFA Euro 2000 final?

2. Which man has scored the most goals for Italy in full internationals?

3. Which Italian won the Golden Boot at the 1990 FIFA World Cup, scoring six goals?

4. Which two players both scored twice for Italy in the 1938 FIFA World Cup final?

5. Italy managers Donadoni and Mancini share which first name?

6. Which former Roma midfielder won 117 caps for Italy between 2004 and 2017?

7. Which man has captained Italy on the most occasions?

8. In which United States city did Italy lose the 1994 FIFA World Cup final on penalties to Brazil?

9. Who captained Italy to 1982 FIFA World Cup glory at the age of 40?

10. Which striker scored nine FIFA World Cup goals for Italy between 1998 and 2002?

11. Who managed Italy from 1975 to 1986, leading them to FIFA World Cup glory in 1982?

12. Who is this famous Italian midfielder in anagram form – Danear Oilpr?

13. Which fellow European nation did Italy lose to in the quarter-final of the 2019 FIFA Women's World Cup?

14. Who scored Italy's winning penalty in the 2006 FIFA World Cup final shoot-out against France?

15. Which country did Italy beat 7-1 in their first-ever FIFA World Cup match in 1934?

16. Which man holds the record for the most FIFA World Cup appearances for Italy with 23?

17. Who scored Italy's third goal in the 1982 FIFA World Cup final?

18. Who in 1994 became the first Italian goalkeeper to be sent off in a FIFA World Cup match?

19. Which Italian played in the 1962 FIFA World Cup and managed his country at the 1998 FIFA World Cup?

20. Who scored a hat-trick for Italy against Jamaica at the 2019 FIFA Women's World Cup?

21. Who played in four successive FIFA World Cups for Italy from 1982 to 1998?

22. Who scored 27 goals for Italy from 1995 to 2008?

23. Which country eliminated Italy from the 1986 and 1998 FIFA World Cups?

24. Italy internationals Dino and Roberto share which surname?

25. At which FIFA World Cup did Italy fail to win a single match for the first time?

26. In 2018 Italy did not participate in the FIFA World Cup for the first time since which year?

27. Who was Italy's captain from 2002 to 2010?

28. Which country which comes third alphabetically in the list of UEFA nations did Italy beat 9-1 in a European Championship qualifier in November 2019?

29. Italy won the Olympic Games men's football gold medal in Berlin. In which year was this?

30. Which Italian, who won two FIFA World Cups, has a stadium in Milan named after him?

JAPAN

1. Which player, who shares his surname with a make of car, has scored the most FIFA World Cup goals for Japan?

2. In which year did Japan win the FIFA Women's World Cup?

3. Which player with the initials Y.E. has won the most international caps for Japan, winning 152 from 2002 to 2015?

4. Which European nation beat Japan in the 2001 FIFA Confederations Cup final?

5. Which former Salzburg player scored in five successive games for Japan from September to November 2019?

6. How did Japan finish ahead of Senegal in their group at the 2018 FIFA World Cup?

7. Who was the only member of Japan's 2014 FIFA World Cup squad playing his club football for Manchester United at the time?

8. Which famous Brazilian coached Japan from 2002 to 2006?

9. Which English Premier League player won his 100th cap for Japan in November 2019?

10. Which Caribbean country did Japan score their first-ever FIFA World Cup goal against?

11. Japan were due to host the Olympic Games football tournaments in 2020, but in which year did they previously host the tournaments?

12. What bird is depicted on Japan's national team emblem?

13. Who scored two of Japan's goals at the 2018 FIFA World Cup?

14. In which year did Japan co-host the FIFA World Cup with the Korea Republic?

15. Which player with the initials K.K. scored a national record 80 goals for Japan from 1964 to 1977?

16. In January 2020 Takumi Minamino became the first Japanese to play for which famous club?

17. Which country did Japan beat at the 2002 FIFA World Cup to record their very first win in the competition?

18. What was Japan's mascot at the 2014 FIFA World Cup?

19. In 1999 Japan became the first nation from outside the Americas to compete in which major tournament?

20. Seven of Japan's 2018 FIFA World Cup squad played their club football in which European country?

21. Which country has Japan faced in each of its two FIFA Women's World Cup final appearances?

22. Which Frenchman coached Japan at the 2002 FIFA World Cup?

23. Which nation has Japan played against on the most occasions?

24. In which year did Japan first participate at the FIFA World Cup?

25. What is the name of Japan's national stadium in Tokyo?

26. Which South American nation beat Japan in a penalty shoot-out at the 2010 FIFA World Cup?

27. What is Japan's national team's most common nickname?

28. Japan has only ever scored more than two goals in a FIFA World Cup match. Against which nation did they score three?

29. Who played for Japan at six FIFA Women's World Cup tournaments?

30. Which former Juventus and AC Milan coach managed Japan from 2010 to 2014?

KOREA REPUBLIC

1. Which former Manchester United player won 100 Korea Republic caps from 2000 to 2011?

2. Who was the Korea Republic's coach at the 2002 FIFA World Cup?

3. What is the colour of the Korea Republic's first-choice shirt?

4. In which year did the Korea Republic first participate at a FIFA World Cup?

5. Who made his international debut for the Korea Republic at the age of 18 in 2010?

6. Which former PSV Eindhoven, Tottenham and Dortmund player won 127 caps for the Korea Republic from 1999 to 2011?

7. Which former Celtic and Newcastle midfielder was the Korea Republic's captain at the 2018 FIFA World Cup?

8. Which wild animal is on the Korea Republic's emblem?

9. Which Italian club was Ahn Jung-Hwan playing for when he scored the Korea Republic's golden goal winner against Italy at the 2002 FIFA World Cup?

10. Which South American nation did the Korea Republic score their first FIFA World Cup goal against?

11. In which year did the Korea Republic win the Asian Cup on home soil – 1960, 1980 or 2000?

12. What is the name of the Korea Republic's home stadium?

13. Who was the only member of the Korea Republic's 2018 FIFA World Cup squad who was playing their club football in Italy. He was playing for Hellas Verona?

14. Who has made the most FIFA World Cup appearances for the Korea Republic, with 16 from 1990 to 2002 He ended his playing career at LA Galaxy?

15. Which is the only non-European nation that the Korea Republic has beaten at the FIFA World Cup?

16. What is the name of the Korea Republic's official supporter group. Manchester United and Belgium spring to mind?

17. In which year did the Korea Republic women's team reach the FIFA Women's World Cup knockout stage for the first and so far only time – 2007, 2015 of 2019?

18. Who is the Korea Republic's most capped goalkeeper?

19. It was not until 2002 that the Korea Republic first won a FIFA World Cup match. Which nation did they beat?

20. Which Portuguese was appointed the Korea Republic's manager in August 2018?

21. What is the Korea Republic's three letter FIFA code?

22. When was the last year the Korea Republic did not participate at a FIFA World Cup?

23. Which former Monaco and Arsenal striker was the Korea Republic's top scorer in 2014 FIFA World Cup qualifying with six goals?

24. Who is the Korea Republic's all-time record goalscorer. He was a member of Bayer Leverkusen's 1988 UEFA Cup-winning team?

25. In what tournament did the Korea Republic win the gold medal on home soil in 2014?

26. Which nation beat the Korea Republic 9-0 in what was the Asians' first-ever FIFA World Cup match?

27. Who scored and was sent off in the Korea Republic's 1998 FIFA World Cup defeat to Mexico?

28. Seol Ki-Hyeon was one of only two members of the Korea Republic's 2002 FIFA World Cup squad playing their club football in Europe at the time. Which Belgian club was he playing for?

29. Which nation beat the Korea Republic 5-0 in what was the Asians' first FIFA Confederations Cup match in 2001?

30. Which former German international and Real Madrid player was the Korea Republic's manager from 2014 to 2017?

MEXICO

1. Mexico hold the record for the most ever defeats in FIFA World Cup history. How many – 27, 29 or 25?

2. Who scored for Mexico in the 2010, 2014 and 2018 FIFA World Cups?

3. Who has made a record 19 FIFA World Cup appearances for Mexico?

4. Which Swede was coach of Mexico from 2008 to 2009?

5. Mexico have made it to the knockout stages of the FIFA World Cup nine times. How many knockout games have they won?

6. Mexico conceded the first-ever FIFA World Cup goal, but against which country?

7. When was the last year Mexico reached the FIFA World Cup quarter-finals?

8. What FIFA World Cup record did Mexico's Jesus Gallardo set against Sweden in 2018?

9. Who scored four goals for Mexico at the 1998 FIFA World Cup?

10. Which player, who shares his surname with a Uruguayan Luis, won 177 caps for Mexico from 1992 to 2006?

11. Which former FIFA World Cup-winning manager was Mexico's coach from 1991 to 1992?

12. Which country eliminated Mexico from the 2006 and 2010 FIFA World Cups?

13. Who coached Mexico at the 1986 FIFA World Cup – one of five nations he has coached at the tournament?

14. Which goalkeeper won his 100th cap for Mexico in 2018?

15. In their previous 16 FIFA World Cup appearances on how many occasions has Mexico reached the semi-finals?

16. Which Mexican won the Golden Ball Award at the 2019 Gold Cup?

17. In 1986 Mexico as a country became the first to do what?

18. Which South American nation did Mexico beat 4-3 in the 1999 FIFA Confederations Cup final?

19. Rafael Marquez and which other Mexican has played in a competition record equalling five FIFA World Cups?

20. One player in Mexico's 2006 FIFA World Cup squad, Jared Borgetti, was playing his club football in England at the time. For which club?

21. What FIFA World Cup record does the Azteca Stadium in Mexico City hold?

22. Which striker with the initials O.P. scored ten goals in Mexico's 2014 FIFA World Cup qualifying campaign?

23. Mexico hold the record for the most consecutive defeats in FIFA World Cup history. How many – eight, nine or ten?

24. Which player who was once on Manchester City's books scored a hat-trick for Mexico against Cuba at the 2019 Gold Cup?

25. Which round has Mexico been eliminated in their last seven FIFA World Cup appearances?

26. Which nation did Mexico beat 9-3 on aggregate in the 2014 FIFA World Cup Inter-confederation play-offs?

27. In which year did Mexico win the Olympic Games men's football tournament?

28. Which nation did Mexico beat in the 2019 Gold Cup final?

29. Which animal is depicted at the top of Mexico's badge?

30. Which player whose surname means white in Spanish scored for Mexico in the 1998, 2002 and 2010 FIFA World Cups?

NETHERLANDS

1. Which winger known for his dribbling skills scored 37 goals in 96 appearances for the Netherlands from 2003 to 2017?

2. In which city did the Netherlands win the UEFA Euro 88 final?

3. The Netherlands has lost to which two hosts in FIFA World Cup finals?

4. Which Dutch goalkeeper won the UEFA European Championship and the European Cup in 1988?

5. At which FIFA World Cup did the Netherlands play seven matches and never lose in normal time?

6. Who scored four goals for the Netherlands in the knockout stage of the 2010 FIFA World Cup?

7. Which country did the Netherlands play in their first and last game at UEFA Euro 88?

8. Which neighbouring country did the Netherlands play their first international match against in 1905?

9. Who was the last non-Dutchman to coach the Netherlands national team?

10. Which country eliminated the Netherlands from the 1994 and 1998 FIFA World Cups?

11. Who scored the Netherlands' extra-time winner against Sweden in the 2019 FIFA Women's World Cup semi-final?

12. Which Dutchman top scored in the UEFA section of 2014 FIFA World Cup qualification with 11 goals?

13. Which surname connects father and son Dutch internationals Danny and Daley?

14. In which city did the Netherlands lose the 2019 UEFA Nations League final?

15. Which country did the Netherlands beat 11-0 in 2011 to record their biggest ever win?

16. Who is the only Dutchman to have scored in six different FIFA World Cup matches?

17. Which former Liverpool player made 15 FIFA World Cup appearances for the Netherlands from 2006 to 2014?

18. Who scored a hat-trick for the Netherlands against Iran at the 1978 FIFA World Cup?

19. In which year was the Netherlands ranked number one in the FIFA World Rankings – 2011, 2014 or 2016?

20. Which country beat the Netherlands in the 2019 FIFA Women's World Cup final?

21. Dutch internationals Siem and Luuk share which surname?

22. Against which country did Marco van Basten score a hat-trick for the Netherlands at UEFA Euro 88?

23. Which man coached the Netherlands to a runners-up spot at the 1974 FIFA World Cup and won the 1988 UEFA European Championship?

24. Who scored eight goals for the Netherlands in UEFA Euro 2020 qualification?

25. Who has had two spells as Netherlands coach, from 1994 to 1998 and from 2014 to 2015?

26. In which year did the Netherlands reach the FIFA World Cup knockout stage despite not winning a group match?

27. Who scored twice for the Netherlands in the 2017 UEFA Women's European Championship final?

28. Who is the Netherlands' most capped defender, winning 112 caps from 1990 to 2004?

29. Which man has scored the most FIFA World Cup goals for the Netherlands, scoring seven from 1974 to 1978?

30. Dutch internationals Rob and Richard share which surname?

NIGERIA

1. Nigeria has only beaten European nations at the FIFA World Cup – true or false?

2. Which West African nation with two words did Nigeria beat in the 2013 Africa Cup of Nations final?

3. In which year did Nigeria make their FIFA World Cup debut?

4. Which 1974 FIFA World Cup winner as a player was Nigeria's manager from 2007 to 2008?

5. Nnamdi Oduamadi scored a hat-trick for Nigeria in a 6-1 win against which Pacific island at the 2013 FIFA Confederations Cup?

6. Which former Ajax, Inter Milan and Arsenal striker won 87 caps for Nigeria from 1994 to 2011?

7. Which nation has Nigeria been drawn in the same FIFA World Cup group with on an incredible five occasions, losing each time?

8. What is Nigeria's nickname?

9. Who was Nigeria's manager at the 1998 FIFA World Cup – the fourth different country he had managed at a FIFA World Cup at the time?

10. Which nation did Nigeria lose to in the last 16 at the 2019 FIFA Women's World Cup?

11. Which nation was Nigeria minutes from beating in normal time before losing after extra time at the 1994 FIFA World Cup?

12. Who became the first Nigerian to be sent off in a FIFA World Cup match, doing so against Greece in 2010?

13. Nigeria has only ever lost all three group stage matches at a FIFA World Cup once before – true or false?

14. Which former Lille goalkeeper won 101 caps for Nigeria from 2002 to 2015?

15. Which former West Ham striker was Nigeria's top scorer at the 2008 Olympic Games men's football tournament?

16. What is the name of Nigeria's home stadium in the capital Abuja?

17. Which Nigerian international joined Chelsea in 2012 and has been on loan at Liverpool and West Ham amongst other clubs?

18. Who scored two of Nigeria's three goals at the 2010 FIFA World Cup?

19. What were the names of the two brothers who played for Newcastle United. One of them played for Nigeria's senior team and the other for their Under-20 team?

20. Which former Everton defender has made the most FIFA World Cup appearances for Nigeria?

21. Which Nigerian international was sent off for Inter Milan in the 1998 UEFA Cup final?

22. In which year did Nigeria win the Olympic Games gold medal in the men's football tournament?

23. Which Frenchman was Nigeria's manager briefly in 1997 – one of five African nations he has been a manager of?

24. Which is the only nation Nigeria has beaten on more than one occasion at the FIFA World Cup?

25. Which former English Premier League striker scored 21 goals for Nigeria from 2000 to 2012?

26. Which Nigerian international won the FA Cup with Chelsea in 2000?

27. Which North African nation did Nigeria lose 4-0 to in the 2018 African Nations Championship final?

28. Who is the only player to have appeared for Nigeria at the 1994, 1998 and 2002 FIFA World Cups?

29. Which former Everton striker has both played for and managed Nigeria?

30. Who scored twice for Nigeria at both the 2014 and 2018 FIFA World Cups?

NORTHERN IRELAND

1. What is the name of Northern Ireland's home stadium?

2. Who scored five goals for Northern Ireland at the 1958 FIFA World Cup?

3. Which midfielder, who shares his surname with a famous golfer, was Northern Ireland's captain at the 1986 FIFA World Cup?

4. Who played his last international for Northern Ireland on his 41st birthday?

5. Which nation did Northern Ireland beat to record their first UEFA European Championship victory?

6. Who is Northern Ireland's most capped defender?

7. Which former Luton Town and Manchester United defender was sent off for Northern Ireland against Spain at the 1982 FIFA World Cup?

8. Who scored two minutes into his Northern Ireland debut, against Israel in September 2018?

9. Which nation did Northern Ireland lose 4-0 to in the 1958 FIFA World Cup quarter-final?

10. Who was Northern Ireland's manager at the 1982 and 1986 FIFA World Cups?

11. Which now defunct nation has Northern Ireland beaten twice at a FIFA World Cup?

12. Which player, who shares his first name with an American singer-songwriter who wrote 'Uptown Girl', scored Northern Ireland's first-ever FIFA World Cup goal?

13. Who is Northern Ireland's record scorer, netting 36 goals from 2000 to 2013?

14. What is the common name given to Northern Ireland's fans?

15. Two players with the surname Lafferty played together for Northern Ireland in 2012. Can you name them both?

16. Which former Rangers and Norwich striker scored seven goals in Northern Ireland's UEFA Euro 2016 qualifying campaign?

17. Who scored two goals against Northern Ireland for Brazil at the 1986 FIFA World Cup?

18. Which tournament did Northern Ireland win in 1984 – the last one ever held?

19. Who scored three of Northern Ireland's five goals at the 1982 FIFA World Cup?

20. Northern Ireland internationals Danny and Kevin share which surname?

21. Who scored Northern Ireland's first-ever UEFA Nations League goal, against Bosnia and Herzegovina in 2018? He has a song named after him.

22. Who scored Northern Ireland's very first UEFA European Championship goal?

23. Name either of the two players who won their 50th Northern Ireland caps against Germany in November 2019.

24. Which nation did Northern Ireland beat in their first-ever FIFA World Cup match?

25. What were the first names of the two Blanchflower brothers who both played for Northern Ireland?

26. Which former Republic of Ireland manager was Northern Ireland's captain at the 1982 FIFA World Cup?

27. Which nation did Northern Ireland lose to in the 2018 FIFA World Cup qualifying play-offs?

28. Which Englishman was Northern Ireland's manager from 1998 to 1999?

29. Which player, who shares his surname with science fiction writer Arthur C., scored a hat-trick for Northern Ireland against the Faroe Islands in September 1991?

30. Northern Ireland's David Healy was the top scorer in UEFA Euro 2008 qualification, but how many goals did he score – 13, 14 or 15?

POLAND

1. Who scored six goals in Poland's UEFA Euro 2016 qualifying campaign?

2. How many former FIFA World Cup finalists did Poland beat at the 1974 FIFA World Cup?

3. Which Caribbean island did Poland beat 7-0 at the 1974 FIFA World Cup?

4. Which goalkeeper was sent off for Poland against Greece at UEFA Euro 2012?

5. Who scored nine goals in Poland's UEFA Euro 2008 qualifying campaign?

6. Two Poles have scored in three different FIFA World Cups. Grzegorz Lato is one. Can you name the other?

7. Poland played their UEFA Euro 2012 matches in Warsaw and in which other Polish city?

8. In 1974 and in which other year did Poland finish third at the FIFA World Cup?

9. Twins Michal and Marcin both played for Poland internationally. What was their surname?

10. Who scored Poland's two goals at the 2006 FIFA World Cup, both in a 2-1 win over Costa Rica?

11. Three of Poland's 2018 FIFA World Cup squad were playing for a Serie A club in Genoa at the time. Which one?

12. Poland beat which country 10-0 in 2009 to record their biggest ever win?

13. Who scored 41 goals for Poland from 1968 to 1978 and played for Manchester City?

14. Poland won only once at the 2018 FIFA World Cup. Which country did they beat?

15. All three of Poland's goalkeepers in their UEFA Euro 2016 squad played their club football in England at some stage. Szczesny and Fabianski were two, but who was the other?

16. With which country were Poland co-hosts at UEFA Euro 2012?

17. Which former AC Milan striker scored in three of Poland's four opening UEFA Euro 2020 qualifiers?

18. Which country did Poland beat in 2016 to record their first-ever UEFA European Championship win?

19. Which defender with the initials W.Z. made a national record 21 FIFA World Cup appearances for Poland from 1974 to 1986?

20. Which country did Poland beat in the 1974 FIFA World Cup third place match?

21. Which former FIFA World Cup-winning nation did Poland eliminate in 1974 qualification?

22. Poland has beaten only one country more than once at the FIFA World Cup. Which country?

23. Who missed their penalty in Poland's UEFA Euro 2016 quarter-final shoot-out defeat to Portugal?

24. When was the last year Poland reached the knockout stage of the FIFA World Cup?

25. Which European Cup winner with Juventus in 1985 scored a hat-trick in Poland's 3-0 win over Belgium at the 1982 FIFA World Cup?

26. Who was sent off for Poland against Germany at the 2006 FIFA World Cup?

27. Who scored a hat-trick against Poland at the 1986 FIFA World Cup?

28. Who equalled a UEFA European Championship qualifying record by scoring 13 goals during 2016 qualification?

29. Father and son Wlodzimierz and Ebi both played for Poland. What was their surname?

30. In which year did Poland win the men's Olympic Games gold medal in football – 1952, 1972 or 1992?

PORTUGAL

1. Which resort city provided the southernmost venue for the 2004 UEFA European Championship in Portugal?

2. How many goals did Eusebio score when he won the Golden Boot at the 1966 FIFA World Cup?

3. Who scored Portugal's winner in the 2019 UEFA Nations League final against the Netherlands?

4. Which country did Portugal play in their first and last match at UEFA Euro 2004?

5. What FIFA World Cup record does Cristiano Ronaldo share with Pele, Uwe Seeler and Miroslav Klose?

6. What colours are their shirts and shorts in their second strip?

7. Which country has eliminated Portugal from three major tournament semi-finals?

8. Which Portuguese was the top scorer in UEFA qualification for the 2006 FIFA World Cup?

9. What was different about Portugal's result over Wales at UEFA Euro 2016 compared to their other results at the tournament?

10. Portuguese internationals Rui and Jorge share which common name?

11. Which Sporting Lisbon goalkeeper played for Portugal for 1969 to 1986 but won only 29 caps?

12. Two players named Pinto scored at UEFA Euro 96. Can you name them?

13. Who was sent off for Portugal against Spain at the 2010 FIFA World Cup?

14. Who scored a hat-trick for Portugal against Germany at UEFA Euro 2000?

15. Which country beat Portugal on penalties in the semi-final of the FIFA Confederations Cup in 2017?

16. Portugal's best FIFA World Cup finish is third, but in which year did they achieve this?

17. Which defender scored for Portugal at both UEFA Euro 2008 and UEFA Euro 2012?

18. What FIFA World Cup record does Eusebio share with Rob Rensenbrink and Gabriel Batistuta?

19. Which Portuguese striker scored at UEFA Euro 2004, 2008 and 2012, but netted only once at each tournament?

20. Who scored four goals for Portugal at UEFA Euro 2000?

21. Against which country has Portugal scored 12 goals in two FIFA World Cup matches?

22. Who was Portugal's manager at UEFA Euro 2004?

23. Which defender played for Portugal at UEFA Euro 2016 at the age of 38?

24. Which Portuguese in 2016 became the youngest ever player to appear in a UEFA European Championship final?

25. Which former FIFA World Cup runners-up did Portugal beat at the 1966 FIFA World Cup to record their first-ever win at a major tournament?

26. Which goalkeeper saved and scored a penalty against England at UEFA Euro 2004?

27. Which legendary player scored 32 goals in 127 caps for Portugal from 1991 to 2006?

28. Portugal played their UEFA Euro 2004 matches in Lisbon and in which other city?

29. At which FIFA World Cup did Portugal fail to qualify for the knockout stage despite winning their first match?

30. Who had two spells as Portugal coach, from 1991 to 1993 and from 2008 to 2010?

REPUBLIC OF IRELAND

1. In which year did the Republic of Ireland last participate at the FIFA World Cup?

2. How many of the Republic of Ireland's penalty kicks in their shoot-out defeat to Spain at the 2002 FIFA World Cup were missed?

3. Ray Houghton scored two 1-0 winners for the Republic of Ireland at major tournaments. One was against Italy at the 1994 FIFA World Cup, but who was the other against, and at which tournament?

4. How many of the Republic of Ireland's 13 FIFA World Cup matches have ended in draws (not including penalty shoot-outs)?

5. Who scored the Republic of Ireland's final two goals at UEFA Euro 2016?

6. Which Italian coached the Republic of Ireland from 2008 to 2013?

7. Who has made a national record 13 FIFA World Cup appearances for the Republic of Ireland?

8. Which central defender won 118 caps for the Republic of Ireland from 2001 to 2018?

9. Which Republic of Ireland player was sent home by manager Mick McCarthy prior to the 2002 FIFA World Cup?

10. Who was sent off for the Republic of Ireland against Italy at UEFA Euro 2012?

11. What is the name of the Republic of Ireland's national stadium?

12. Which nation controversially beat the Republic of Ireland in the 2010 FIFA World Cup qualifying play-offs?

13. Which goalkeeper played in all of the Republic of Ireland's matches at the 1990 and 1994 FIFA World Cups?

14. The Republic of Ireland has won only two FIFA World Cup matches in normal time – against Italy and which other nation?

15. How many of the players in the Republic of Ireland's starting line-up against England at the 1990 FIFA World Cup were born in the United Kingdom – seven, eight or nine?

16. The Republic of Ireland reached the quarter-finals of the 1990 FIFA World Cup without doing what?

17. Who had his penalty saved in normal time for the Republic of Ireland against Spain at the 2002 FIFA World Cup?

18. Who is the Republic of Ireland's most capped goalkeeper?

19. Who scored the Republic of Ireland's only goal at UEFA Euro 2012?

20. Only one member of the Republic of Ireland's UEFA Euro 2016 squad, Robbie Keane, was not playing their club football in England. Who was Keane playing for?

21. Which nation did the Republic of Ireland beat in the play-offs to qualify for UEFA Euro 2016?

22. Republic of Ireland internationals Steven and Andy share which surname?

23. In which Yorkshire town was Republic of Ireland manager Mick McCarthy born?

24. Who scored the Republic of Ireland's winning penalty kick in their shoot-out win over Romania at the 1990 FIFA World Cup?

25. Which country beat the Republic of Ireland in the last 16 at the 1994 FIFA World Cup?

26. Who was sent off for the Republic of Ireland against France at UEFA Euro 2016?

27. Which midfielder was the Republic of Ireland's captain at the 1994 FIFA World Cup?

28. Who scored 21 goals for the Republic of Ireland from 1986 to 2002?

29. Which winger won his 100th cap for the Republic of Ireland at UEFA Euro 2012?

30. How many goals did the Republic of Ireland score in normal time in their five matches at the 1990 FIFA World Cup?

RUSSIA
(INCORPORATING SOVIET UNION AND CIS)

1. In which year did Russia compete as CIS at the UEFA European Championship?

2. Who was sent off for Russia against Uruguay at the 2018 FIFA World Cup?

3. Which now defunct country did the Soviet Union beat in the UEFA Euro 60 final?

4. Who scored twice in Russia's opening match of the 2018 FIFA World Cup?

5. Which legendary goalkeeper played in three FIFA World Cups for the Soviet Union from 1958 to 1966?

6. In which year did the Soviet Union/CIS/Russia reach their one and only FIFA World Cup semi-final to date?

7. Who scored a record five goals in Russia's 6-1 win over Cameroon at the 1994 FIFA World Cup?

8. Which country beat Russia in the UEFA Euro 2008 semi-finals?

9. What was unusual about the Soviet Union's defeat to Italy in the UEFA Euro 68 semi-final?

10. Who scored nine goals in Russia's UEFA Euro 2020 qualifying campaign?

11. In which city did the Soviet Union lose the UEFA Euro 72 final?

12. Which country did Russia beat 9-0 in UEFA Euro 2020 qualifying to record their biggest ever win as Russia?

13. Which famous Italian coached Russia from 2012 to 2015?

14. Who scored a hat-trick in the Soviet Union's match against Belgium at the 1986 FIFA World Cup?

15. Which goalkeeper was sent off for Russia against Portugal at UEFA Euro 2004?

16. Who scored 30 goals for Russia from 2002 to 2016?

17. Two Dutchmen have coached Russia in the past. Guus Hiddink is one. But who is the other?

18. Which country beat Russia 7-1 in FIFA World Cup qualifying in October 2004, with Petit amongst the scorers with two?

19. Who scored for Russia after just 67 seconds against Greece at UEFA Euro 2004?

20. Russia lost only once in normal time at the 2018 FIFA World Cup, but to which country?

21. To which country did the Soviet Union lose in the UEFA Euro 72 final?

22. Who scored three of Russia's five goals at UEFA Euro 2012?

23. Who scored four of Russia's six goals at the 1970 FIFA World Cup?

24. The last time Russia beat a European country in normal time at the FIFA World Cup was back in 1986. Against which former FIFA World Cup runners-up?

25. Who coached Russia to the semi-finals at UEFA Euro 2008?

26. Who scored four goals for Russia over two UEFA European Championships (2008 and 2012)?

27. Which former Chelsea player was sent off for Russia against Mexico in the 2017 FIFA Confederations Cup?

28. Which defender is Russia's most capped player, winning 127 caps from 2002 to 2018?

29. What is the surname of the twins Aleksei and Vasili who were both Russian internationals?

30. Prior to 2018, when was the last year that Russia/Soviet Union/CIS reached the FIFA World Cup knockout stage?

SCOTLAND

1. When was the last year Scotland participated at the FIFA World Cup?

2. Who is the only man to have won over 100 caps for Scotland?

3. What is the name of Scotland's national stadium?

4. To which country did Scotland lose in their opening match at both the Women's UEFA Euro 2017 and 2019 FIFA Women's World Cup?

5. Who scored twice in Scotland's 3-2 win over the Netherlands at the 1978 FIFA World Cup?

6. What flower is depicted on the national team's emblem?

7. Who was sent off for Scotland against Morocco at the 1998 FIFA World Cup?

8. Which goalkeeper has made a national record nine FIFA World Cup appearances for Scotland?

9. Which unwanted FIFA World Cup record does Scotland hold?

10. Who scored Scotland's only goal at UEFA Euro 96?

11. Scotland has failed to beat countries from which continent in eight previous FIFA World Cup matches?

12. Kenny and Willie, who both won over 60 caps for Scotland, share which surname?

13. In which year did England and Scotland play the world's first international match?

14. Who had a penalty saved in the Scotland against England match at UEFA Euro 96?

15. Kenny Dalglish shares the record for most goals for Scotland with which other player?

16. Scotland's last FIFA World Cup win came in 1990, but against which country?

17. Which former German FIFA World Cup winner was Scotland's manager from 2002 to 2004?

18. Who scored two hat-tricks in Scotland's UEFA Euro 2016 qualifying campaign?

19. What is the name of Archie Gemmill's son, who also played for Scotland?

20. What animal is depicted on the national team's emblem?

21. Who is the only man to have scored for Scotland at three different FIFA World Cups?

22. Which goalkeeper, born in Sutton, England, won 28 caps for Scotland?

23. Which two players scored on their debuts in a UEFA Euro 2020 qualifier against San Marino in October 2019?

24. Who was Scotland's manager at the 1986 FIFA World Cup?

25. Which tournament did Scotland win on 24 occasions, most recently in 1977?

26. Two former Scotland managers Brown and Levein share which first name?

27. Three of Scotland's 1998 FIFA World Cup squad played for a Lancashire club. Which one?

28. Scotland has won only twice at the UEFA European Championship. Name either of the countries they have beaten.

29. Who scored a hat-trick in Scotland's 6-0 win over San Marino in October 2019?

30. What are the Scotland supporters collectively known as?

SPAIN

1. In which year did Spain reach its first-ever FIFA World Cup semi-final?

2. Who scored nine FIFA World Cup goals for Spain from 2006 to 2014?

3. Which country did Spain beat 6-1 at the 1998 FIFA World Cup?

4. Spain won the 2010 FIFA World Cup despite losing their opening match to which country?

5. Which goalkeeper played 16 FIFA World Cup matches for Spain from 1986 to 1998?

6. Who played for Spain in two FIFA World Cups in the 1980s and managed the side at the 2002 FIFA World Cup?

7. Who scored four goals in Spain's 5-1 win over Denmark at the 1986 FIFA World Cup?

8. By what score did Spain, the defending champions at the time, lose to the Netherlands at the 2014 FIFA World Cup?

9. Which island country did Spain beat 10-0 at the 2013 FIFA Confederations Cup?

10. In which Spanish city did Spain play their 1982 FIFA World Cup group stage matches?

11. Which former captain scored ten penalties for Spain in an international career from 1989 to 2002?

12. Who scored on his international debut for Spain after coming on as a substitute against England in November 2016?

13. Who scored three goals for Spain at the 2019 FIFA Women's World Cup?

14. Which former Barcelona striker was sent off for Spain against Bulgaria at Euro 96?

15. Spain has won only one penalty shoot-out at a FIFA World Cup. Against which country?

16. Which country did Spain lose to in the 2013 FIFA Confederations Cup final?

17. In which year did Spain host the European Championship for the first, and so far only, time?

18. Spain has lost two quarter-final penalty shoot-outs to host countries at major tournaments. Korea Republic at the 2002 FIFA World Cup is one. Name the other country.

19. Which classy midfielder won 131 caps for Spain from 2006 to 2018?

20. Which country beat Spain in a quarter-final penalty shoot-out at the 1986 FIFA World Cup?

21. Who scored seven goals for Spain in the 2018-19 season?

22. Which country eliminated Spain from the 1934 and 1994 FIFA World Cups, as well as at Euro 2016?

23. Who scored for Spain in the final at both UEFA Euro 2008 and UEFA Euro 2012?

24. In which year did Spain first reach number one in the FIFA World Rankings – 1994, 2002 or 2008?

25. Between November 2007 and June 2009 Spain was unbeaten, but for how many games – 25, 35 or 45?

26. Which South American country did Spain beat in their first-ever FIFA World Cup match in 1934?

27. Who scored a hat-trick in Spain's win over Korea Republic at the 1990 FIFA World Cup?

28. In which city did Spain win the Euro 2008 final?

29. Which country did Spain lose to in the round of 16 at the 2019 FIFA Women's World Cup?

30. Which country did Spain beat in the UEFA Euro 64 final?

SWEDEN

1. Who won a record 148 caps for Sweden from 1999 to 2013?

2. In which major tournament was Sweden eliminated despite not losing any of their four matches in normal time?

3. Who scored six UEFA European Championship goals for Sweden but never scored in the FIFA World Cup?

4. Which African country eliminated Sweden at the 2002 FIFA World Cup?

5. Which Swede was President of UEFA for 27 years?

6. In which year did Sweden lose all of their matches at a FIFA World Cup?

7. Which nation did Sweden beat on penalties in the 1994 FIFA World Cup quarter-final?

8. Who scored in three of Sweden's four matches at UEFA Euro 92?

9. Which player, who shares his first name with a type of children's bear, was sent off for Sweden against Germany at the 2006 FIFA World Cup?

10. Which former Dortmund striker became Sweden's youngest scorer when he netted against Slovakia in 2017 at the age of 17 years, three months and 22 days?

11. Who scored two penalties for Sweden at the 2018 FIFA World Cup?

12. In which year did Sweden win the men's Olympic Games football tournament in London?

13. Who is the only man to have scored for Sweden in three different FIFA World Cups?

14. In which year did Sweden finish runners-up in the FIFA Women's World Cup?

15. Which English manager was in charge when Sweden finished runners-up at the 1958 FIFA World Cup?

16. Which coach led Sweden to third place at the 1994 FIFA World Cup?

17. Which South American country did Sweden beat to win their first-ever FIFA World Cup match in 1934?

18. Who scored five goals for Sweden at the 1994 FIFA World Cup?

19. Which European country eliminated Sweden from the 1934 and 2006 FIFA World Cups?

20. Which former AC Milan player scored for Sweden in the 1958 FIFA World Cup final at the age of 35?

21. Which nation did they beat in the third place match at the 2019 FIFA Women's World Cup?

22. Which island country did Sweden beat 8-0 at the 1938 FIFA World Cup?

23. Who top scored for Sweden in UEFA Euro 2020 qualification with five goals?

24. How many goals did Swedish players score in their three matches at UEFA Euro 2016?

25. In which year did Sweden host the UEFA European Championship?

26. How many of Sweden's 2018 FIFA World Cup squad played their club football in Sweden?

27. Who is Sweden's most capped goalkeeper, winning 143 caps from 1981 to 1997?

28. Who made a record 13 FIFA World Cup appearances for Sweden?

29. Which player, who shares his first name with a famous Swedish tennis player, captained Sweden on 92 occasions from 1967 to 1978?

30. Who played for Sweden at the 1978 FIFA World Cup and was then their manager at the 1990 FIFA World Cup?

SWITZERLAND

1. Who was the only member of Switzerland's 2018 FIFA World Cup squad who was playing their club football in Switzerland (for Basel)?

2. In which year did Switzerland host the FIFA World Cup?

3. Who won his 100th cap for Switzerland in June 2018?

4. Who scored Switzerland's decisive goal in their win over Northern Ireland in the 2018 FIFA World Cup play-offs?

5. Who is Switzerland's record goalscorer, netting 42 goals from 2001 to 2011?

6. Which Englishman coached Switzerland from 1992 to 1995?

7. Which is the only non-European country to have eliminated Switzerland in the knockout stage of a major tournament?

8. Switzerland had two players sent off at UEFA Euro 2004. Name either.

9. Switzerland played who in the opening match at UEFA Euro 96?

10. Which Swiss became the youngest ever scorer at the UEFA European Championship in 2004, netting against France at the age of 18 years and 141 days?

11. Switzerland failed to win any of their opening eight UEFA European Championship matches. Which country did they finally beat in 2008?

12. Which striker with the initials E.D. scored a hat-trick in Switzerland's 5-3 friendly win over Germany in 2012?

13. Who scored a hat-trick in Switzerland's 5-2 win over Belgium in the UEFA Nations League in November 2018?

14. What was the surname of the brothers Max and Andre who scored 63 goals for Switzerland between them?

15. Which country were Switzerland's co-hosts at the 2008 UEFA European Championship?

16. Who was Switzerland's manager from 2008 to 2014?

17. Which country did Xherdan Shaqiri score a hat-trick for Switzerland against at the 2014 FIFA World Cup?

18. Switzerland was eliminated by which country in a penalty shoot-out at UEFA Euro 2016?

19. Who played for Switzerland at the 1966 FIFA World Cup and also coached them at the 2006 FIFA World Cup?

20. Which player, who shares his first name with a famous German goalkeeper from the 1970s, scored six goals for Switzerland at the 1954 FIFA World Cup?

21. One of Switzerland's nicknames is Rossocrociati. What does this mean in English?

22. Which former Lazio, West Ham and Napoli midfielder was sent off for Switzerland against Chile at the 2010 FIFA World Cup?

23. Which Austrian, who shares his first name with the famous fashion designer Lagerfeld, was Switzerland's manager at three FIFA World Cups, in 1938, 1954 and 1962?

24. Switzerland won twice at the 1954 FIFA World Cup – against which country on both occasions?

25. What was the surname of the brothers Hakan and Murat who played together for Switzerland at the 2004 UEFA European Championship?

26. Alexander Frei and which Zaire-born striker, who shares his first name with a 2018 FIFA World Cup winner, scored five goals in 2010 FIFA World Cup qualifying?

27. Eleven of the 23 players in Switzerland's UEFA Euro 2016 squad played their club football in which country?

28. How many penalties did Switzerland score in their shoot-out against Ukraine at the 2006 FIFA World Cup?

29. Who missed the decisive penalty in Switzerland's penalty shoot-out defeat to England in the 2019 UEFA Nations League third place match?

30. What was the surname of the twins Philipp and David who both played for Switzerland?

TURKEY

1. Which country did Turkey beat 3-2 after being two goals behind at UEFA Euro 2008?

2. Who in 2002 scored for Turkey 11 seconds after kick-off to record the fastest ever FIFA World Cup goal?

3. Which nation has Turkey beaten twice at the FIFA World Cup – in 1954 to record their first-ever win in the tournament and in 2002 in the third place match?

4. Who scored Turkey's golden goal against Senegal at the 2002 FIFA World Cup?

5. In which year did Turkey finish third in the FIFA Confederations Cup?

6. Which former Atletico Madrid and Barcelona midfielder captained Turkey at UEFA Euro 2016?

7. At which major tournament did Turkey lose all three matches and fail to score?

8. Who scored in three of Turkey's five matches at UEFA Euro 2008?

9. When was the last time Turkey participated at a FIFA World Cup?

10. Which country did Turkey lose to in the UEFA Euro 2008 semi-final?

11. Which midfielder made his Turkey debut in 2000 and won his 100th cap in 2019?

12. Who coached Turkey to third place at the 2002 FIFA World Cup?

13. Who scored five goals in Turkey's 2018 FIFA World Cup qualifying campaign?

14. Which country has twice inflicted an 8-0 defeat on Turkey, back in 1984 and in 1987?

15. What two objects from the sky are depicted on Turkey's national emblem?

16. Which Dutchman was briefly Turkey's coach from 2010 to 2011?

17. Which goalkeeper is Turkey's most capped player, winning 120 caps from 1994 to 2012?

18. Turkey qualified for the 1950 FIFA World Cup but were forced to withdraw. Why?

19. Which former Besiktas and Aston Villa defender was sent off for Turkey at UEFA Euro 2000 and at the 2002 FIFA World Cup?

20. Which country did Turkey beat in the UEFA Euro 2000 qualifying play-offs?

21. Which goalkeeper was sent off for Turkey against the Czech Republic at UEFA Euro 2008?

22. Turkey has won all of its matches against Asian countries at the FIFA World Cup. Korea Republic and China are two countries they've beaten. Who is the other?

23. Which country has beaten Turkey on three occasions at the UEFA European Championship – in 1996, 2000 and 2008?

24. Who has had four spells as Turkey's coach, most recently from 2013 to 2017?

25. Which country beat Turkey 1-0 at both UEFA Euro 96 and at UEFA Euro 2016?

26. Which former Galatasaray striker missed a penalty for Turkey against Portugal at UEFA Euro 2000?

27. Who scored seven goals in Turkey's 2006 FIFA World Cup qualifying campaign?

28. Burhan Sargun is the only Turk to have done what at a major tournament, doing so against the Korea Republic at the 1954 FIFA World Cup?

29. Who scored twice for Turkey near the end of the game against the Czech Republic at UEFA Euro 2008?

30. Which country beat Turkey twice at the 1954 FIFA World Cup, scoring 11 goals against them in the process?

UKRAINE

1. Which player with the initials V.V. was sent off for Ukraine against Spain at the 2006 FIFA World Cup?

2. Who is Ukraine's most capped player, winning 144 caps from 2000 to 2016?

3. Which country beginning with the letter 'S' did Ukraine beat in the UEFA Euro 2016 qualifying play-offs?

4. Which goalkeeper started all of Ukraine's 2006 FIFA World Cup matches?

5. In which city did Ukraine play two of their three matches at UEFA Euro 2012?

6. In which year did Ukraine play its first international – 1990, 1991 or 1992?

7. Who scored a hat-trick in Ukraine's 8-0 win in San Marino in October 2013?

8. Only one member of Ukraine's UEFA Euro 2016 squad played his club football west of Turkey (for Sevilla). Who was he?

9. Which UEFA Nations League group did Ukraine win in 2018?

10. Who scored Ukraine's first-ever FIFA World Cup goal, against Saudi Arabia in 2006?

11. Which stadium has Ukraine played the most internationals in?

12. Which former UEFA European Championship winners did Ukraine lose to in the 2010 FIFA World Cup qualifying play-offs?

13. Which legendary Ukrainian manager coached the Soviet Union on three occasions, as well as Ukraine, and has a stadium named after him?

14. Which major youth tournament did Ukraine win in 2019?

15. In which major youth tournament did they finish runners-up to the Netherlands in 2006?

16. Which former Liverpool player won 74 caps for Ukraine from 2002 to 2012?

17. Who top scored for Ukraine in their UEFA Euro 2020 qualifying group stage campaign with four goals?

18. Who in 2019 became Ukraine's most capped goalkeeper?

19. Which former Tottenham player scored 15 goals in 75 caps for Ukraine from 1992 to 2006?

20. How many goals did Ukraine score at UEFA Euro 2016?

21. What colour is Ukraine's first-choice kit?

22. Who scored both of Ukraine's goals at UEFA Euro 2012?

23. In which country will Ukraine play two of their three group stage matches at UEFA Euro 2020?

24. Which former Soviet Union international striker was Ukraine's coach when they reached the quarter-finals of the 2006 FIFA World Cup?

25. Which country did Ukraine lose to in the 2014 FIFA World Cup qualifying play-offs?

26. Who scored Ukraine's final penalty in their shoot-out win over Switzerland at the 2006 FIFA World Cup?

27. Which Ukrainian international defender joined Manchester City in 2016?

28. Which country did Ukraine lose 4-0 to in their opening match at the 2006 FIFA World Cup?

29. Which former Arsenal defender captained Ukraine on 39 occasions?

30. Which former Dortmund player scored six goals in Ukraine's 2018 FIFA World Cup qualifying campaign?

URUGUAY

1. Which Uruguayan finished joint top scorer at the 2010 FIFA World Cup with five goals?

2. In terms of size what FIFA World Cup record does Uruguay hold?

3. Two of Uruguay's defenders in their 2018 FIFA World Cup squad played for which Spanish club?

4. Who scored Uruguay's final three goals at the 2018 FIFA World Cup?

5. What new FIFA World Cup record did Uruguay set in 2010?

6. Which Asian nation did Uruguay beat in the 2014 FIFA World Cup Inter-confederation play-offs?

7. Uruguay last beat a fellow South American nation at the FIFA World Cup in 1962. Which nation did they beat?

8. Uruguay's Jose Batista holds the record for the fastest sending off in FIFA World Cup history in 1986. After how many seconds was he dismissed – 49, 56 or 67?

9. Who is only man to have coached Uruguay in over 50 internationals?

10. Which player, who shares his first name with a famous movie award, scored eight FIFA World Cup goals for Uruguay from 1950 to 1954?

11. Which tournament did Uruguay win in 1980 to commemorate the 50th anniversary of the first FIFA World Cup?

12. Who was Uruguay's 1950 FIFA World Cup-winning captain?

13. Which country beat Uruguay in the 1970 and 2010 FIFA World Cup third place matches?

14. Who was sent off for Uruguay against Costa Rica at the 2014 FIFA World Cup?

15. Who scored in every game for Uruguay at the 1950 FIFA World Cup?

16. What did Uruguay achieve in both the 2010 and 2018 FIFA World Cup group stages?

17. Which former Argentine FIFA World Cup-winning captain coached Uruguay from 2000 to 2001?

18. Uruguay has won all of its four FIFA World Cup matches against countries from which continent?

19. Uruguay lost their semi-final and third place match at the 2010 FIFA World Cup by what same scoreline?

20. When was the last year Uruguay did not participate in a FIFA World Cup?

21. Which former Atletico Madrid defender captained Uruguay at the 2018 FIFA World Cup?

22. Which goalkeeper made 16 FIFA World Cup appearances for Uruguay from 2010 to 2018?

23. Uruguay has won two gold medals in the Olympic Games men's football tournament. In which decade did they win both?

24. What is the name of Uruguay's national stadium?

25. What did Uruguay achieve for the first time ever in the group stage at the 2018 FIFA World Cup?

26. Uruguay was unbeaten in their first eleven FIFA World Cup matches. Which former FIFA World Cup runners-up eventually beat them for the first time in 1954?

27. Against which country did Uruguay come back from three goals down to draw 3-3 at the 2002 FIFA World Cup?

28. Uruguay has been eliminated by the eventual champions in the FIFA World Cup knockout stage on three occasions. Which of these nations eliminated them from the last 16?

29. Which country has Uruguay faced in three of their last four FIFA World Cup appearances, and has failed to score against them in this time?

30. Uruguay's nickname is 'La Celeste'. What is this translated into English?

USA

1. What is the common name of the biennial football championship of North America, Central America and the Caribbean that the USA compete in?

2. Which American has made the most ever FIFA Women's World Cup appearances with 30?

3. Which 18-year-old scored the 1-0 winner against Costa Rica on his international debut for the United States in February 2020?

4. Which country did the USA lose 3-2 to in the 2009 FIFA Confederations Cup final despite being two goals ahead?

5. Who won 164 caps for the USA men's team from 1992 to 2004?

6. The USA had two players sent off against Italy at the 2006 FIFA World Cup. Can you name either?

7. In which stadium did the USA play two of their three group stage matches at the 1994 FIFA World Cup?

8. Which American won the Golden Boot and Golden Ball at the 2019 FIFA Women's World Cup?

9. Which nation did the USA lose to in their final match of their 2018 FIFA World Cup qualifying campaign – a result which meant they did not reach the finals?

10. Who scored the USA's only goal at the 1998 FIFA World Cup?

11. In which year did the USA finish third at the FIFA World Cup?

12. Who scored in the USA's opening two FIFA World Cup matches in 2014?

13. Which American was top scorer at the 1991 FIFA Women's World Cup with ten goals?

14. Which country were the USA's first FIFA World Cup opponents in 1930, and also their most recent opponents in 2014?

15. Who played in a national record four FIFA World Cups for the USA from 2002 to 2014?

16. Who has scored the most FIFA World Cup goals for the USA with five?

17. Which neighbouring country has the USA played the most internationals against?

18. Which country did the USA famously beat 1-0 at the 1950 FIFA World Cup?

19. Who was the USA's first-choice goalkeeper at the 2010 and 2014 FIFA World Cups?

20. Who has scored the most goals for the USA at the FIFA Women's World Cup with 14 goals?

21. Who is the only man to have coached the USA at two FIFA World Cups?

22. Since 2002 the USA's only two FIFA World Cup wins have come against African nations. Can you name either of the African nations they have beaten?

23. Since 1950 the USA has beaten only one European nation at the FIFA World Cup. Which nation?

24. In which stadium did the USA win the 2012 Olympic Games women's football final?

25. The USA will co-host the 2026 FIFA World Cup with two other nations – name either.

26. Two of the USA's FIFA World Cup wins have come in which South American city?

27. Who scored five goals in USA's 13-0 win over Thailand at the 2019 Women's World Cup?

28. The USA has lost all three matches at a FIFA World Cup on two occasions – in 1998 and in which other year?

29. The USA has never won a FIFA World Cup match in Europe – true or false?

30. Which Caribbean country did the USA beat in the 2017 Gold Cup final?

WALES

1. In which year did Wales make their first, and so far only, appearance at a FIFA World Cup?

2. Which Northern Ireland player scored an own goal to hand Wales their win at UEFA Euro 2016?

3. What is Wales's nickname?

4. Against which Asian nation did Gareth Bale score a hat-trick for Wales in March 2018?

5. Which two players with the surname Charles played for Wales at the 1958 FIFA World Cup?

6. Which are the only two nations Wales has played more than 100 internationals against?

7. Who scored twice in Wales's only FIFA World Cup appearance?

8. Who was the last non-Welshman to manage Wales?

9. Whose Wales international career spanned 25 years, from 1895 to 1920?

10. Name either of the two players who scored four goals in Wales's UEFA Euro 2004 qualifying campaign. One was playing for Celtic at the time, while the other was playing for Tottenham.

11. Which two Wales players with the surname Williams played for them at UEFA Euro 2016?

12. Which now defunct nation did Wales lose to in the UEFA Euro 76 qualifying quarter-finals?

13. Whose Wales national goalscoring record did Gareth Bale surpass in 2018?

14. Which tournament did Wales win on 12 occasions?

15. Which Wales legend managed his country alongside Mark Hughes for one match as caretaker manager in 1999?

16. Who scored Wales's opening goal in their UEFA Euro 2016 win over Russia?

17. Former Wales internationals Bryn and Cliff share which surname?

18. Which two former Wales managers had the first name Mike?

19. Which is the only nation Wales has beaten in a FIFA World Cup match?

20. Which player, who shares his surname with a famous Welsh rugby union player called Gareth, once scored four goals in Wales's 7-0 win over Malta in 1978?

21. Which country did Wales beat 4-1 in their first-ever UEFA Nations League match in 2018?

22. Which former Norwich and Nottingham Forest striker scored a hat-trick in Wales's 4-0 friendly win over Scotland in February 2004?

23. In which Welsh town did they beat England 4-1 in 1980?

24. Who scored in both of Wales's wins against Slovakia and Belgium at UEFA Euro 2016?

25. Only two of Wales's squad members at UEFA Euro 2016 played their club football in Wales. Can you name them both?

26. Which Liverpool youth player made his Wales debut at the age of 16 years and 207 days in 2013?

27. Who scored Wales's first-ever goal at a major tournament?

28. Which man, who shares his surname with an actor in the film *Beverly Hills Cop*, was Wales's manager at the 1958 FIFA World Cup?

29. Who came on as a substitute to score in Wales's UEFA Euro 2016 quarter-final win over Belgium?

30. Which player who won the League and Cup double with Tottenham in 1961 scored Wales's 2-1 winner against Hungary at the 1958 FIFA World Cup?

OTHER AFRICAN NATIONS

1. Which nation did Egypt beat in the 2010 Africa Cup of Nations final?

2. Which two-time FIFA World Cup semi-finalist as a player with France has been manager of Mali, Senegal and Tunisia?

3. Mohamed Kader scored which African nation's only previous FIFA World Cup goal, against the Korea Republic in 2006?

4. Which nation lost 1-0 to a Lothar Matthaus goal against Germany at the 1986 FIFA World Cup?

5. Which is the only nation to have reached the FIFA Women's World Cup quarter-final?

6. Which African nation did Brazilian Carlos Alberto Parreira manage over two spells?

7. Which country produced the 1995 FIFA World Cup Player of the Year?

8. Which nation is Pierre-Emerick Aubameyang the record goalscorer of?

9. Which nation's nickname is 'The Wild Beasts'?

10. Who is the Ivory Coast's all-time record goalscorer with 65 goals?

11. The man who scored the 1-0 winner in the 1973 FA Cup final went on to manage Zambia and Zimbabwe. Can you name him?

12. Which nation lost to England in the last 16 of the 2019 Women's World Cup?

13. Which North African nation plays its home matches at the Stade Olympique de Rades?

14. Which former Paris St Germain player is Benin's most capped player and record goalscorer?

15. In which year did Angola play at the FIFA World Cup?

16. Which nation is Peter Ndlovu the most capped player and record goalscorer of?

17. In which year was the first Africa Cup of Nations held – 1957, 1967 or 1977?

18. Which Central African nation's nickname is 'The Cranes'?

19. Which African nation has played in the most FIFA World Cups with seven appearances?

20. Which nation will host the 2023 Africa Cup of Nations?

21. Which nation beginning with the letter 'S' won the 1970 Africa Cup of Nations on home soil?

22. Name three of the six African nations Henri Michel has coached in his career.

23. What is the nickname of South Africa's men's football team?

24. Which former English Premier League striker scored South Africa's first-ever FIFA World Cup goal, against Denmark in 1998?

25. Which Mali international had spells in the English Premier League with West Ham and Tottenham?

26. Which African nation has yet to record a win in seven previous FIFA World Cup matches?

27. Which North African nation qualified for the FIFA World Cup knockout stage for the first time in 2014?

28. Which Central African nation plays its home matches at the Stade des Martyrs?

29. Which African nation was Sven-Goran Eriksson manager of in 2010?

30. Which two nations contested the 2019 Africa Cup of Nations final?

OTHER ASIAN NATIONS

1. Which former Belgian international player and manager had a brief spell as Iran's boss in 2019?

2. Which South-East Asian nation plays its home matches at the My Dinh National Stadium?

3. In which year did Iraq win the Asian Cup – 2007, 2011 or 2015?

4. Which Asian nation has the nickname 'The Cedars'?

5. Which three nations did China lose to at the 2002 FIFA World Cup?

6. Name either of the two Asian nations that former Tottenham player Graham Roberts was manager of.

7. For the first time in FIFA Women's World Cup history no Asian nation qualified for the quarter-finals in 2019 – true or false?

8. Which nation won the Asian Cup for the first time in 2019?

9. In which year did the United Arab Emirates participate in the FIFA World Cup?

10. Which two Asian nations played the bronze medal match at the 2012 Olympic Games men's tournament and who won the bronze medal?

11. Which nation reached the round of 16 in its first-ever Asian Cup in 2019?

12. Which Asian nation has Javad Nekounam as its most capped player with 151 caps?

13. Which Asian nation lost 7-0 to Portugal at the 2010 FIFA World Cup?

14. Which nation did North Korea famously beat at the 1966 FIFA World Cup?

15. German Bernd Stange has managed four Asian nations. Can you name two of them?

16. Which was the only Asian nation to reach the knockout stage at the 2018 FIFA World Cup?

17. Which Qatar player with the same second name as the most famous heavyweight boxer in history was top scorer at the 2019 Asian Cup with nine goals?

18. Which nation beginning with the letter K won the 1980 Asian Cup on home soil?

19. Which Iranian player appeared in his fourth Asian Cup tournament in 2019?

20. Which Asian nation has the nickname 'The Green Falcons'?

21. Ahmed Khalil scored 16 goals in 2018 FIFA World Cup qualifying for which Asian nation?

22. Which former England captain was manager of Thailand from 2009 to 2011?

23. Hamza Al-Dardour scored four goals for which nation in a 5-1 win over Palestine at the 2015 Asian Cup?

24. Which nation will host the Asian Cup in 2023?

25. Who won 184 caps for Egypt from 1995 to 2012?

26. Which nation beat China in the final of the women's football tournament at the 1996 Olympic Games?

27. Who scored 109 goals for Iran from 1993 to 2006?

28. Which nation, now part of UEFA, won the Asian Cup in 1964?

29. Which South American country did Saudi Arabia lose to in the 1992 FIFA Confederations Cup final?

30. Which Asian nation beginning with the letter O plays its home matches at the Sultan Qaboos Sports Complex?

OTHER EUROPEAN NATIONS

1. What is the name of Norway international Erling Braut Haaland's father, who played in England for Nottingham Forest, Leeds United and Manchester City?

2. Which European nation was managed by John Toshack from 2011 to 2012?

3. Who scored Albania's only goal at UEFA Euro 2016?

4. Which UEFA European Championship-winning nation did Bosnia & Herzegovina lose to in the UEFA Euro 2012 qualifying play-offs?

5. Which island nation play their home matches at the GSP Stadium?

6. Which nation joined UEFA in 1994, having previously been part of the Oceania and Asian Football Confederations?

7. Who scored ten goals in Finland's UEFA Euro 2020 qualifying campaign?

8. Which nation competed in UEFA European Championship qualification for the first time in 2019?

9. Michael Mifsud is the all-time leading appearance-maker and record goalscorer for which European nation?

10. Which European nation has competed in the most FIFA World Cup qualifying campaigns without ever making it to the finals?

11. In which year did Romania reach the UEFA European Championship quarter-finals?

12. Which European nation played its first international in November 2013?

13. Which European nation is nicknamed 'La Serenissima'?

14. Which Baltic nation plays its home matches at the Lillekula Stadium?

15. Who scored ten goals in Serbia's UEFA Euro 2020 qualifying campaign?

16. In which city did Iceland beat England at UEFA Euro 2016?

17. Which European nation did David Beckham make his England debut against in 1996?

18. In which year did Latvia compete in the UEFA European Championship?

19. Which nation did Kazakhstan beat 3-0 at the start of their UEFA Euro 2020 qualifying campaign?

20. Which nation beat Moldova in October 2019 to claim its first-ever UEFA European Championship qualifying win?

21. Which European nation reached the last 16 in its FIFA World Cup and UEFA European Championship debuts in 2010 and 2016 respectively?

22. Which nation finished runners-up to Kosovo in UEFA Nations League Group D3 in 2018 and was promoted to League C?

23. In which year did Belarus play its first international – 1992, 1993 or 1994?

24. Which European nation beginning with the letter L plays its home matches at the Rheinpark Stadion?

25. Which European nation has Henrikh Mkhitaryan as its all-time leading scorer?

26. Which European country reached its first FIFA World Cup in 2002, losing to Spain, South Africa and Paraguay?

27. Which nation won five and drew one of its six matches in UEFA Nations League D1 in 2018?

28. Which European nation usually plays its home internationals in the city of Podgorica?

29. Which former Celtic and Aston Villa midfielder is Bulgaria's most capped player, winning 105 caps from 1998 to 2013?

30. Which former Ballon d'Or winner was manager of the Faroe Islands for seven years?

OTHER NORTH AMERICAN NATIONS

1. Which nation's nickname is 'The Canal Men'?

2. In which year did Canada finish fourth at the FIFA Women's World Cup – 1995, 1999 or 2003?

3. Who scored Jamaica's first-ever FIFA World Cup goal?

4. Which former Trinidad & Tobago international who also played for Porto and Rangers was appointed Barbados manager in 2019?

5. Which CONCACAF nation has the most words in it?

6. Which Canadian scored at her fifth FIFA Women's World Cup in 2019?

7. Deon McCaulay was the top scorer in CONCACAF 2014 World Cup qualifying with 11 goals. Which nation did he represent?

8. What does CONCACAF stand for?

9. Which nation plays its home matches at the Andre Kamperveen Stadion in Paramaribo?

10. Which nation beat the United States in a penalty shoot-out in the quarter-finals at the 2016 Olympic Games women's football tournament?

11. Which former Nottingham Forest, Birmingham, Coventry and Southampton striker is Trinidad and Tobago's record goalscorer?

12. Which nation has Maynor Figueroa as its most capped player?

13. Who scored Panama's first-ever FIFA World Cup goal in 2018?

14. Which nation lost 10-1 at the 1982 FIFA World Cup?

15. In which year did Jamaica first compete at the FIFA World Cup?

16. In which city did the 2015 FIFA Women's World Cup final take place?

17. Jonathan David won the Golden Boot at the 2019 CONCACAF Gold Cup. Which country does he represent?

18. Which Caribbean island beginning with the letter 'A' lost 15-0 to Trinidad and Tobago in November 2019?

19. Which nation plays its home matches at the Hasely Crawford Stadium?

20. Which three nations co-hosted the 2019 CONCACAF Gold Cup?

21. Phil Woosnam had a brief spell as the United States manager in 1968. Who is his famous cousin?

22. Which medal did Canada win at the 2012 and 2016 Olympic Games women's football tournaments?

23. Which Caribbean island beginning with the letter H won the CONCACAF Championship in 1973?

24. Which nation has won the most CONCACAF Gold Cups?

25. Who captained Trinidad & Tobago at the 2006 FIFA World Cup?

26. Carlos Ruiz was the top scorer in CONCACAF 2018 World Cup qualifying with nine goals. Which nation did he represent?

27. Which nation beat Scotland in their first-ever FIFA World Cup match in 1990?

28. Which women's national team is known as the 'Reggae Girlz'?

29. Which CONCACAF nation reached the semi-finals at the 2016 Olympic Games men's football tournament?

30. Which nation's nickname is 'The Lions of the Caribbean'?

OTHER SOUTH AMERICAN NATIONS

1. Which South American nation plays its home matches at the Estadio Olimpico Atahualpa in Quito?

2. Which is the only CONMEBOL nation to have not played at the FIFA World Cup?

3. Which South American country won its 15th Copa America in 2011?

4. Which South American nation plays its home matches at the Estadio Defensores del Chaco in Asuncion?

5. Who scored ten FIFA World Cup goals for Peru?

6. Renato Tapia was the only member of Peru's 2018 FIFA World Cup squad that was playing his club football in the Netherlands. Which club was he playing for?

7. Who was the top scorer in CONMEBOL 2018 World Cup qualifying with ten goals?

8. Which South American country has yet to win any of its six FIFA World Cup matches, drawing one and losing the other five?

9. Which Asian nation did Uruguay beat in the AFC-CONMEBOL FIFA World Cup play-off in 2014?

10. Which South American nation is nicknamed 'The Green'?

11. How many South American nations are there in CONMEBOL?

12. Who was manager of Argentina at the 2006 FIFA World Cup and was boss of Colombia at the 2014 and 2018 FIFA World Cups?

13. Which South American nation played in its first-ever FIFA Women's World Cup in 2019?

14. Which nation did Uruguay lose to in a penalty shoot-out in the OFC-CONMEBOL FIFA World Cup play-off in 2006?

15. Which South American nation lost its first two FIFA World Cup matches 4-0 in 1930?

16. Which Colombian was the top scorer at the 2014 FIFA World Cup?

17. Which player, who shares his surname with a famous Chilean player, has scored Bolivia's only FIFA World Cup goal, doing so against Spain in 1994?

18. Two of Panama's 2018 FIFA World Cup squad were on the books of which Belgian top division club at the time?

19. Which South American nation lost only one of their 18 FIFA World Cup qualifiers in the 2002 qualifying campaign?

20. For which South American nation is Salomon Rondon record goalscorer?

21. Which nation did Peru beat in the OFC-CONMEBOL FIFA World Cup play-off in 2018?

22. Which former Bayern Munich striker is Paraguay's record goalscorer?

23. Which player with a distinctive hairstyle won 111 caps for Colombia from 1985 to 1998?

24. Which player, who shares his surname with a Spanish city, scored all of Ecuador's goals at the 2014 FIFA World Cup?

25. Chile failed to qualify for the 2018 FIFA World Cup by losing 3-0 to which nation in the final round of qualifying?

26. Who was the top scorer in CONMEBOL 2014 World Cup qualifying with 11 goals?

27. Which South American nation was Marcelo Bielsa manager of from 2007 to 2011?

28. Can you name the only member of Colombia's 2018 FIFA World Cup squad that was on Barcelona's books at the time?

29. Which nation did Ecuador lose to in their only previous FIFA World Cup knockout stage match?

30. Which South American nation is nicknamed 'The Coffee Growers'?

LEGENDARY PLAYERS

Pele, Maradona, Cruyff, Messi, Ronaldo… the list goes on and on, but these are players who are known and revered in every corner of the globe, simply because of the feats they have performed on the football pitch. This section celebrates the greatest footballers to have ever played the game, and you will have to be an expert on all of their greatest achievements – both on and off the pitch – if you are to answer everything correctly.

ALFREDO DI STEFANO

1. Which three countries did he win caps for?

2. Apart from Real Madrid, with which other Spanish club did he have more than one spell as manager?

3. With which Argentine club did he begin his professional career in 1945?

4. Against which club did he score a hat-trick on his Real Madrid debut?

5. Which England defender did he beat into second place in the 1957 Ballon d'Or Award?

6. In 1983 the Real Madrid side he was manager of finished runners-up in which three major competitions?

7. In which country was he born?

8. What trophy did he win as Valencia manager in 1970-71?

9. Which UEFA award did he receive in 2007?

10. Against which Spanish club did he score four goals in a European Cup quarter-final match in 1958?

11. How many times did he finish as La Liga's top scorer – five, six or seven?

12. Against which Swiss club did he score twice in Real Madrid's first-ever European home game in 1955?

13. Apart from him, who also scored for Real Madrid in the 1956 and 1958 European Cup finals?

14. Against which country did he score his only hat-trick for Spain in 1957?

15. He was included in the World Team of the 20th Century. Who was the other Argentinian international in the team?

16. What major tournament did he win with Argentina in 1947?

17. Which European trophy did he win as a manager?

18. Against which South American country did he score his only hat-trick for Argentina in 1947?

19. Which Uruguayan club did he score against in the 1960 Intercontinental Cup?

20. Which FIFA award did he receive in 1994?

21. Which club did he score a hat-trick against in a European Cup final?

22. With which club did he win the Argentine Primera Division as manager in 1969?

23. In which year did he win the League and Cup double with Real Madrid?

24. What was the only trophy he won as Real Madrid manager?

25. Name either of the other two players that won five European Cups in a row with Real Madrid from 1956 to 1960.

26. With which club did he end his professional career in 1966?

27. How many consecutive European Cup finals did he score in for Real Madrid?

28. In which decade did he die?

29. His nickname was 'Saeta rubia'. What is this translated into English?

30. Which Austrian club did he score four goals against in a European Cup quarter-final match in 1959?

SIR BOBBY CHARLTON

1. Which country did he score against on his England debut in the British Home Championship in 1958?

2. In which decade was he born?

3. Which BBC award did he receive in 2008?

4. Which country did he score against at the 1962 FIFA World Cup?

5. How many goals did he score for Manchester United – 249, 259 or 269?

6. He scored twice in the 1968 European Cup final against Benfica. What was the score before extra time?

7. What major trophy did he win with Manchester United in 1963?

8. In which competition did he score twice in a 3-3 draw against Tottenham in August 1967?

9. In which year did he win his last England cap?

10. Which English club did he score twice against in a Cup Winners' Cup match in 1963?

11. Is Jack his younger brother or elder brother?

12. In which year did he win the Ballon d'Or Award?

13. Which Manchester United goalkeeper rescued him from the 1958 Munich air crash?

14. Which club was he manager of from 1973 to 1975?

15. Who surpassed his Manchester United appearance record in 2008?

16. Against which country did he score an England hat-trick in an 8-1 win in 1963?

17. Which German club did he score a hat-trick against in an Inter-Cities Fairs Cup match in 1964?

18. In which English county was he born?

19. Against which South American country did he score his 49th and final goal for England in 1970?

20. From 1978 to 1980 he played for three clubs from which country?

21. What did his daughter Suzanne present at the BBC in the 1990s?

22. Which Irish club did he briefly play for in 1976?

23. Which country did he score against in the group stage of the 1966 FIFA World Cup?

24. In 2009 he was granted the freedom of which city?

25. Who surpassed his England and Manchester United goalscoring records?

26. In which year was his last game for Manchester United?

27. He was the second man to reach 100 England caps. Who was the third?

28. Who was his first England manager?

29. Which club did he manage on a caretaker basis in 1983?

30. Which country did he score against at UEFA Euro 68?

BOBBY MOORE

1. Against which European country did he score his first England goal in 1966?

2. Which club did his West Ham team lose to in the 1966 League Cup final?

3. Who surpassed his England caps record for an outfield player in 2009?

4. Which vacant manager's position did he apply for in 1977?

5. In 1975 he played in the FA Cup final for which club against his former club West Ham?

6. In which county was he born?

7. In the 1996 song 'Three Lions' what reference is made to Moore in the lyrics?

8. In which year did he first captain England?

9. In 2008 what did West Ham officially retire in his honour?

10. Which future Premier League manager was his assistant at Oxford City?

11. Only two players have made more West Ham appearances than him. Can you name them?

12. In 1966 he became the first footballer to win what BBC Award?

13. Which club manager's job did he almost get in 1977, which went to Graham Taylor instead?

14. How many times did he captain England – 70, 80 or 90?

15. He managed Eastern AA in the early 1980s. Which country is this club from?

16. Which club did his West Ham team beat in the 1964 FA Cup final?

17. Which Danish club did he play for in 1978?

18. How old was he when he first captained England?

19. Which radio station did he work for as an analyst and commentator?

20. In 2016 he was the first footballer to be honoured with what outside his home?

21. Which club was he manager of from 1984 to 1986?

22. He provided two assists for England in the 1966 FIFA World Cup final. Which goals did he assist – the first, second, third and/or fourth?

23. Which German international said he was the best defender in the history of the game?

24. What was he accused of stealing in Colombia in 1970?

25. What was his character's name in the 1981 film *Escape to Victory*?

26. Which South American country did he make his England debut against in 1962?

27. Name two of the three North American Soccer League teams he played for.

28. What achievement award did he receive in 1967?

29. In which year did he die of bowel and liver cancer?

30. Which German club did his West Ham team beat in the 1965 Cup Winners' Cup final?

CRISTIANO RONALDO

1. On which Portuguese island was he born?

2. Against which Italian club did he make his professional debut, for Sporting Lisbon, in a UEFA Champions League qualifier in August 2002?

3. Against which European country did he make his international debut for Portugal in August 2003?

4. Against which club was he sent off in European competition for the first time in 2018?

5. In which season did he score 17 UEFA Champions League goals, including one in the final?

6. Who was the only player who appeared alongside him on his Real Madrid debut in 2009 to still be at the club when he left in 2018?

7. Against which club did he score his first professional hat-trick for Manchester United in 2008?

8. He scored 450 goals for Real Madrid, but in how many games – 438, 458 or 478?

9. Whom did he replace when he came on as a substitute to make his Manchester United debut?

10. At UEFA Euro 2016 he equalled which player's record of most goals scored in the competition's history?

11. Even though they finished fourth at the 2006 FIFA World Cup, he scored only once for Portugal at that tournament. Against which country?

12. Which club did he score against in the 2004 FA Cup final?

13. How many hat-tricks did he score for Real Madrid – 34, 44 or 54?

14. What squad number did he wear when he signed for Real Madrid?

15. Which club did he score against on his Real Madrid debut in 2009?

16. At the 2006 FIFA World Cup which player was he involved with in an incident that saw that player being sent off?

17. Against which country did he score his first hat-trick for Portugal? It came in September 2013 in a FIFA World Cup qualifier.

18. Against which south of England-based club did he score his first Manchester United goal?

19. In scoring a hat-trick against Spain in 2018, what new FIFA World Cup record did he set?

20. Which club did he score four goals against in a UEFA Champions League match in 2015?

21. Which Portuguese club did he score twice against on his league debut in October 2002?

22. Which English club did he almost join instead of Manchester United?

23. Against which club did he score UEFA Champions League hat-tricks in 2017 and in 2019?

24. What was the most goals he ever scored in one season at Real Madrid – 61, 63 or 65?

25. In which season did he first win the European Golden Shoe with 31 Premier League goals?

26. Which club did he score the most goals against as a Real Madrid player – Atletico Madrid, Sevilla or Getafe?

27. He scored his first goal for Portugal at UEFA Euro 2004, but against which country?

28. After scoring a hat-trick in Serie A for Juventus in 2020, how many different competitions had he scored hat-tricks in – 10, 11 or 12?

29. Who was his international team-mate for two seasons at Manchester United?

30. At which major tournament did he win his 150th cap for Portugal?

DIEGO MARADONA

1. Which player surpassed his Napoli goalscoring record in 2017?

2. How old was he when he made his international debut for Argentina?

3. Which German club did his Napoli side beat in the 1989 UEFA Cup final?

4. In which season, while at Napoli, was he Serie A's top scorer?

5. He scored two European hat-tricks for Barcelona. Can you name either of the two teams he scored them against? One was Cypriot and the other was German.

6. Which FIFA World Cup record did he set in 1994 that is still a record today?

7. Against which country was one of his goals voted 'Goal of the Century' by FIFA.com voters in 2002?

8. Which Argentine club appointed him as their manager in September 2019?

9. Which Belarus club named him as chairman in 2018?

10. He scored eight FIFA World Cup goals. Which other Argentine scored eight goals in the competition?

11. Which European country did he score his only international hat-trick against in 1980?

12. In which year did he win his second Serie A title with Napoli?

13. At which UK stadium did he score his first international goal in 1979?

14. In which year was he born?

15. From 2018 to 2019 he managed Dorados de Sinaloa. Which country is this club from?

16. Against which country did he score his first FIFA World Cup goals in 1982?

17. Which are the two nations he scored twice against at the 1986 FIFA World Cup?

18. What is his middle name?

19. In which year did he coach Argentina at the FIFA World Cup?

20. Which Spanish club did he play for in the 1992-93 season?

21. Which club did his Napoli side beat in the 1987 Italian Cup final?

22. Against which club did he score in both legs for Barcelona in the 1983 Spanish League Cup final?

23. Which Argentine FIFA World Cup-winning coach won the Spanish Cup alongside him in 1983?

24. Which FIFA tournament did he win with Argentina in 1979?

25. He was given the nickname 'El Pibe de Oro'. What is this translated into English?

26. Which country did he score against in the 1986 FIFA World Cup group stage?

27. Against which country at the 1994 FIFA World Cup did he win his final cap for Argentina?

28. Which club did his Napoli side beat 5-1 in the 1990 Italian Super Cup final?

29. Which nation did he score against at the 1994 FIFA World Cup?

30. With which club did he make his professional debut in 1976?

DINO ZOFF

1. Six other men whose surname begins with the letter Z have played for Italy at major tournaments since him. Can you name four of them?

2. Which Spanish club did his Juventus side beat in the 1977 UEFA Cup final?

3. Which major tournament did he win with Italy on home soil?

4. Which club did he begin his career with?

5. How many FIFA World Cups did he play in?

6. With which club did he have three spells as manager?

7. How many consecutive Serie A appearances did he make – 132, 232 or 332?

8. Who is the only goalkeeper to have won more caps for Italy than him?

9. In which year did he make his international debut for Italy?

10. In which decade was he born?

11. Name either of the Serie A records he held for more than 20 years.

12. Which goalkeeper with the initials E.A. was he understudy to at the 1970 FIFA World Cup?

13. At which major tournament did he coach Italy?

14. In 1982 he became the second goalkeeper to captain a FIFA World Cup-winning side. Who was the first – another Italian?

15. Who surpassed his Italy caps record in 2000?

16. Which English club did his Juventus side lose to in the 1980 Cup Winners' Cup semi-final?

17. Can you name either of the clubs he lost to in European Cup finals?

18. He helped the men's team qualify for which year's Olympic Games?

19. How many minutes did he go without conceding a goal in UEFA European Championship matches (including qualifiers) from 1975 to 1980 – 784, 884 or 984 minutes?

20. Whom did he replace as Lazio boss in 2000?

21. Which legendary player did he finish runner-up to in the 1973 Ballon d'Or award?

22. With which club did he end his managerial career in 2005?

23. What Italy record does he still hold? It is connected to honours.

24. How many Serie A titles did he win as a Juventus player – four, five or six?

25. In which year did he win the UEFA Cup as Juventus manager?

26. In which competition did he make his European debut with Napoli in 1967?

27. How old was he when he last played in a European Cup final?

28. Which record did he set while playing for Italy from 1972 to 1974?

29. Which club did he play for between 1963 and 1967?

30. In which year did he make his final professional appearance?

EUSEBIO

1. How many goals did he score at the 1966 FIFA World Cup?

2. In which African country, then a Portuguese colony, was he born?

3. The English were so impressed by his performances at the 1966 FIFA World Cup that what was made in London?

4. An avenue in front of which stadium was renamed in his honour after his death in 2014?

5. Which club from Coimbra did he score an extra-time winner against in the 1969 Portuguese Cup final?

6. In which year did he win the Ballon d'Or Award?

7. How many goals did he score for Benfica in 440 matches – 423, 453 or 473?

8. Teams from which city beat his Benfica side in the 1963 and 1965 European Cup finals?

9. How many league titles did he win with Benfica – an all-time record – 9, 10 or 11?

10. He scored only two hat-tricks for Portugal. One was against North Korea at the 1966 FIFA World Cup. Can you name the European country he scored the other against?

11. In which year did he win his last cap for Portugal?

12. Which other legend of the game did he play against in the 1962 Intercontinental Cup against Santos?

13. In the 1964-65 season he was the European Cup's top scorer with nine goals alongside which Benfica team-mate whose surname he shares with an ex-Atletico Madrid, Liverpool and Chelsea striker?

14. In 1968 he was the first-ever recipient of which goalscoring award?

15. He won the Bola de Prata on a record seven occasions. What is this?

16. What was his full name?

17. In which decade did he die?

18. What BBC Award did he receive in 1966?

19. Name any of the three clubs he played for in the North American Soccer League.

20. Who was the only player to have scored more European Cup goals than him in the pre-UEFA Champions League era?

21. Which striker surpassed his Portugal national team goalscoring record in 2005?

22. Which club did he score twice against in the 1962 European Cup final?

23. In which year did he win the Soccer Bowl, scoring in the final against Minnesota Kicks – 1976, 1977 or 1978?

24. Two of his nicknames began with the word 'black'. Black what?

25. Apart from Benfica, which other club did he play for in Portugal's top division?

26. In which stadium did he score four goals against North Korea at the 1966 FIFA World Cup?

27. Which Slovenian club did he score five goals against in a Cup Winners' Cup match in 1970?

28. Which Italian club almost signed him before he joined Benfica?

29. How many penalties did he score at the 1966 FIFA World Cup?

30. Which small European country beginning with the letter L did he score against on his international debut in 1961?

FERENC PUSKAS

1. In which Hungarian city was he born?

2. Which Asian country did he manage from 1976 to 1977?

3. What was his surname at birth?

4. In which year did he win Olympic gold in the men's football tournament?

5. Which central European country did he score against on his international debut in 1945?

6. Which club did he guide to the 1971 European Cup final?

7. In terms of age, which decade was he in when he joined Real Madrid – 20s or 30s?

8. Which Liverpool player won the Puskas Award in 2018?

9. Which Spanish club did he score three goals against over two legs in a European Cup semi-final in 1960?

10. Which Dutch club did he once score four goals against in a European Cup match in 1965?

11. Can you name any of the three Spanish clubs he was manager of?

12. Which European country beginning with the letter A did he once score four goals against in 1950?

13. How many European Cup winners' medals did he win with Real Madrid?

14. In 1947 he won a trophy with Hungary, scoring three goals in the process. Which trophy did they win?

15. As well as playing for Hungary, which other country did he play for?

16. He scored only one European goal for Honved, in 1956. Which Spanish club did he score it against?

17. He missed two European Cup final wins with Real Madrid. Can you name both years?

18. He scored in two European Cup finals. How many goals did he score in those two finals – six, seven or eight?

19. In which major final did he score both goals in a 2-1 win over Sevilla in 1962?

20. Against which Luxembourg club did he score his first hat-trick in Europe in 1959?

21. Which nation was he manager of for four games in 1993?

22. How many European Cup goals did he score in the 1959-60 season – 12, 13 or 14?

23. Which nation did he help Hungary beat 6-3 and 7-1 in 1953 and 1954 respectively, scoring twice in each game?

24. Which now defunct nation did he score against in the 1952 Olympic Games final?

25. What injury was he playing with during the 1954 FIFA World Cup final?

26. Which Asian country did he score his first FIFA World Cup goals against?

27. For how many seasons did he finish as La Liga's top scorer – four, five or six?

28. He scored in all three of his appearances at the 1954 FIFA World Cup. Against which country did he score twice?

29. Against which Spanish club did he score his first European goal for Real Madrid in a European Cup semi-final in 1959?

30. How many goals did he score for Honved in the 1947-48 season – 40, 50 or 60?

FRANZ BECKENBAUER

1. Which American club did he join after Bayern Munich?

2. Which French club did he score against in a European Cup semi-final match in 1975?

3. What was his nickname?

4. Name either of the years he was named European Football of the Year.

5. Which country did he score twice against in his first FIFA World Cup appearance in 1966?

6. Can you name his son who was also a professional footballer?

7. In 1990 he became the first man to win the FIFA World Cup as both captain and as a manager. Can you name the second man to achieve this feat?

8. Which French club was he manager of briefly in 1990?

9. Which European country did he score his first two international goals against in 1966?

10. What injury did he sustain in the 1970 FIFA World Cup semi-final against Italy?

11. What unique trophy treble record did he set in 1974?

12. Which Brazilian club did his Bayern side beat in the 1976 Intercontinental Cup?

13. What was his position on the field as a youngster?

14. Name either of the two international awards he received in 2012.

15. In which year did he make his international debut?

16. Which European trophy did he win as Bayern Munich manager?

17. What was his first honour as a Bayern Munich player, winning it in 1966?

18. Against which Greek club did he score his first European goal in 1967?

19. Whom did he replace as West Germany's national team manager in 1984?

20. Which major honour did he win three times with the New York Cosmos?

21. Which club did he score against in the 1971 German Cup final?

22. Which was the first European trophy he won as a Bayern Munich player?

23. What role on the pitch is he often credited as having invented?

24. Which German newspaper did he work for as a columnist?

25. What is his middle name? A clue – his initials are 'F.A.B.'.

26. Which other German club did he play for?

27. In which city did he score against the Soviet Union in the 1966 FIFA World Cup semi-final?

28. Which Scottish club did his Bayern side beat in the 1967 Cup Winners' Cup final?

29. Which country did he score against at the 1970 FIFA World Cup?

30. Which Munich club did he support as a boy?

GARY LINEKER

1. How many FIFA World Cup goals did he score?

2. In which European competition did he score four goals for Barcelona in the 1988-89 season?

3. Which nation did he score twice against in the round of 16 at the 1986 FIFA World Cup?

4. Which club did he begin his professional career with?

5. Which manager signed him when he joined Barcelona in 1986?

6. Who saved his penalty in the 1991 FA Cup final?

7. Which near neighbour did he make his international debut against in 1984?

8. Which trophy did he win with Leicester City?

9. What is his middle name, named after a famous British prime minister?

10. With which club did his Tottenham side share the FA Charity Shield in 1991?

11. Which country did he miss a penalty against at Wembley Stadium in 1992?

12. In which season was he the First Division's top scorer with 30 goals, doing so with Everton?

13. Which club did he famously score a hat-trick against for Barcelona in January 1987?

14. Against which near neighbour did he score his first international goal in 1985?

15. What other sport did he excel at, captaining the team at Leicestershire Schools level?

16. Which England manager made him captain for the first time?

17. Which Welshman was his team-mate at Barcelona?

18. Which former Nottingham Forest player did he replace when making his England debut as a substitute in 1984?

19. He never received a yellow or red card in his career – true or false?

20. How many UEFA European Championship matches did he win in his six appearances in the competition?

21. Against which two countries did he score four goals in an England shirt?

22. In which year did his Everton side lose to Liverpool in the FA Cup final?

23. With which club did he win the most England caps – Leicester or Everton?

24. Which Basque side did his Barcelona team beat in the 1988 Spanish Cup final?

25. Name either of the two domestic awards he received in the 1985-86 season.

26. Only one British player has scored more Spanish La Liga goals than him. Can you name him?

27. Which trophy did he win with England in 1988, scoring in the final game against Colombia?

28. Which Japanese club did he play for?

29. What is the name of the English Premier League highlights show he presents every Saturday night on the BBC?

30. Which country did he make his final international appearance against, at UEFA Euro 92?

GEORGE BEST

1. Which goalscoring feat did he achieve in the 1967-68 season?

2. Against which island nation did he score four of his nine international goals?

3. How old was he when he made his Manchester United debut in 1963?

4. What nickname did the Portuguese media give him in 1966?

5. Against which club did he score an FA Cup record six goals in 1970?

6. Who was his last manager at Manchester United?

7. Which Scottish club did he play for from 1979 to 1980?

8. Name either of the two teams he scored twice for Manchester United against in European Cup matches in the 1965-66 season – one was Finnish and the other was Portuguese.

9. What was the name of the bar he opened in California in the 1970s (initials B.B.C.)?

10. Which goalkeeper did he cheekily score past in a Northern Ireland versus England match in 1971?

11. He scored his last European goals for Manchester United against which Austrian club in a European Cup quarter-final in 1969?

12. Which domestic award did he win in 1967-68, becoming its youngest ever recipient?

13. Which English south coast club did he join in 1982?

14. He played for two clubs called Sea Bee and Rangers in 1982. Which Asian country were they from?

15. Which club from the Midlands did he make his Manchester United league debut against in 1963?

16. Which East Belfast club beginning with the letter G did he support as a boy?

17. What do he and Cristiano Ronaldo both have named in their honour?

18. Against which club, one of their fiercest rivals, did he score for Manchester United in the 1965 FA Charity Shield?

19. How many league titles did he win with Manchester United?

20. Name one of the three clubs he played for in the United States.

21. What was the reason why his local club rejected him as a boy?

22. Against which Swedish side did he score his first goal in Europe, in an Inter-Cities Fairs Cup match in 1964?

23. How old was he when he died?

24. In which decade was he born?

25. Which English club did he support as a boy?

26. In which major cup final in 1968 was he sent off?

27. When he scored in the 1968 European Cup final, what score did he make it at the time?

28. He played for a club called Jewish Guild after leaving Manchester United. Which country are they from?

29. What was the name of the nightclub he opened in Manchester in 1973? The first word is another word for lazy and the second word is the name of a fictional character in Wonderland.

30. Which famous club did he score the 1-0 winner against for Manchester United in the first leg of their European Cup semi-final in 1968?

GERD MULLER

1. In which year did he score twice in a European Cup final?

2. What was his nickname?

3. Who surpassed his Germany goalscoring record in 2014?

4. Which award did he receive in 1970?

5. Can you name any of the four nations he scored four goals against in an international match? All of them are European.

6. From which club did he join Bayern Munich in 1964? It was also his birthplace.

7. Which South American nation did he score a hat-trick against at the 1970 FIFA World Cup?

8. In which European competition did he score eight goals in his first season in continental competition?

9. Which south-eastern European country did he make his international debut against in 1966?

10. In 1972 he scored a then record 85 goals in a calendar year. Who surpassed that record in 2012?

11. He and which other player, who shares his first name with a German philosopher, both scored hat-tricks in Bayern Munich's UEFA Cup match against Mjondalen in 1977?

12. Against which club from the Ruhr Valley did he score both goals in a 2-1 German Cup final win in 1969?

13. Which game was his last for West Germany?

14. Can you name the four major finals he scored in for club and country?

15. Which Cypriot club did he once score five goals against in a European Cup match in 1972?

16. In which season did he win the German League and Cup double with Bayern Munich – 1966-67, 1967-68 or 1968-69?

17. On how many occasions was he the Bundesliga's top scorer – six, seven or eight?

18. Who surpassed his FIFA World Cup scoring record with his 15th goal in the competition in 2006?

19. He scored ten goals at the 1970 FIFA World Cup. Since then how many times has a player managed to score a double-figure amount of goals at one tournament?

20. Which Belgian club did he score three goals against over two legs in the 1976 UEFA Super Cup?

21. Which North American Soccer League club did he play for?

22. In which European competition did he score a hat-trick at Sparta Rotterdam in 1970?

23. In which season did he score 11 goals in five European Cup appearances – 1972-73, 1973-74 or 1974-75?

24. In what division was Bayern Munich when he joined the club?

25. He scored his first European hat-trick in a Cup Winners' Cup semi-final in 1967. Against which Belgian club?

26. Against which Brazilian club did he score in the 1976 Intercontinental Cup?

27. How many goals did he score for West Germany in his 62 caps?

28. How many Bundesliga goals did he score in his career – a record – 365, 375 or 385?

29. Which near neighbour did he score twice against in the UEFA Euro 72 semi-final?

30. Against which African nation did he score his first-ever FIFA World Cup goal, a 2-1 winner in 1970?

JOHAN CRUYFF

1. In which season did he score a high of 41 goals in all competitions for Ajax – 1966-67, 1967-68 or 1968-69?

2. In which three years did he win the Ballon d'Or?

3. Which nation did he score twice against at the 1974 FIFA World Cup?

4. What did he win on four occasions as an Ajax player?

5. With which club did he win a League and Cup double in 1984?

6. How old was he when he scored on his Ajax debut in 1964?

7. Name either of the two North American clubs he played for.

8. Which European trophy did he win as a manager with two different clubs?

9. A feint he executed at the 1974 FIFA World Cup became known as what?

10. How many times did the Netherlands lose when he scored?

11. What is the name of his son who played professionally?

12. What unwanted Dutch international record did he set in his second international against Czechoslovakia in 1966?

13. What is his full name?

14. As a player he helped Barcelona win the league title in 1974. It was their first league title in how many years?

15. Which future Barcelona manager did he give a first-team debut to in 1990?

16. Which small central European nation did he score his only international hat-trick against in 1971?

17. Apart from Barcelona which other Spanish club did he play for?

18. What was the Barcelona team he managed more commonly known as? The United States basketball team from the 1992 Olympics was also known as this.

19. Which club beginning with the letter G did he score against on his Ajax debut in 1964?

20. Which German side did his Barcelona team beat in the 1992 UEFA Super Cup?

21. Throughout his career he became synonymous with a playing style known as what?

22. In which year did he play in his first European Cup final with Ajax?

23. Which team did his Barcelona side lose 4-0 to in the 1994 UEFA Champions League final?

24. Against which English club did he score his first goal in Europe in 1966?

25. In 1978 he captained Barcelona to which major trophy?

26. Which club did his Barcelona side beat in both the 1989 Cup Winners' Cup and 1992 European Cup finals?

27. Which former FIFA World Cup runners-up did he score against on his international debut in 1966?

28. He won the European Cup as Barcelona manager in 1992. Name three of the other four Dutchmen to have won this trophy as a manager.

29. Which shirt number was he synonymous with?

30. Against which club did he score both goals for Ajax in the 1972 European Cup final?

LEGENDARY WOMEN

1. With which Swedish club beginning with the letter U did Marta win the UEFA Women's Cup in 2004?

2. Against which country did Alex Morgan score in the 2018 Gold Cup final?

3. Who scored her 50th goal for her country in the 2019 FIFA Women's World Cup final?

4. Who is the leading all-time international scorer for men and women?

5. Against which country did Homare Sawa score a hat-trick at the 2011 FIFA Women's World Cup?

6. Which nation did Marta score two penalties against in Brazil's 5-0 win in the 2007 Pan American Games final?

7. Against which South American country did Christine Sinclair score four goals in a Gold Cup match in 2010?

8. Who is Norway's record goalscorer in FIFA Women's World Cup matches with ten goals?

9. In which major tournament did Cristiane once score 12 goals in 2006?

10. Which American played at five FIFA Women's World Cups from 1999 to 2015?

11. Who won 354 caps for the United States and also played in five FIFA Women's World Cups?

12. In which year did Cristiane make her debut for Brazil at the age of 18?

13. How many goals did Marta score in Brazil's 7-0 win over Canada at the 2007 Pan American Games?

14. Kristine Lilly scored in three successive games at the 2004 Olympic Games. Can you name two of the three nations she scored against in that run? Two are Asian and one is European.

15. Who scored all of Canada's goals in their 4-3 defeat to the USA at the 2012 Olympic Games?

16. Against which country did Carli Lloyd score the 1-0 extra-time winner in the 2008 Olympic Games final?

17. In which round of the tournament did Alex Morgan score the 4-3 extra-time winner against Canada at the 2012 Olympic Games?

18. How many FIFA Women's World Cup goals have Marta and Cristiane scored between them?

19. Birgit Prinz once scored four goals in a match against China at which major tournament?

20. Who in 2019 became the first woman to score in six FIFA Women's World Cup matches in a row?

21. Against which country did Abby Wambach score four goals in the 2014 Gold Cup final?

22. In which major Games final did Cristiane score the 2-1 winner against Canada in 2003?

23. How many goals did Birgit Prinz score for Germany – 128, 138 or 148?

24. In which major final did Kristine Lilly score the 120th minute penalty winner against Canada in 2006?

25. Homare Sawa scored twice in an Asian Games match against Jordan in 2006. What was the final score?

26. Who scored the 100th goal for her country against Australia in April 2019?

27. Which nation did Carli Lloyd score twice against in the 2012 Olympic Games final?

28. Against which nation did Christine Sinclair score the 1-0 winner in the 2010 Gold Cup final?

29. In which year was Marta the top scorer at a FIFA Women's World Cup tournament?

30. Which country did Birgit Prinz score twice against in the UEFA Euro 2009 final?

LIONEL MESSI

1. Which near neighbouring club did he make his Barcelona first-team debut against?

2. In which two cities did he score his first two UEFA Champions League final goals?

3. Who was his international team-mate for eight seasons at Barcelona?

4. Against which Greek club did he score his first goal in Europe in 2005?

5. What age-related record did he set at the 2018 FIFA World Cup?

6. In 2019-20 he became the first player to score in how many successive seasons in the UEFA Champions League?

7. In 2018 he scored his 100th UEFA Champions League goal in his 123rd appearance in the competition. What record did he set here?

8. In which round of the competition did he score four goals in a UEFA Champions League match against Arsenal in April 2010?

9. Which European nation did he first captain Argentina against in a FIFA World Cup match in 2010?

10. In 2019 he scored which milestone hat-trick number of his career?

11. Which nation did he score a hat-trick against at the 2016 Copa America?

12. Which Basque club did he score against in the 2009, 2012 and 2015 Copa del Rey finals?

13. Which manager handed him his Barcelona first-team debut?

14. Which competition's hat-trick record did he break in the 2011-12 season?

15. In 2015 he scored in seven different official competitions. Can you name them all?

16. Which future Barcelona player did he play opposite in the 2011 FIFA Club World Cup final?

17. Which country was he sent off against on his international debut in August 2005?

18. In which season did he finish as the UEFA Champions League top scorer with 14 goals?

19. Against which English club did he score his first hat-trick in Europe when he scored four goals against them in 2010?

20. Against which club beginning with the letter 'A' did he score his first senior goal in May 2005?

21. In which major youth tournament did he score both goals in the final against Nigeria?

22. Whose Argentina national goalscoring record did he surpass in 2016?

23. Which nation did he lose to on penalties in the 2015 and 2016 Copa America finals?

24. Against which now defunct European nation did he score his first FIFA World Cup goal?

25. Which Argentine clubs did he score against in the 2009 and 2015 FIFA Club World Cup finals?

26. Which country was he sent off against at the 2019 Copa America?

27. Which club did he score his first senior hat-trick against in March 2007?

28. How many goals did he score for club and country in the calendar year in 2012 – 71, 81 or 91?

29. In which season did he help Barcelona win the treble for the first time?

30. He has scored more than one goal in just one FIFA World Cup match. Which is the only country he has scored twice against?

LOTHAR MATTHAUS

1. Which FIFA World Cup record does he still hold?

2. What award was he the first recipient of in 1991?

3. Apart from the 1990 FIFA World Cup, which other major tournament did he win with West Germany?

4. Against which African country did he score his first FIFA World Cup goal in 1986?

5. He and one other player are the only two to have played over 2,000 minutes at the FIFA World Cup. Can you name the other player?

6. With which club did he begin his professional career?

7. Which Italian club did he score against in the 1991 UEFA Cup final?

8. How many caps did he win for West Germany/Germany?

9. How many major tournaments did he play in for West Germany/Germany – a national record?

10. What is his middle name? It is the same name as the Arsenal manager who won two league titles in the 1930s.

11. In which year did he win the UEFA Cup with Bayern Munich?

12. Which other German international joined him at Inter Milan in 1988?

13. With which Austrian club did he begin his managerial career in 2001?

14. Which near neighbouring country did he make his international debut against at UEFA Euro 80?

15. His three goals in Europe for Monchengladbach were all scored against fellow German clubs. Can you name two of them?

16. He appeared in five FIFA World Cups. Can you name the five years he played in the tournament?

17. Which club did his Bayern Munich side lose to in the 1987 European Cup final?

18. In which 1980 European final did he score in?

19. Name the two countries he was manager of.

20. His last international goal came against New Zealand in 1999. In which tournament?

21. Which club did his Partizan side eliminate on penalties in the UEFA Champions League third qualifying round in 2003?

22. At which stage of the tournament did he score against the Netherlands at UEFA Euro 88?

23. Who is the only other outfield player to have appeared at five FIFA World Cups?

24. During his international career in which two years did he miss the UEFA European Championship?

25. Against which club did he score two penalties for Bayern Munich in a European Cup semi-final match in 1987?

26. Name either of the two seasons he won the League and Cup double with Bayern Munich.

27. Which club did he play for in the United States?

28. In 1990, which nation did he score West Germany's 1-0 penalty winner against in the FIFA World Cup quarter-final?

29. Which Israeli club did he manage from 2008 to 2009?

30. Which major tournament was his last in a German shirt?

MARCO VAN BASTEN

1. How old was he when he played his last game as a professional – 28, 29 or 30?

2. In 1985-86 he won which major goalscoring award, netting 37 league goals for Ajax?

3. Which European island nation did he make his international debut against in 1983?

4. Which club beginning with the letter 'N' did he score against on his Ajax first-team debut in 1982?

5. Which striker scored 28 goals in his only season in charge of Ajax (2008-09)?

6. Which two FIFA World Cup-winning nations did his Netherlands side beat 3-0 and 4-1 respectively at UEFA Euro 2008?

7. How many goals did he once score in a UEFA Cup match for Ajax against Red Boys Differdange in 1984?

8. In which two major tournaments did he manage the Netherlands?

9. Against which Scandinavian nation was his first match as Netherlands manager in 2004?

10. Which Barcelona player did he beat into second place in winning the 1992 Ballon d'Or?

11. Which manager signed him at AC Milan?

12. He never scored a FIFA World Cup goal – true or false?

13. Who was his assistant during his reign as the Netherlands national team manager?

14. Which German club did he score the 1-0 winner against in the 1987 Cup Winners' Cup final?

15. Name either of the two clubs he scored against in the 1988 and 1992 Italian Super Cup finals.

16. Against which European island nation did he once score five goals in an international in 1990?

17. Which club was he manager of between 2012 and 2014?

18. Which striker joined Real Madrid midway through his season in charge of Ajax (2008-09)?

19. For how many successive seasons was he the Eredivisie's top scorer – four, five or six?

20. Which country did he score the 2-1 winner against at UEFA Euro 88?

21. He was Serie A's top scorer twice. Who became the next AC Milan player to be Serie A's top scorer?

22. He was an assistant to which Dutch manager from 2015 to 2016?

23. His brother was rejected as an Ajax player. What is his name? He shares his name with the director of the film *2001: A Space Odyssey*.

24. Which nation eliminated his Netherlands side at the 2006 FIFA World Cup?

25. He and which other Dutchman scored twice in the 1989 European Cup final?

26. Which club was he manager of briefly in 2014?

27. Which club from the capital of the province of South Holland did he score two goals against in the 1987 Dutch Cup final?

28. Which near neighbouring nation did he score his first international goal against in 1983?

29. What record did he set during the 1992-93 UEFA Champions League season?

30. What was his last match for AC Milan?

MICHEL PLATINI

1. Against which English club did he score twice for Juventus in a European Cup quarter-final match in 1983?

2. Against which nation did he score his first FIFA World Cup goal?

3. Which UEFA president did he succeed in 2007?

4. In which tournament did he represent France in 1976?

5. What was the first honour he won as a player, with Nancy in 1975?

6. He played for France at the 1978 FIFA World Cup. It was France's first FIFA World Cup since what year?

7. Against which club from the south did he score Nancy's 1-0 winner in the 1978 French Cup final?

8. In which European competition did he score five goals for St Etienne in the 1979-80 season?

9. Which two nations did he score hat-tricks against at UEFA Euro 84?

10. Which Argentine club did he score against in the 1985 Intercontinental Cup?

11. What is his middle name? It is the same name as France's president from 1981 to 1995.

12. Against which now defunct European nation did he score on his international debut in 1976?

13. Name any of the three midfielders which he formed the 'magic square' with for France in the 1980s.

14. For which Asian nation did he play one international in 1988?

15. Which football magazine voted him as the French Player of the 20th century in 1999?

16. In which three years in succession did he win the Ballon d'Or?

17. Which club did his Juventus side lose to in the 1983 European Cup final?

18. Who scored France's only two goals when Platini was their manager at UEFA Euro 92?

19. In 1984-85 he was the European Cup's joint top scorer. How many goals did he score that season?

20. Which European trophy did he win first with Juventus, and in which year?

21. Whom did he succeed as France's boss in 1988?

22. He was the first former player to become UEFA president – true or false?

23. What was his nickname?

24. Which Danish club did he score his first European goals for Juventus against in 1982?

25. Which player once said of him, 'When I was a kid and played with my friends, I always chose to be Platini'?

26. Which French club did he score against for Juventus in a European Cup semi-final match in 1985?

27. Who surpassed his France national scoring record in 2007?

28. Against which nation did he score France's extra-time winner in the UEFA Euro 84 semi-final?

29. He scored his last international goal at the 1986 FIFA World Cup on his birthday. How old was he?

30. Against which Asian nation did he score at the 1982 FIFA World Cup?

PELE

1. In which decade was he born?

2. How many goals did he score for Brazil in the Copa America?

3. What landmark did he set with his goal in the 1970 FIFA World Cup final?

4. Which is the only country to concede two Pele international hat-tricks?

5. Which 1994 FIFA World Cup venue was his home stadium in the 1970s?

6. Against which team did he try to score from the halfway line in the 1970 FIFA World Cup?

7. In which two successive years in the 1960s did he and Santos win the Copa Libertadores?

8. How many goals did he score in FIFA World Cup qualifying matches?

9. How many FIFA World Cup goals did he score?

10. To whom did he pass for the last goal of the 1970 FIFA World Cup final?

11. Against which country did he make his full international debut in the 1957 Roca Cup?

12. What was his given name?

13. Against which European team did he make his FIFA World Cup debut?

14. How many times did he win the Copa America?

15. How many players have the same number of FIFA World Cup winners' medals as him?

16. In which country did he make his Copa America debut?

17. What was the league in which he played when he moved to the United States?

18. At which stadium did he make his FIFA World Cup debut?

19. How many of Santos's eight goals did he score in the 1962 Intercontinental Cup defeat of Benfica?

20. How many FIFA World Cup qualifying competitions did he play in?

21. His only match in London was a 1973 club friendly for Santos against which West London club?

22. In which position did he and Brazil finish in the 1959 Copa America?

23. How many goals did he score in official internationals and how many caps did he win?

24. Which club made him Honorary President in 2010?

25. When Brazil played England in the 1970 FIFA World Cup who made the 'save of the century' from his header?

26. How many Copa America tournaments did he play in?

27. Who were the opponents when he scored his first FIFA World Cup goal?

28. His only Brazilian club Santos is based around 50 miles (80km) from which city?

29. How many international hat-tricks did he score in friendlies and competitive matches?

30. In 1999 he was named joint World Player of the Century with whom?

RIVALDO

1. Who was his first manager at Barcelona?

2. Against which nation did he score his first FIFA World Cup goal?

3. In which year did he win the Ballon d'Or?

4. With which club did he win his first honour, the Brazilian Serie A in 1994?

5. He scored his first-ever goal in Europe for Barcelona in the 1997 UEFA Super Cup, but against which club?

6. Which CONCACAF nation did he score the 1-0 winner against on his international debut in 1993?

7. He scored more than one goal in only one FIFA World Cup match. Against which nation did he score twice?

8. Which club did he score against in AC Milan's Italian Cup final win in 2003?

9. Which South American nation did he score his last international goal against in 2003?

10. Which was the only Asian nation he scored against at the FIFA World Cup?

11. At the 2002 FIFA World Cup how many consecutive matches did he score in?

12. Which club from Thessaloniki did he score against for Olympiacos in the 2005 Greek Cup final?

13. Which nation did he score twice against in the 1999 Copa America final?

14. In which year did he win a UEFA Champions League winners' medal?

15. Who was the only other Brazilian playing for AC Milan on the day he made his debut for the club in 2002?

16. Against which nation did he score a late 2-1 penalty winner for Brazil at the 2002 FIFA World Cup?

17. Himself and which other Brazilian scored in Barcelona's 3-3 UEFA Champions League draw at Manchester United in 1998?

18. Which Spanish club did he join Barcelona from?

19. Which tournament staged in England did he win with Brazil in 1995?

20. He was the Spanish Cup's top scorer in 1997-98 with Barcelona. How many goals did he score that season?

21. Which Greek club was the last European club he played for?

22. He played for a club called Bunyodkor from 2008 to 2010. Which country is the club from?

23. How many goals did he score in official internationals, and how many caps did he win?

24. How many FIFA World Cup goals did he score?

25. Which Brazilian club did he rejoin 20 years after leaving in 1994?

26. Name either of the two clubs he scored European hat-tricks against. One was Italian and the other was Polish.

27. Against which English club did he score his first UEFA Champions League goal for Olympiacos?

28. In which year did he win an Olympic Games bronze medal?

29. In which three countries did he win a League and Cup double?

30. Which nation did he score his only international hat-trick against in 1999?

RONALDINHO

1. With which Brazilian club did he begin his professional career?

2. Which Austrian club did he score his first European goals against, for Paris St Germain in 2001?

3. How many goals did he score in official internationals, and how many caps did he win?

4. Which fellow Brazilian came on as a substitute when he made his AC Milan debut in 2008?

5. What does the word 'inho' mean in English?

6. Name either of the two nations he scored international hat-tricks against.

7. In which two consecutive years was he voted FIFA World Player of the Year?

8. Can you name the two English grounds he scored at in European competitions?

9. Which Slovakian club did he score a Barcelona hat-trick against in a UEFA Cup match in 2003?

10. Apart from England, which was the only other nation he scored against at the FIFA World Cup?

11. Which major youth tournament did he win with Brazil in 1997?

12. He scored his first goal for Brazil at the 1999 Copa America – against which nation?

13. Which English club expressed an interest in signing him in 2001?

14. In which major tournament did he score twice against New Zealand in 2008?

15. How many goals did he score in Barcelona's 2005-06 UEFA Champions League-winning campaign – five, six or seven?

16. In which year did he make his final international appearance for Brazil, and against which nation?

17. He won the 2005 Ballon d'Or. Which two Englishmen did he finish ahead of?

18. Which former Tottenham manager scored when he made his Paris St Germain debut in 2001?

19. Against which Baltic nation did he make his international debut in 1999?

20. Which individual award did he win in 2013?

21. Can you name either of the Spanish clubs he both scored and was sent off against in the same La Liga game?

22. In which FIFA competition did he score a record nine goals?

23. He scored only one La Liga hat-trick in his career – true or false?

24. Which club did he win the Copa Libertadores with in 2013?

25. Against which club beginning with the letter S did he score his only AC Milan hat-trick in January 2010?

26. Which Brazilian club did he and Barcelona lose to in the 2006 FIFA Club World Cup final?

27. Against which nation did he score for Brazil in the 2005 FIFA Confederations Cup final?

28. Why did he wear shirt number 49 at Atletico Mineiro?

29. Which England goalkeeper did he memorably score past at the 2002 FIFA World Cup?

30. Against which club did he score his only UEFA Champions League hat-trick, for Barcelona in 2005?

RONALDO

1. Against which Baltic nation did he score his first international hat-trick in 1996?

2. In 1996 he was the first Brazilian to win the FIFA World Player of the Year Award – true or false?

3. In which city did he score Barcelona's 1-0 penalty winner against Paris St Germain in the 1997 Cup Winners' Cup final?

4. How many goals did he score in official internationals, and how many caps did he win?

5. With which club did he begin his professional career?

6. In which Cup final did he score for Corinthians against Internacional in 2009?

7. Against which Paraguayan club did he score for Real Madrid in the 2002 Intercontinental Cup?

8. How many FIFA World Cup goals did he score for Brazil?

9. He was Real Madrid's top scorer in each of his four full seasons at the club – true or false?

10. In which year was he a member of Brazil's FIFA World Cup squad but did not play?

11. Against which nation did he score in the 1997 Copa America final?

12. He scored for AC Milan in a 3-1 win over Messina in April 2007. Which other Brazilian scored in that game?

13. He is the last player to score more than once in a FIFA World Cup final – true or false?

14. Against which fellow Italian club did he score for Inter Milan in the 1998 UEFA Cup final?

15. Which fellow Brazilian finished second behind him in the 1997 FIFA World Player of the Year Award?

16. Which club beginning with the letter 'S' did he score twice against on his first start for AC Milan in February 2007?

17. He once scored four goals for PSV against MyPa in a UEFA Cup match in 1995. Which country are MyPa from?

18. In which year was he the joint top scorer with Rivaldo at the Copa America with five goals?

19. Against which German club did he score a hat-trick for PSV in a UEFA Cup match in 1994 – his first-ever goals in Europe?

20. Against which European island nation did he score his first international goal?

21. How many Copa America goals did he score – 10, 11 or 12?

22. Which was the only South American nation he scored twice against in a FIFA World Cup match?

23. Which club was he sent off against in a UEFA Champions League match in March 2005?

24. He and which other player both scored hat-tricks in Brazil's 1997 FIFA Confederations Cup final win over Australia?

25. At which stadium did he score his only UEFA Champions League hat-trick?

26. In which tournament in 1997 did he score against Italy?

27. Against which Basque club did he score twice on his Real Madrid debut in October 2002?

28. Which two other Brazilian players formed a partnership known as Ka-Pa-Ro at AC Milan?

29. Name either of the African nations he scored a FIFA World Cup goal against.

30. Which Brazilian striker was his team-mate at Inter Milan in the 2001-02 season?

ZICO

1. What was his common nickname?

2. With which Brazilian club did he spend the majority of his career?

3. Which club did he manage to a league title in 2007?

4. Which was the only nation he scored two goals against for Brazil in a FIFA World Cup match?

5. Which FIFA award did he receive in 1996?

6. Which European club did he play for?

7. Name both of the national teams he has managed.

8. With which Japanese club did he end his playing career, and was also briefly their manager?

9. He had a spell as manager of Al-Gharafa. Which country is this club from?

10. What was his given name?

11. What government position did he hold in 1990?

12. He played in only one season of club football in Europe in his career – true or false?

13. Which tournament did he win with Brazil in 1995 and 1996?

14. How many goals did he score for Flamengo – 408, 508 or 608?

15. Which Brazilian club did he form in 1999?

16. Which fellow South American nation did he score against on his international debut in 1976?

17. He finished as Serie A's second top scorer in 1983-84 with 19 goals. Who beat him to top spot, scoring 20 goals that season?

18. Against which South American country did he score his first FIFA World Cup goal in 1978?

19. How many of Flamengo's four goals did he score in their three finals matches at the 1981 Copa Libertadores, a tournament they won?

20. Which nation did his Japan side lose 4-1 to at the 2006 FIFA World Cup?

21. Which club did his Flamengo side beat in the 1981 Intercontinental Cup?

22. Which was the only European nation he scored a FIFA World Cup goal against?

23. Which now defunct nation did he score an international hat-trick against in 1986?

24. Which nation did he miss a penalty against in regulation time at the 1986 FIFA World Cup?

25. Which Russian club was he briefly manager of in 2009?

26. Which major tournament did he win as Japan's manager in 2004?

27. What nickname did the Japanese fans commonly give him?

28. Which football magazine named him World Player of the Year in 1983?

29. Which nation did he score four goals against in a World Cup qualifier in 1977?

30. In which tournament in 1979 did he score in two of his three appearances?

ZINEDINE ZIDANE

1. He scored twice in the 1998 FIFA World Cup final. Who was the last player before him to score more than one goal in a FIFA World Cup final?

2. With which club did he begin his professional career?

3. Which other French international was on the pitch when he made his Real Madrid debut in 2001?

4. In which city did he and Juventus lose the 1998 UEFA Champions League final?

5. Which European club trophy did he win first as a player?

6. How many times did he win the FIFA World Player of the Year Award?

7. Which club did he and Juventus lose to in the 1997 UEFA Champions League final?

8. In which city did he score for Real Madrid in the 2002 UEFA Champions League final?

9. Which game was his last match for France?

10. How many major tournaments (FIFA World Cup and UEFA European Championship) did he play in for France?

11. Against which club beginning with the letter 'S' did he score his only Real Madrid hat-trick?

12. Clubs from which three countries did his Real Madrid side beat in the 2016, 2017 & 2018 UEFA Champions League finals?

13. In 2006 he became the fourth player to score in two different FIFA World Cup finals. Can you name the three other players?

14. How many caps did he win for France, and how many goals did he score?

15. Which country did he score two injury-time goals against at UEFA Euro 2004?

16. In which year was he born?

17. Which nations did he score penalties against in shoot-outs at UEFA Euro 96?

18. He won the Ballon d'Or in 1998. Who was the last French winner before him?

19. What was the transfer fee in euros when he moved from Juventus to Real Madrid in 2001 – a world record fee at the time?

20. Against which country was he sent off for France at the 1998 FIFA World Cup?

21. In which competition did he make his Real Madrid debut in 2001?

22. In which city in the south of France was he born?

23. Which Greek club did he score his first brace against as a Real Madrid player, in a UEFA Champions League match in October 2002?

24. Which two clubs did his Real Madrid side beaten in the 2016 and 2017 FIFA Club World Cup finals?

25. Can you name either of the sides he was sent off against while playing for Real Madrid?

26. Which club did he and Real Madrid beat in the 2002 UEFA Super Cup?

27. Which nation did he score twice against on his international debut in 1994?

28. In 2001 he was voted the Serie A Footballer of the Year for a second time. Which other Frenchman won the award the following year?

29. In which city did he win his first European match as a manager, for Real Madrid in 2016?

30. Against which country did he score a golden goal at UEFA Euro 2000?

THE GREAT CLUBS

The world of football would not be what it is today without the domestic game. This section celebrates the clubs who have millions of fans tuning in to watch them play each week. While they may not be able to compete for the FIFA World Cup, the domestic leagues and cups they strive to win can be just as important to both clubs and fans alike. To answer these questions you will need to know about everything from their greatest successes and longest-serving player to the rivalries, mascots and managers who make each club special.

AC MILAN

1. Which club record does Gunnar Nordahl hold?

2. Who coached them to successive European Cup triumphs in 1989 and 1990?

3. Which team did they beat in Athens to win a UEFA Champions League final?

4. Who scored 104 goals for the club over two spells, from 2003 to 2009 and from 2013 to 2014?

5. In which stadium did they win the 2003 UEFA Champions League final?

6. Who is their oldest ever first-team player, appearing in 2007 at the age of 41 years and 25 days?

7. Who was their top scorer in 2018-19 with 11 goals, despite only joining them in January 2019?

8. Which club have they beaten in two European Cup finals?

9. Which Slovakian international midfielder was sent off three times for the club during the 2016-17 season?

10. Who scored a hat-trick in their 5-1 UEFA Europa League win over Austria Vienna in 2017?

11. Which English club did they beat in the 1973 UEFA Cup Winners' Cup final?

12. Which fellow Italian club did they beat in the 1990 UEFA Super Cup?

13. Which former player also had three spells as their manager?

14. In 1974 they were attempting to win back-to-back UEFA Cup Winners' Cups but lost in the final to which German club?

15. In which year were they formed?

16. Who scored twice in their 1994 UEFA Champions League final win over Barcelona?

17. What did they achieve for the first time in the 1991-92 Serie A season?

18. Who missed the decisive penalty in their shoot-out defeat to Liverpool in the 2005 UEFA Champions League final?

19. Which Brazilian goalkeeper played for the club from 2000 to 2010?

20. Against which club do they play the 'Derby della Madonnina'?

21. Who scored their winning goal in the 1990 European Cup final?

22. Herbert Kilpin was the founding father of the club and their first manager. Which country was he from?

23. Which Argentine club did they beat in the FIFA Club World Cup final in December 2007?

24. Which former player from 1960 to 1979 was also a former Member of the European Parliament?

25. What club record does Filippo Inzaghi hold?

26. Who scored twice in normal time in the 2005 UEFA Champions League final against Liverpool?

27. Which striker, with the same first name as Germany's 2014 FIFA World Cup final scorer, netted 33 goals in 77 games for the club over two spells, from 2013 to 2014 and from 2015 to 2016?

28. Who is their longest serving and most successful manager, winning two Serie A titles and two European Cups?

29. Which Italian was their top scorer in 2017-18 with 18 goals at the age of only 20?

30. Which Paraguayan club did they beat in the 1990 Intercontinental Cup?

AJAX

1. Which Greek god is depicted on their emblem?

2. Who scored their winning goal in the 1995 UEFA Champions League final?

3. Which Spanish club did they beat in the 1995 UEFA Super Cup?

4. In which year did they win their only UEFA Cup, beating Torino in the final?

5. Which Ajax player was the Eredivisie's joint top scorer in 2018-19 with 28 goals?

6. Which Finn is their highest ever scorer in Europe with 26 goals?

7. Which player was sold to Juventus for €75m in July 2019?

8. Which German club did they beat in the 1987 Cup Winners' Cup final?

9. How many games did they play in Europe in total in 2016-17 in reaching the UEFA Europa League final?

10. Who has been their mascot since 2000?

11. Which club squad number did they retire in 2007?

12. Who is known as Mr Ajax, who made a club record 603 appearances for the club?

13. What is the name of Daley Blind's father who coached them and was a UEFA Champions League winner with them?

14. Which Moroccan international joined them from Twente for €11m in 2016?

15. Which Ajax player was the Eredivisie's top scorer for three successive seasons from 1991 to 1993?

16. Who won 71 of his 83 caps for the Netherlands while playing for Ajax from 1968 to 1980?

17. Who in 1993 became their youngest scorer at the age of 16 years and 361 days?

18. Who in 2018 became their youngest ever player at the age of 16 years and 130 days?

19. Which Ajax player represented Argentina at the 2018 FIFA World Cup?

20. Who scored 49 goals in all competitions for the club in the 2009-10 season?

21. Which Luxembourg club did they beat 14-0 in a UEFA Cup match in 1984?

22. Which club did they beat in the 1996 UEFA Champions League semi-final despite losing the first leg 1-0 at home?

23. In which Dutch city did they win the 1972 European Cup final?

24. What was the name of the twins who played for the club in the 1990s?

25. A meeting between Ajax and which other Dutch club is known as 'The Classic'?

26. Which attacking midfielder won the Dutch Footballer of the Year award in 2016?

27. In which three consecutive years did they win the European Cup?

28. Who was the only Ajax player to represent the Netherlands at UEFA Euro 2012?

29. Which legendary Dutch manager won league titles as their manager from 1966 to 1970?

30. Who once scored six goals for the club in a Dutch Cup tie in September 2014?

ARSENAL

1. In 2003-04 they became the first side since which team in 1888-89 to go unbeaten throughout a whole season in England's top division?

2. Who scored a hat-trick in their 4-2 win at Werder Bremen in the UEFA Cup in 2000?

3. In which city did they win the 1994 Cup Winners' Cup final?

4. In which year did they move from Highbury to the Emirates Stadium?

5. Which club did they beat in the 1993 FA Cup and League Cup finals?

6. Who scored their 1-0 winner at Old Trafford in May 2002 to clinch the Premier League title?

7. Which club beat them in the 1994 UEFA Super Cup?

8. Which manager led them to two league titles in the 1930s?

9. Who scored a hat-trick in their 3-2 Premier League win at Chelsea in October 1999?

10. Arsene Wenger's first match in charge of the club was a 2-0 win at which club in October 1996?

11. Who in 2003 became Arsenal's youngest ever player at the age of 16 years and 177 days?

12. Who scored after 20 seconds of their UEFA Champions League match at PSV Eindhoven in 2002?

13. Who won 77 of his 86 England caps while playing for the club?

14. Whom did Ian Wright surpass as their record scorer in 1997?

15. Who missed the decisive penalty in their 1980 Cup Winners' Cup final shoot-out defeat to Valencia?

16. George Graham and which other man has been manager of both Arsenal and Tottenham?

17. Who finished as their top scorer in the 2007-08 season with 30 goals in all competitions?

18. Who was the first Arsenal player to play in a FIFA World Cup final?

19. To which club did they lose 4-2 at home in their very first Premier League match in 1992?

20. Which future manager scored on his debut for the club against Manchester United in September 1998?

21. Who scored their late winner against Manchester United in the 1979 FA Cup final? His surname is the name of an English club.

22. Which Cameroonian played 241 games for the club from 2000 to 2006?

23. Who scored all four goals in their 4-4 draw at Anfield in April 2009?

24. Who had two spells as their caretaker manager in the 1990s?

25. Which Irish defender has made the most appearances for the club?

26. Which club ended their 49-match Premier League unbeaten run in October 2004?

27. Only two foreign players are in the top ten of their all-time goal-scoring list. Thierry Henry is one, but who is the other?

28. Who scored their winner in the 1993 League Cup final?

29. Against which European club did Thierry Henry score in 2005 to become their record scorer?

30. Which club did they beat in the 1970 Inter-Cities Fairs Cup final?

ATLETICO MADRID

1. Which teenager joined them from Benfica for £113m in July 2019?

2. To which club did they lose in a replay in the 1974 European Cup final?

3. What wild animal are they associated with?

4. Who was their top scorer for five successive seasons from 2002 to 2007?

5. Who was their coach before Diego Simeone?

6. Which club did they beat 4-1 in the 2012 UEFA Super Cup?

7. Who scored 133 goals for the club from 2014 to 2019?

8. Which major final did their Metropolitano Stadium host in 2019?

9. Which Dutch international scored 33 goals in all competitions for the club in 1999-2000?

10. Which controversial politician and businessman was their president from 1987 to 2003?

11. Who missed the only penalty in their 2016 UEFA Champions League final shoot-out defeat to Real Madrid?

12. Who had four spells as their coach and is also their record scorer?

13. Which Argentine club did they beat in the Intercontinental Cup in 1974?

14. What was the name of their former stadium before they moved to the Metropolitano in 2017?

15. Which goalkeeper came up through the youth ranks at the club and spent two seasons in the first team from 2009 to 2011 before moving to England?

16. Which European trophy did they win first?

17. What did they achieve for the first time in 1996?

18. Which Brazilian-born striker scored 36 goals in all competitions for the club in the 2013-14 season?

19. What did Jose Eulogio Garate achieve for three seasons in a row at the club from 1968 to 1971?

20. Who has been their honorary president since 2003?

21. Which club did they beat in the 2018 UEFA Europa League final?

22. Which Spanish international made his first-team debut in 2009 and has made over 400 appearances for the club?

23. To which club did they lose in the UEFA Champions League round of 16 in 2018-19 despite being two goals ahead in the first leg?

24. Who scored 12 goals in their 2011-12 UEFA Europa League campaign?

25. Which club did Thibaut Courtois, Felipe Luis, Diego Costa, Alvaro Morata and Fernando Torres also play for apart from Atletico?

26. Which England international joined them in 2019?

27. Which Italian was La Liga's top scorer in 1997-98 while playing for the club?

28. Which Ukrainian club beat them in the 1986 Cup Winners' Cup final?

29. Which goalkeeper has played for both Atletico and Real Madrid since 2014?

30. Who scored both goals in their 2010 UEFA Europa League final win over Fulham?

BARCELONA

1. Which classy midfielder made 767 appearances for the club from 1998 to 2015?

2. Against which club do they contest the 'El derbi Barceloni'?

3. What club record does Carles Rexach hold?

4. In which year did they first win the treble of Spanish League, Spanish Cup and UEFA Champions League?

5. In the 1998-99 season eight Dutchmen played for the club. Can you name five of them?

6. Which Barcelona player won the Zamora Trophy for the best goalkeeper in La Liga in 2014-15?

7. Which Spanish international scored a nine-minute hat-trick for the club against Getafe in December 2013?

8. Name the four Brazilians who have won the FIFA World Player of the Year Award while playing for the club.

9. Which European trophy did Bobby Robson win as their coach?

10. Three players have won four UEFA Champions League trophies with the club. Lionel Messi and Xavi are two – who is the other?

11. What club record does Hans Krankl hold?

12. How many goals were scored in all competitions by Messi, Neymar and Luis Suarez in the 2015-16 season – 121, 131 or 141?

13. In the 2009-10 season how many different official club competitions did Pedro score in?

14. Which club did Lionel Messi score five goals against in a UEFA Champions League match in 2012?

15. Who scored the winning goal in the 2006 UEFA Champions League final against Arsenal – his only goal for the club?

16. Who preceded Pep Guardiola as their manager?

17. How many goals did Laszlo Kubala score for the club in a league game against Sporting Gijon in 1952 – a La Liga record – six, seven or eight?

18. How many penalties out of four did they miss in their shoot-out defeat to Steaua Bucharest in the 1986 European Cup final?

19. Who won the Ballon d'Or while playing for the club in 1994?

20. How many goals did Lionel Messi score in all competitions in the 2011-12 season – 53, 63 or 73?

21. Which Serbian was briefly their manager in 2003?

22. Who was the only member of France's 2018 FIFA World Cup-winning squad on their books?

23. Which Barcelona player was the UEFA Champions League's joint top scorer in 1993-94 with eight goals?

24. They beat two English sides in their first two Inter-Cities Fairs Cup finals. Can you name either?

25. In the 2012-13 season they gained the most points ever in a La Liga season. How many points?

26. Which Argentine club did they beat in the 2015 FIFA Club World Cup final?

27. Who signed for the club for an initial £97m from Borussia Dortmund in 2017?

28. What is the surname of the father and son who played in goal for the club – the father from 1966 to 1973 and the son from 2000 to 2002?

29. What is the name of Rafael Nadal's paternal uncle who played for the club from 1991 to 1999?

30. Who was La Liga's top scorer in 2005-06 with 26 goals while playing for the club?

BAYERN MUNICH

1. Who won the Ballon d'Or in 1980 and 1981 while playing for the club?

2. Who had two spells as their manager, from 1998 to 2004 and from 2007 to 2008?

3. In which European Cup final did Franz Roth score their 1-0 winner?

4. What did they achieve for the first time in the 2019-20 UEFA Champions League group stage?

5. Which Frenchman won the UEFA Men's Player of the Year Award in 2013 as a Bayern player?

6. Who was the only member of West Germany's 1954 FIFA World Cup-winning squad who was playing for the club at the time?

7. In which year did they start playing at the Allianz Arena – 2005, 2006 or 2007?

8. Who is their longest serving manager, being in charge for almost nine years over two spells?

9. Which club are their main city rivals?

10. Which Brazilian scored 139 goals for them from 1997 to 2003?

11. Which European trophy did they win first (in 1967)?

12. Who scored after ten seconds, the fastest ever UEFA Champions League goal, playing for the club against Real Madrid in 2007?

13. Which Italian once scored four goals in their UEFA Cup win over Aris Salonika in 2007?

14. In which city did they beat Leeds United in the 1975 European Cup final?

15. Which brothers played together at the club at the start of the century?

16. Who scored 15 goals in their 1995-96 UEFA Cup-winning campaign?

17. Who was their 2001 UEFA Champions League-winning captain?

18. Which Bayern player was top scorer in the 1981-82 European Cup season?

19. The colours in the centre of their emblem are the colours of which German state?

20. Which Portuguese club did they beat 12-1 on aggregate in the UEFA Champions League round of 16 in 2009?

21. Which Bayern player was the Bundesliga's top scorer in the 2010-11 season?

22. Which Frenchman was their caretaker manager for nine days in 2017?

23. Who was the only member of France's 1998 FIFA World Cup-winning squad who was playing for the club at the time?

24. Who scored their winning goal in the 2013 UEFA Champions League final against Borussia Dortmund?

25. Who scored in both legs of their 1996 UEFA Cup final win over Bordeaux?

26. Who was their club captain from 2011 to 2017?

27. Which goalkeeper is their record appearance maker?

28. Who scored their goal in the 1999 UEFA Champions League final against Manchester United?

29. Which Croatian was their top scorer in the 2012-13 and 2013-14 seasons with 22 and 26 goals in all competitions respectively?

30. Which Dane in 2012 became their youngest ever player at the age of 17 years and 10 days?

BENFICA

1. In which consecutive years did they win the European Cup?

2. Which club do they play against in the 'O Clássico'?

3. Which former England manager was their boss from 1989 to 1992?

4. Who has made the most appearances for the club, playing 575 games from 1968 to 1986?

5. Which team from southern Spain beat them in their very first European match in 1957?

6. Who is the only non-Portuguese player in their top ten list of all-time top scorers with 172 goals?

7. From which club did they sign Julian Weigl in January 2020?

8. Which Brazilian was their top scorer in the 2013-14 season with 21 goals?

9. Which club did they lose to in a penalty shoot-out in the 2014 UEFA Europa League final?

10. What did they achieve for the first time in the 2013-14 season?

11. Who was their manager for only 11 matches in 2000?

12. Who scored their goal in the 1968 European Cup final?

13. Which Brazilian has made the most appearances in Europe for the club?

14. What nickname do they share with English club Crystal Palace?

15. Bela Guttmann won two European Cups as their manager. What nationality was he?

16. Which Luxembourg club did they once beat 10-0 in a European Cup match in 1965?

17. What feat did they achieve in the 1972-73 league season?

18. Sheu scored their only goal against which club in the 1983 UEFA Cup final?

19. Which Greek international was their top scorer in the 2016-17 season with 27 goals?

20. Who was their manager for six years from 2009 to 2015?

21. Who scored a UEFA Europa League hat-trick for the club against Eintracht Frankfurt in 2019 at the age of 19?

22. Which Uruguayan club did they lose to in the 1961 Intercontinental Cup?

23. Which Belgian was sold to Zenit St Petersburg for 40 million euros in 2012?

24. Name either of the two players who scored for the club in both the 1961 and 1962 European Cup finals.

25. Which Brazilian scored 37 goals in all competitions for the club in the 2017-18 season?

26. Which team did they beat 6-2 in the 2016 League Cup final?

27. Who scored 166 goals for the club over two spells, most recently from 2002 to 2011?

28. What unwanted thing did Antonio Veloso do in the 1988 European Cup final?

29. Which Swede with the initials M.M. scored 84 goals for the club from 1987 to 1992?

30. Which club do they play against in the 'Derby de Lisboa'?

BORUSSIA DORTMUND

1. In which year did they win the UEFA Champions League?

2. Who in August 2005 became the youngest player to appear in the Bundesliga when he played for the club against Wolfsburg at the age of 16 years and 335 days?

3. Which goalkeeper spent 16 years at the club from 2002 to 2018?

4. In which year did they achieve the League and Cup double for the first time in their history?

5. What is the nickname of their 24,454-capacity South Bank terrace at their stadium?

6. Who scored 79 goals in five seasons for the club from 2001 to 2006?

7. Who joined them on loan from Juventus in January 2020 – his third German club as a professional?

8. Who scored a hat-trick in their 5-2 Cup final win over Bayern Munich in 2012?

9. Who returned in 2019 after previously being at the club from 2008 to 2016?

10. Which club did they beat in the 1966 Cup Winners' Cup final?

11. Which Brazilian was the Bundesliga's top scorer while at the club in the 2001-02 season with 18 goals?

12. Who had two spells at the club with a spell at Manchester United sandwiched in between?

13. Who in 1997 became the only non-German to win a major trophy as their manager?

14. What is the first name of Eden Hazard's younger brother who joined the club in 2019?

15. Who is the only non-German to appear in the club's list of top ten all-time appearance makers, playing 398 games from 1998 to 2011?

16. Which three letters are the club simply known as?

17. Who made a club record 463 appearances for them from 1981 to 1998?

18. Who was the only member of Germany's 2018 FIFA World Cup squad who was playing for the club at the time?

19. Who scored twice in a UEFA Champions League final for the club before joining Liverpool?

20. Which team did they beat 8-4 in a UEFA Champions League match in November 2016?

21. Which Swiss scored 123 goals for the club from 1991 to 1999?

22. Who scored four goals for the club in the 2019-20 UEFA Champions League group stage?

23. Can you name the two Dutchmen who have been their manager?

24. Who scored their goal in the 2013 UEFA Champions League final?

25. Who was their top scorer in the 2009-10 and 2010-11 seasons with 23 and 21 goals respectively?

26. Which Brazilian club did they beat in the 1997 Intercontinental Cup?

27. Who scored 14 goals in their 1965-66 Cup Winners' Cup campaign, including six in one game?

28. Who joined the club from Shakhtar Donetsk for £23.6m in July 2013?

29. Which manager led them to two Bundesliga titles in the 1990s?

30. Which club did they lose to in the 2002 UEFA Cup final?

CELTIC

1. Which flower is depicted on their emblem, above?

2. Which club did they beat in the 1967 European Cup final?

3. Which Englishman scored 31 goals in all competitions for the club in the 2012-13 season?

4. In which city did they lose the 2003 UEFA Cup final to Porto?

5. Only two Englishmen have been their manager. Can you name them?

6. Which Mark once scored a three-minute hat-trick for the club against Jeunesse Esch in the UEFA Cup in 2000?

7. Who in May 2016 became their youngest ever goalscorer at the age of 16 years and 71 days?

8. Which Celtic player in December 2019 became the youngest ever to play for a Scottish team in European competition?

9. Their stadium lies in which area of Glasgow, and the stadium is often called this name by the fans?

10. What is the collective name for Celtic and Rangers?

11. From May 2016 to December 2017 they went a UK professional club record number of domestic games unbeaten. How many games was it – 59, 69 or 79?

12. What club record does Henrik Larsson hold?

13. Which club did they beat a record 9-0 in a Scottish Premiership match in November 2010?

14. Who is their most successful manager since the Second World War, winning ten League titles, eight Scottish Cups, six Scottish League Cups and one European Cup?

15. Which English club did they beat in the quarter-finals of the 2002-03 UEFA Cup?

16. Which Dutch club beat them in the 1970 European Cup final?

17. Who scored both goals in their 2019 Scottish Cup final win over Hearts?

18. Which Norwegian was their manager from 2014 to 2016?

19. Which former English Premier League striker became their oldest debutant when he played in 2006 at the age of 36?

20. Up to and including the 2018-19 season how many successive Scottish Premiership titles had they won?

21. Which former English Premier League winner scored 86 goals for the club from 2000 to 2005?

22. What is the nickname given to the team that won the 1967 European Cup final?

23. What is the name of their weekly magazine, the oldest club magazine in football, having been launched in 1965?

24. Which Wales international joined them from Coventry City for £6m in 2001?

25. Which midfielder made his 500th appearance for the club in December 2018?

26. Which Argentine club beat them in the 1967 Intercontinental Cup?

27. Who is the only Scot to have managed them on a full-time basis this century?

28. Which Dutch player was sold by them to Southampton for £11.5m in 2015?

29. Which former Tottenham striker scored 16 goals in 19 games for the club in the second half of the 2009-10 season?

30. What is their official nickname?

CHELSEA

1. Who in May 2014 became their oldest player at the age of 41 years and 218 days?

2. Which two Dutchmen have been their manager?

3. Which German club did they beat in the 1997 Cup Winners' Cup final?

4. Who has made the most appearances for the club, playing 795 games from 1961 to 1980?

5. Against which Norwegian club did Gianluca Vialli score a hat-trick in the Cup Winners' Cup in 1997?

6. Which Serb scored the third goal in their 2005 League Cup final win over Liverpool?

7. Can you name all of their five Italian managers?

8. Which two players joined them from Porto in 2004?

9. In winning the UEFA Europa League in 2013 what English first did they achieve in Europe?

10. They won the FA Cup for the first time in 1970. Which team did they beat after a replay in the final?

11. Who scored 78 goals in six seasons with them before joining Barcelona?

12. What was their first European trophy, winning it in 1971?

13. What animal is depicted on their crest?

14. In 2019 Frank Lampard became the first English manager of the club since whom in 1996?

15. Who scored their last-minute winner against Benfica in the 2013 UEFA Europa League final?

16. Which player, known as 'The Cat', made the most appearances for the club as a goalkeeper, playing 729 games from 1959 to 1979?

17. They won the League title in 2005, but in which year did they last win the League before this – 1953, 1954 or 1955?

18. Which renowned England international striker scored 41 league goals for the club in the 1960-61 season?

19. Who scored a hat-trick in their 1986 Full Members' Cup final win over Manchester City?

20. Who scored eleven goals in their 2018-19 UEFA Europa League-winning campaign?

21. How many goals did Didier Drogba score for the club in cup finals – eight, nine or ten?

22. Who is the only manager to have won the League and Cup double in his first season in charge at the club?

23. Whose club scoring record did Frank Lampard surpass?

24. Who is their record scorer in European competitions with 36 goals?

25. Who is the only foreign player in the top ten of their all-time appearance list?

26. Who had his penalty saved in their shoot-out defeat to Manchester United in the 2008 UEFA Champions League final?

27. Who once scored five goals in their 13-0 Cup Winners' Cup win over Jeunesse Esch in 1971?

28. Name either of the two clubs that Frank Lampard scored four goals for the club against in a Premier League match.

29. Who scored for the club after just 42 seconds of the 1997 FA Cup final against Middlesbrough?

30. In the mid-2000s two players who shared the same first name were in the team – one a German international and the other a Ghanaian international. What was their first name?

CLUB AMERICA

1. What is the name of their home stadium?

2. Which club do they play against in the 'El Super Clasico'?

3. In which CONCACAF tournament did they beat fellow Mexican club Tigres in the final in 2016?

4. Why do they have the word 'America' in their name?

5. Which Argentine side beat them in the 2007 Copa Sudamericana final?

6. Who has made the most appearances for the club?

7. Percy Clifford was manager of the club in the late 1920s. What nationality was he?

8. In which year did their stadium host the Summer Olympic Games?

9. What is the nickname shared by both of the father and son duo who rank fourth and first respectively on the club's all-time top scorers list?

10. By what score in the penalty shoot-out did they beat Tigres in the 2019 Campeon de Campeones?

11. Which tournament did they win twice, in 1978 and in 1991?

12. Which side beat them in the semi-finals of the 2016 FIFA Club World Cup?

13. Which former Real Madrid and Inter Milan striker played for the club from 2001 to 2003?

14. Who scored their famous golden goal winner against Club Necaxa in the 2002 league final?

15. Which club do they play against in the 'Clasico Joven'?

16. Who had three spells as their manager, from 2001 to 2003, in 2006 and from 2010 to 2011?

17. Name either of their two players who were joint top scorers in the 2014-15 CONCACAF Champions League.

18. Jorge Solari was briefly their manager in 1997. What is the name of his nephew, who both played for and managed Real Madrid?

19. Which Ecuadorian international striker was their top scorer for three league seasons in a row from 2011 to 2013?

20. Who scored both goals in their 2005 Campeon de Campeones win over Pumas?

21. Who scored both goals for the club in the 2018 Apertura final against Cruz Azul?

22. Which club did they beat in the Clausura 2019 Copa MX Final?

23. Which Ecuadorian club beat them in the semi-finals of the 2008 Copa Libertadores?

24. From which club did Hugo Sanchez join them in 1992?

25. Which former Cameroonian international played for the club for three years?

26. Which Paraguayan international striker was the top scorer at the 2007 and 2008 Copa Libertadores while playing for the club?

27. Which club do they play against in the 'Clasico Capitalino'?

28. Which former Netherlands, Ajax and Real Madrid manager was their boss from 1994 to 1995?

29. Which team beat them in the semi-finals of the 2006 FIFA Club World Cup?

30. Which United States side did they beat in the 2001 CONCACAF Giant Cup final?

INDEPENDIENTE

1. In which city are they based?

2. Which future Argentine international striker made his debut for the club as a 15-year-old in 2003?

3. Name either of the two Uruguayan clubs they've beaten in a Copa Libertadores final.

4. In which competition did they lose to Brazilian club Internacional in 2011?

5. Which club did they beat in the 1984 Intercontinental Cup?

6. Who scored twice in the second leg of their Copa Sudamericana final against Goias in 2010?

7. They won four Copa Libertadores in a row in the 1970s. Do you know which years?

8. Which former Argentine international defender had two spells as a player with the club and was also briefly their manager in 2016?

9. Which Italian club did they beat in the 1973 Intercontinental Cup?

10. Which club do they play against in the Avellaneda derby?

11. Who is their all-time top scorer, netting 293 goals from 1933 to 1946?

12. Name either of the two Brazilian clubs they've beaten in a Copa Libertadores final.

13. What colour are their home shirts?

14. What is the name of their former player and manager who scored Argentina's 3-2 winner in the 1986 FIFA World Cup final?

15. In which year were they officially formed – 1905, 1915 or 1925?

16. Which Japanese club did they beat in the 2018 Suruga Bank Championship?

17. Which Brazilian club did they beat in the 2017 Copa Sudamericana final?

18. Name either of the two Chilean clubs they've beaten in a Copa Libertadores final.

19. One of their nicknames is 'Los Diablos Rojos'. What does this mean in English?

20. What is the name of their stadium?

21. Which FIFA World Cup-winning manager had four spells as their boss?

22. They are one of Argentina's 'big five' clubs. Can you name three of the other four?

23. Which player did they sell to Ajax in 2018?

24. Which of their former goalkeepers had a brief spell at Sunderland in 2014?

25. Which former Valencia and Liverpool defender was their manager from 2015 to 2016?

26. Which Argentine club did they lose to at the quarter-final stage of the 2018 Copa Libertadores?

27. In which district of Buenos Aires were they originally founded?

28. Which striker did they sell to Manchester United in 2002?

29. In which city did they win the 1973 Intercontinental Cup?

30. Which Italian club did they lose to in the 1964 and 1965 Intercontinental Cups?

INTER MILAN

1. Who won the Ballon d'Or in 1990 while he was on their books?

2. Who scored both goals in their 2010 UEFA Champions League final win over Bayern?

3. What club record does Alessandro Altobelli hold?

4. Which Argentine club did they beat in both the 1964 and 1965 Intercontinental Cups?

5. Which Inter player was Serie A's joint top scorer in 2017-18 with 29 goals?

6. Which Argentine scored five goals in their 2019-20 UEFA Champions League campaign?

7. Who was their top scorer for five successive seasons from 1999 to 2004?

8. Who was the only member of France's 1998 FIFA World Cup-winning squad who was playing for the club at the time?

9. They have never been relegated from the top division – true or false?

10. Who is their record goalscorer and has their stadium named after him?

11. Which club do they play against in the 'Derby d'Italia'?

12. Who scored eight goals in their 1996-97 UEFA Cup campaign? He also went on to play for AC Milan.

13. Their main nickname is 'I Nerazzurri'. What is this translated into English?

14. Which player on loan at the club was sent off on his full debut in September 2019?

15. Which Congolese club did they beat in the 2010 FIFA Club World Cup final?

16. Which Brazilian scored two UEFA Champions League hat-tricks for the club in 2005, one against Porto and the other against Artmedia?

17. In which city did they win the 1965 European Cup final against Benfica?

18. Which entrepreneur with the initials M.M. was their president from 1995 to 2004 and from 2006 to 2013?

19. Which fellow Italian club did they beat in the 1998 UEFA Cup final?

20. Geoffrey Kondogbia joined them for 31 million euros from Monaco in June 2015. Which two nations has he played for internationally?

21. Who was their manager when they won the UEFA Cup in 1991? He also won two UEFA Cups as Juventus boss.

22. What did they achieve in 2010, becoming the first-ever Italian club to do so?

23. Which Argentine has made the most appearances for the club, with 858 from 1995 to 2014?

24. Which club did they beat in the final to win their first European Cup in 1964?

25. Which Englishman had two spells as their manager during the 1990s?

26. Which former Barcelona striker scored 37 goals in all competitions for the club in the 2010-11 season?

27. Which Inter player was Serie A's top scorer in 2008-09 with 25 goals?

28. Who scored eight goals in their 1993-94 UEFA Cup-winning campaign?

29. Which two members of Italy's 2006 FIFA World Cup-winning squad were playing for the club at the time?

30. Who has made the most appearances for the club as a goalkeeper? He made 473 appearances from 1982 to 1994.

JUVENTUS

JUVENTUS

1. Who was their captain when they won the 1996 UEFA Champions League final?

2. What was the name of their stadium for 16 years, from 1990 to 2006?

3. Which major European trophy did they win first (in 1977)?

4. Which Argentine scored 32 goals in all competitions for the club in the 2016-17 season?

5. What is their most common nickname?

6. Who was their most successful manager, winning 14 trophies in his 13 years in charge over two spells?

7. In 1985 they were the first club to achieve what feat in European football?

8. Who has managed them in the most UEFA Champions League matches?

9. Which club do they play against in the 'Derby della Mole'?

10. In which year did they move into their current stadium, the Juventus stadium?

11. Which Serb scored ten goals in their UEFA Cup campaign in 1999-2000?

12. Which Welshman scored 109 goals for the club from 1957 to 1962?

13. Which Argentine was their top scorer in the 2013-14 and 2014-15 seasons with 21 and 29 goals respectively?

14. Who is the only Dutchman to have played over 200 games for the club?

15. Who is their all-time leading scorer, netting 290 goals from 1993 to 2012?

16. In which two years in the 1990s and 2010s did they lose to Real Madrid in UEFA Champions League finals?

17. Which fellow Italian club did they beat in the 1990 UEFA Cup final?

18. Name either of the two Juventus players to have won the FIFA World Cup Golden Boot.

19. Who won the Ballon d'Or in 2003 whilst he was a Juventus player?

20. Which European trophy did they win in 1999?

21. Who scored three goals over the two legs of their 1993 UEFA Cup final win over Dortmund?

22. Two players with the first name Roberto are in the top ten of their all-time goalscoring list. Roberto Baggio is one, but who is the other?

23. Which Portuguese club did they beat in the 1984 Cup Winners' Cup final?

24. Which defender made his 500th appearance for the club in 2019?

25. Up to and including the 2018-19 season, how many successive Serie A titles had they won?

26. Which fellow Italian club did they lose to in the 1995 UEFA Cup final?

27. Who scored their winning goal in the 1985 European Cup final?

28. Who was the only member of France's 2018 FIFA World Cup-winning squad who was playing for the club at the time?

29. Which club did they beat 9-2 on aggregate in the 1996 UEFA Super Cup?

30. Who once scored five goals in their UEFA Cup match against CSKA Sofia in 1994?

LIVERPOOL

1. Who is their record league goalscorer with 245 goals?

2. Who was their manager for only 31 matches?

3. Who scored 18 goals for the club as a substitute from 1975 to 1983?

4. Who scored in both legs of their 1976 UEFA Cup final win over Club Bruges?

5. Who scored their winning penalty in their 1984 European Cup shoot-out win over Roma?

6. Who has scored the most goals for the club in Europe, with 41 to his name?

7. Which club did they beat in the 2005 UEFA Super Cup?

8. From which club did Naby Keita join them for £48 million in 2018?

9. What is the name of their famous anthem?

10. Against which club did Robbie Fowler score a hat-trick in 4 minutes and 33 seconds in 1994?

11. How many goals did the trio of Mo Salah, Sadio Mane and Roberto Firmino score in all competitions for them in the 2017-18 season – 71, 81 or 91?

12. Who has made the most appearances for the club, playing 857 games from 1960 to 1978?

13. Name either of the two England internationals who played 665 games for the club.

14. Who in 2002 became the first non-British player to play in a FIFA World Cup final while being on the club's books?

15. Against which club did Michael Owen score on his first-team debut in May 1997?

16. In which year did they win the FA Cup, League Cup and UEFA Cup treble?

17. Who became their youngest scorer in 2016 at the age of 17 years and 45 days?

18. Which defender made 464 appearances for the club from 1999 to 2009?

19. Which club did they beat in the 1973 UEFA Cup and 1977 European Cup finals?

20. Which midfielder scored two hat-tricks in their 1980-81 European Cup-winning campaign?

21. In which city did they win the 1981 European Cup final?

22. Who in 2012 became their youngest ever player at the age of 16 years and 6 days?

23. Three players from the club were in England's 1966 FIFA World Cup-winning squad. Roger Hunt was one – but can you name the other two?

24. Who is the only non-British player in their top ten list of all-time appearance makers, playing 628 games from 1980 to 1994?

25. Which Dutch goalkeeper played 103 games for the club from 1999 to 2001?

26. Who scored on his debut for the club against Fulham in a League Cup match in September 1993?

27. Which club did they beat 8-0 in a Champions League match in 2007?

28. Who made an amazing 417 consecutive appearances for the club from 1976 to 1983?

29. Who scored their winner in the 2019 FIFA Club World Cup final?

30. Which player with the first name Mark scored their first-ever Premier League goal, against Sheffield United in 1992?

MANCHESTER CITY

1. Which club did they beat in the 2011 FA Cup final?

2. Which Frenchman scored on his debut for the club against Charlton Athletic in August 2003?

3. Who was sent off three times for the club in the 2016-17 season?

4. Whose club goalscoring record did Sergio Aguero surpass? His surname is connected with a famous Grand National fence.

5. Who was their manager when they won the 1967-68 League title?

6. Which Spaniard scored a hat-trick in their UEFA Champions League win over CSKA Moscow in November 2013?

7. In 2008 they were taken over by a company from which country?

8. From which club did they sign Aymeric Laporte in 2018?

9. What vessel is depicted on the upper half of the shield on their emblem?

10. Swansea City conceded two goals in August 2011 to a man making his club debut as a substitute. Which man?

11. In which year did they move to the City of Manchester Stadium?

12. Which goalkeeper made 604 appearances for the club from 1967 to 1983?

13. Which club did they draw 1-1 against in their very first Premier League game in 1992?

14. Which player, who shares his surname with a famous actor who played Dracula, scored six goals in their 1969-70 Cup Winners' Cup-winning campaign?

15. Squad number 23 has not been used since 2003 in memory of which former player?

16. Up to and including 2018-19 which three English clubs have eliminated them from European competition?

17. Who was their 1969 FA Cup final-winning captain? His surname is connected to a yellow card.

18. Which club did they beat on penalties to win the Second Division play-off final in 1999?

19. What new English record did they achieve in the 2018-19 season?

20. Which player, who shares his surname with a 1980s pop star called Paul, scored their winning goal in the 1969 FA Cup final against Leicester City?

21. Against which London club did Kevin De Bruyne score on his full debut for the club in September 2015?

22. Which Italian was sent off on his debut for the club against Chelsea in August 2006?

23. What was the name of their previous stadium where they played for 80 years?

24. Which club did they beat in the 1970 Cup Winners' Cup final?

25. Which City player was voted 2017-18 PFA Young Player of the Year?

26. Which player, who shares his first name with the husband of a prime minister, scored their spectacular overhead winner in the 1976 League Cup final?

27. Against which Turkish club did they play in their very first match in Europe, losing to them in the European Cup in 1968?

28. In beating Watford 6-0 in the 2019 FA Cup they achieved the biggest FA Cup final win for how many years – 96, 106 or 116?

29. What is the name of the fans' dance that was inspired by a Polish side?

30. Which Italian scored on his debut for the club against West Ham in August 2007?

MANCHESTER UNITED

1. Which Ecuadorian club did they beat in the FIFA Club World Cup final in December 2008?

2. Which club did they beat in the 1999 FA Cup final to clinch the domestic double?

3. How many Premier League titles did they win under manager Alex Ferguson?

4. Which midfielder scored 155 goals in 718 games for the club from 1994 to 2013?

5. Which Argentine joined them for £59.7 million from Real Madrid in 2014?

6. Which club beat them in their very first Premier League game in August 1992?

7. Which team beat them 6-1 at Old Trafford in the Premier League in October 2011?

8. In which stadium did they beat Benfica in the 1968 European Cup final?

9. Which Scottish manager led them to FA Cup success in 1977?

10. Which player won the Ballon d'Or in 1968 while playing for the club?

11. Against which club did Wayne Rooney score a hat-trick on his debut for the club in 2004?

12. Which United defender became the first player to be sent off in an FA Cup final?

13. Paul Scholes and which other United player were suspended from the 1999 UEFA Champions League final?

14. Who became the first player to win the UEFA European Championship while being on their books?

15. Which Swedish international played 13 games for the club from January to March 2007?

16. In which country did they lose the 2017 UEFA Super Cup final to Real Madrid?

17. Against which Russian club did Peter Schmeichel score in a UEFA Cup match in 1995?

18. Who once scored four goals as a substitute in their 8-1 Premier League win at Nottingham Forest in February 1999?

19. Which goalkeeper did David Beckham score against from the halfway line in a Premier League match against Wimbledon in 1996?

20. Who was sent off more times for the club – Paul Scholes or Roy Keane?

21. Who scored both of their goals in their 1991 Cup Winners' Cup final win over Barcelona?

22. In 2016 Wayne Rooney scored his 39th European goal for the club, setting a new club record. Whose club record did he beat?

23. Which Dutch goalkeeper was at the club from 1996 to 2002?

24. Which club did they fail to beat on the final day of the 1994-95 season, a result which saw them lose their Premier League title to Blackburn?

25. Which winger went in the opposite direction in the Andy Cole transfer deal with Newcastle in January 1995?

26. Which Brazilian club did they beat in the 1999 Intercontinental Cup?

27. Which team did they once beat 10-0 in a European Cup match in 1956?

28. Who was the last foreign player to score 30 goals for the club in a season?

29. Who scored their 3-2 winner against Aston Villa on his first-team debut in April 2009?

30. What was their original name when it was founded?

PARIS ST GERMAIN

1. Which defender made his 300th appearance for the club in 2019?

2. Which European trophy did they win in 2001?

3. Which Paris St Germain player became the first defender to score a UEFA Champions League hat-trick?

4. Who ended his playing career with them in 2013, playing 14 games in all competitions?

5. What club record does Jean-Marc Pilorget hold?

6. Who scored his 200th goal for the club in February 2020?

7. In which year were they formed – 1950, 1960 or 1970?

8. Which Paris St Germain player won the Ligue 1 Player of the Season Award in 1993-94?

9. Against which club do they play 'Le Classique'?

10. Which player whose surname makes up half of the name of a Moscow-based club scored a hat-trick in their Cup Winners' Cup quarter-final, second leg against AEK Athens in 1997?

11. Which Brazilian was their captain from 1996 to 1998?

12. Which Brazilian finished as their top scorer in the 2011-12 season with 27 goals in all competitions?

13. Which club did they famously lose to in Europe over two legs despite winning the first leg 4-0?

14. What famous monument is depicted on their emblem?

15. Who was sent off for them in the 2016 Coupe de la Ligue final against Lille?

16. Who scored four goals in their UEFA Champions League match against Anderlecht in 2013?

17. Which future France national manager led them to their first-ever Ligue 1 title in 1986?

18. Which Brazilian scored his first professional goal on his club debut against Olympiacos in September 2013?

19. Which Reunion-born striker scored their 1-0 winner in the 2010 Coupe de France final against Monaco?

20. Which Portuguese twice won the Ligue 1 Golden Boot whilst at the club in the 2000s?

21. Former players Jerome and Laurent shared which surname?

22. Which player, who shares his first name with a pop star from another planet, scored their winning goal in the 1996 Cup Winners' Cup final against Rapid Vienna?

23. What club first did Dominique Rocheteau achieve in 1987?

24. Which player, who shares his surname with France's most capped goalkeeper, scored and was sent off in their 2003 Coupe de France final defeat to Auxerre?

25. How many goals did the trio of Neymar, Cavani and Mbappe score in all competitions for the club in the 2017-18 season – 80, 90 or 100?

26. Which midfielder made his 300th appearance for the club in 2020?

27. Which club did they lose to in the 1997 Cup Winners' Cup final?

28. From which club did they sign Leandro Paredes for 47 million euros in 2019?

29. Which manager won the Ligue 1 title in each of his three seasons with the club?

30. What is the surname of the father and son who played for the club in the 1970s and 1990s respectively?

RANGERS

1. Who was their last English manager before Steven Gerrard?

2. In which city did they lose the 2008 UEFA Cup final to Zenit St Petersburg?

3. Who was the first Rangers player to score at the UEFA European Championship?

4. Who holds the unofficial club record for most appearances for the club – including friendlies and war-time appearances – playing 940 times between 1925 and 1947?

5. Which Russian club did they beat in the 1972 Cup Winners' Cup final?

6. Who became their first non-Scottish manager in 1998?

7. Which Italian defender scored their winner in the 2003 Scottish Cup final?

8. Who made a club record 755 appearances for the club from 1961 to 1978?

9. Which Northern Ireland international made his debut for the club in November 2018 at the age of 38 years and 338 days?

10. Who once scored four goals for the club in a Cup Winners' Cup match in 1983?

11. Which English club did they beat in the 1961 Cup Winners' Cup semi-final?

12. Which goalkeeper joined them four days after he had been a member of France's 1998 FIFA World Cup-winning squad?

13. Prior to 2019-20 how many league titles had they won – a world record?

14. What British record did they achieve in Europe in 1961?

15. Which of their squad numbers is reserved for the fans?

16. Against which club did Ally McCoist score his last goal for the club in the 1998 Scottish Cup final?

17. Which former Liverpool team-mate of Steven Gerrard's joined them as assistant manager in 2018?

18. Which player, who shares his first name with a British 4x400m relay world champion from 1991, scored a hat-trick on his debut for the club in January 2006?

19. Which defender, who shares his surname with a former Scottish rugby international called Doddie, scored for the club against Kilmarnock in November 2008 at the age of 38 years and 183 days?

20. Which club signed Alan Hutton from the club for £9m in 2008?

21. Who is their most expensive signing, joining them from Chelsea for £12 million in 2000?

22. Which of their players, who shares his name with a famous snooker player, won the 2009-10 Scottish PFA Player of the Year Award?

23. Which Spaniard scored 25 goals in all competitions for the club in his first season in 2004-05?

24. From which club did Andrei Kanchelskis join the club in 1998?

25. Which goalkeeper has made the most Rangers appearances by a non-UK player?

26. Which Rangers player was the first to appear at the UEFA European Championship?

27. Which Rangers player became the first Dutchman to win the Scottish PFA Player of the Year Award?

28. Which player, who played for both Rangers and Celtic, scored their winner in the 2010 Scottish League Cup final?

29. Which German club beat them 12-4 on aggregate in a European Cup semi-final in 1960?

30. Which former player was nicknamed The Hammer?

REAL MADRID

1. Which club did they beat in two of their first four European Cup finals?

2. Which striker who spent 17 years at the club scored eight goals in their 1982-83 Cup Winners' Cup campaign?

3. Which of their players was a member of France's 1998 FIFA World Cup-winning team?

4. From which club did they sign James Rodriguez for £63 million in 2014?

5. Who was the first non-Spanish player to make 500 appearances for the club, playing 527 games from 1996 to 2007?

6. Which manager won the UEFA Champions League in his only season in charge of the club?

7. Which of their players won the Ballon d'Or in 1957 and 1959?

8. Who scored their winner in the 1998 UEFA Champions League final?

9. Who scored in both of their 2014 and 2016 UEFA Champions League finals?

10. Which of their players, a Dutchman, was La Liga's top scorer in the 2006-07 season?

11. Who were considered the six Galacticos who played for the club in the 2003-04 season?

12. Which of their players became the first to be born in the 21st century to score a UEFA Champions League hat-trick, against Galatasaray in November 2019?

13. Which player, whose full name is Francisco Roman Alarcon Suarez, scored on his debut for the club against Real Betis in August 2013?

14. Which Real Madrid player won the Best FIFA Men's Player Award in 2018?

15. Who was the first player to reach 700 appearances for the club, doing so in 2000?

16. Who was their captain for eight years, from 1990 to 1998?

17. Against which club did Cristiano Ronaldo score a hat-trick in the 2016 FIFA Club World Cup final?

18. Who was the first German to play more than 300 games for the club?

19. Who has had two spells as their president, the first from 2000 to 2006 and the second beginning in 2009?

20. Which player has won the most major trophies with the club, winning 23 from 1953 to 1970?

21. Which club did they lose their first European Cup final against, and in which year?

22. Which Mexican won the European Golden Shoe Award while at the club with 38 goals in the 1989-90 season?

23. In the 1980s they lost to two UK clubs in European finals. Can you name both?

24. Which Norwegian became their youngest player in 2015 at the age of 16 years and 157 days?

25. Which of their former goalkeepers won the Ricardo Zamora Trophy in 1991-92?

26. Which former Mallorca player scored on his debut for the club, against Sevilla in the 2016 UEFA Super Cup?

27. Who has scored hat-tricks in two of their European Cup finals?

28. Which club do they play against in the 'Old Classic'?

29. Which of their players was a member of Argentina's 1986 FIFA World Cup-winning team?

30. Which club from Abu Dhabi did they beat in the 2018 FIFA Club World Cup final?

SANTOS

1. Which club did they beat in the 1962 Intercontinental Cup?

2. In which year did Pele make his debut for the club?

3. What is the name of their stadium?

4. Which club do they play the 'Black and White derby' against?

5. Who became their manager in December 2018 – the first non-Brazilian to be in charge for 40 years?

6. Which former Brazilian FIFA World Cup-winning captain played for the club in the mid-1980s?

7. What colour is their regular home shirt?

8. Which club did they beat in the 1962 and 2011 Copa Libertadores final?

9. In 1962 they became the first Brazilian club to win the Copa Libertadores without losing a match – true or false?

10. Who had four spells as their manager as well as being Real Madrid's boss in the mid-2000s?

11. In 2004 which player did they sell to Chelsea?

12. Which former Real Madrid and Manchester City player came up through the youth ranks at the club, making his first-team debut for the club in 2002?

13. In which city did they lose to Barcelona in the 2011 FIFA Club World Cup final?

14. Which club did they beat in the 2010 Copa do Brasil final?

15. Who made his debut for the club as a 17-year-old against Oeste in March 2009?

16. Which Portuguese club did Diego join from Santos in 2004?

17. One of their nicknames is 'Peixe' in Portuguese. What does this mean in English?

18. Which two-time UEFA Cup winner with Sevilla had two spells as their player?

19. What was the nickname for the group of Santos players that won a total of 25 titles between 1959 and 1974?

20. In January 1998 they became the first club to reach a goal milestone. How many goals had they scored in their history?

21. Which Argentine club did they beat in the 1998 Copa CONMEBOL final?

22. Which former Manchester City midfielder began his professional career with them in 2001 and was also briefly their manager in 2017?

23. Which Portuguese was appointed their manager in December 2019?

24. Which club did they beat in the 2012 Recopa Sudamericana?

25. How many of the 15 goals they scored in their 1962 and 1963 Intercontinental Cup matches did Pele score?

26. What was the name of the goalkeeper who won the 1958 and 1962 FIFA World Cups with Brazil and played for the club for eight years from 1961 to 1969?

27. How many official goals did Pele score for the club – 1,071, 1,081 or 1,091?

28. How many major trophies did they win in 1962?

29. Which club do they play the 'Nostalgia derby' against?

30. Which club did they beat in the 1963 Intercontinental Cup?

ANSWERS

1930 FIFA WORLD CUP URUGUAY™

1. 13
2. Youngest team manager (27)
3. Montevideo
4. First countries to win a FIFA World Cup match
5. First player to score a FIFA World Cup hat-trick
6. The ball was provided by Argentina in the first half and by Uruguay in the second half
7. Uruguay 4 Argentina 2
8. Yugoslavia
9. Romania v Peru
10. Jules Rimet
11. First player to score an own goal at the FIFA World Cup (he was also the first to score a penalty which he did in the next match v Argentina)
12. Olympic Games final
13. Estadio Centenario
14. He ended the match six minutes early (he subsequently brought teams back on the pitch later)
15. Alex Thepot (v Chile)
16. It was not played at the weekend (it was played on a Wednesday)
17. Belgian
18. Jose Pedro Cea
19. Jose Leandro Andrade
20. Hector Castro
21. Youngest coach to win the FIFA World Cup (31)
22. First player to be sent off in a FIFA World Cup match
23. He had to take a university exam
24. Manuel Rosas (for Mexico v Argentina)
25. First player to score in a FIFA World Cup final
26. Jose Nasazzi
27. 6-1
28. Belgium
29. Bolivia
30. A broken leg

1934 FIFA WORLD CUP ITALY™

1. First FIFA World Cup match to go to a replay
2. Germany
3. 12
4. Ricardo Zamora
5. Romania
6. Turin
7. They had to qualify for the tournament
8. Spain
9. Mexico
10. They all kicked off at the same time
11. South America (4 from Argentina, 1 from Brazil)
12. Luis Monti (Argentina in 1930 & Italy in 1934)
13. The first-ever FIFA World Cup match to go into extra time
14. In retaliation for Italy's refusal to travel in 1930
15. Hungary
16. United States
17. Edmund Conen
18. Trieste

19. Austria
20. 1990
21. Germany
22. They were both goalkeepers (the only time this has happened in a final)
23. 26
24. Italy 2 Czechoslovakia 1 (after extra time)
25. Egypt
26. England (1966)
27. Eight (the only time this has happened)
28. Vittorio Pozzo
29. Napoli
30. Stadio Flaminio

1938 FIFA WORLD CUP FRANCE™

1. Stade Velodrome
2. Because Austria had been absorbed into Germany before the tournament began
3. Gyorgy Sarosi
4. 1994
5. Silvio Piola
6. Stade Olympique de Colombes
7. Dutch East Indies (now Indonesia)
8. French (only man to referee a World Cup final in his native country)
9. Five
10. 1966 (England 4 West Germany 2) & 2018 (France 4 Croatia 2)
11. Score four times in a FIFA World Cup match
12. 1970 & 1994
13. 24 years (1962)
14. Brazil 4 Poland 4
15. Three
16. Cuba
17. Antibes
18. Czechoslovakia
19. Leonidas
20. Two

21. True
22. First player to score more than one goal in a final
23. Belgium
24. 16 (1934 to 1950)
25. Poland
26. 1974
27. Parc des Princes
28. 20 years (1958)
29. They were given a bye in the round of 16 against Austria
30. Hungary

1950 FIFA WORLD CUP BRAZIL™

1. Antonio Carbajal (Mexico)
2. George Reader (England)
3. Nilton Santos
4. 199,854
5. Telmo Zarra & Estanislau Basora
6. Sweden
7. Germany & Japan
8. True
9. Three (out of four)
10. Brazil
11. Maracana Stadium, Rio
12. Yugoslavia
13. India, Scotland & Turkey
14. 13
15. Uruguay
16. England
17. A win or a draw
18. Bolivia
19. Mexico
20. The Maracanazo (roughly translated as 'The Agony of Maracana')
21. Two
22. None
23. Recife
24. 88
25. 1990
26. Sweden & Spain
27. Walter Winterbottom (England)
28. 1994
29. Porto Alegre

30. Milorad Arsenijevic (1930 as a player and 1950 as a coach, both times for Yugoslavia)

1954 FIFA WORLD CUP SWITZERLAND™

1. Austria 7 Switzerland 5
2. Turkey
3. Scotland, Turkey & Korea Republic
4. True
5. Three
6. Sandor Kocsis
7. 140
8. Germany & Yugoslavia/Serbia
9. Spain
10. Kaiserslautern
11. Geneva
12. Korea Republic
13. England & Belgium
14. Uruguay
15. Sandor Kocsis (Hungary), Erich Probst (Austria), Max Morlock (West Germany) and Josef Hugi (Switzerland)
16. Most goals scored (25) and conceded (14) by the eventual winners
17. West Germany (1974), Argentina (1978) & Spain (2010)
18. Hungary 4 Brazil 2
19. Lugano
20. Eight
21. Tommy Docherty
22. The only time that a team has won without playing any team from outside its own continent
23. 5.4
24. France
25. 11
26. True
27. Helmut Rahn
28. Gerd Muller (West Germany, 1970)
29. St Jakob Stadium, Basel
30. Turkey

1958 FIFA WORLD CUP SWEDEN™

1. Pele
2. Scotland
3. Vava
4. Bobby Robson
5. Uwe Seeler
6. Wales, Northern Ireland & Soviet Union
7. All four
8. Omar Oreste Corbatta
9. Rasunda Stadium
10. Erich Juskowiak
11. Gothenburg
12. 12
13. Harry Gregg
14. Mario Zagallo
15. True
16. Czechoslovakia
17. England
18. Brazil, 2002
19. Sandviken
20. Most goals in a FIFA World Cup final (5)
21. 31
22. Nine
23. 1958 (Brazil 5-2 Sweden), 1970 (Brazil 4-1 Italy), 1998 (France 3-0 Brazil)
24. The northern-most FIFA World Cup matches in history
25. England and Brazil
26. A broken leg
27. Brazil
28. Malmo Stadium, Malmo
29. False (Brazil also lost in 1950)
30. West Germany, third-place match

1962 FIFA WORLD CUP CHILE™

1. Santiago
2. Never
3. Uruguay
4. Alfredo Di Stefano
5. Sepp Herberger (West Germany) & Walter Winterbottom (England)

6. Argentina
7. Bulgaria & Colombia
8. Garrincha (Brazil) & Honorino Landa (Chile)
9. Czechoslovakia
10. Garrincha
11. Eladio Rojas
12. Four
13. Amarildo
14. It was scored directly from a corner
15. Five (1970, 1978, 1986, 1994 & 2002)
16. Vaclav Masek
17. Ron Flowers
18. Chile & Italy
19. Drazan Jerkovic
20. Aymore Moreira
21. Inter Milan
22. Switzerland
23. Leonel Sanchez
24. Earthquake (their largest ever recorded)
25. Colombia
26. Mauro Ramos
27. Czechoslovakia
28. Valentin Ivanov
29. Hungary
30. Mexico

1966 FIFA WORLD CUP ENGLAND™

1. Wolfgang Weber
2. Six
3. 1970 & 1990
4. Second linesman who took no part in Hurst's controversial second goal
5. Kenneth Wolstenholme
6. True
7. Elias Figueroa
8. The youngest ever goalkeeper to play in a FIFA World Cup match
9. Gordon (Banks), George (Cohen) & Geoff (Hurst)
10. 13
11. Helmut Schon (West Germany)

12. Roker Park, Sunderland
13. Africa
14. Uruguay
15. Pickles
16. World Cup Willie, Lion
17. Croatia, 1998
18. White City Stadium
19. 89
20. 30 July
21. Edu
22. They became the first FIFA World Cup-winning team not to win its first game of the tournament
23. Rafael Albrecht (v West Germany) & Antonio Rattin (v England)
24. Roger Hunt
25. The first nation from outside Europe or the Americas to progress from the first stage
26. North Korea
27. Italy (1950), France (2002), Italy (2010), Spain (2014) & Germany (2018)
28. Goodison Park, Liverpool
29. Portugal
30. Helmut Haller

1970 FIFA WORLD CUP MEXICO™

1. Yellow and red cards
2. Jules Rimet Trophy
3. Alan Mullery
4. El Salvador, Israel and Morocco
5. First FIFA World Cup to be staged in North America, and first to be held outside Europe and South America
6. Uwe Seeler
7. Giacinto Facchetti
8. Israel
9. Juanito
10. Brazil
11. Estadio Nou Camp
12. Argentina
13. Teofilo Cubillas

14. 2006
15. Five (Italy 3 West Germany 2)
16. Anatoliy Puzach
17. Karl-Heinz Schnellinger
18. Peter Bonetti
19. Soviet Union and Mexico
20. None (1950 and 1970 are the only years in which no players have been sent off)
21. Carlos Alberto
22. Belgium
23. Eight
24. Gerd Muller (West Germany)
25. Mexico (v Italy)
26. Italy (Karl-Heinz Schnellinger, AC Milan & Helmut Haller, Juventus)
27. West Germany 1 Uruguay 0
28. Jairzinho
29. Egypt
30. Peru

1974 FIFA WORLD CUP WEST GERMANY™

1. True
2. Seven
3. Poland
4. Grzegorz Lato
5. Haiti
6. Spain
7. First player to be sent off with a red card in a FIFA World Cup match
8. Johan Neeskens
9. 2018
10. Poland and Netherlands
11. Tip and Tap
12. Poland
13. Hamburg
14. Scotland
15. Jan Tomaszewski
16. Haiti & Zaire
17. East Germany
18. Italy
19. West Germany (1954)

20. Australia
21. Ralf Edstrom
22. Argentina & Italy
23. Brazil
24. Real Madrid
25. Zaire (now Democratic Republic of Congo)
26. Jack Taylor
27. Andrzej Szarmach
28. Poland
29. Third place play-off match
30. Dusan Bajevic

1978 FIFA WORLD CUP ARGENTINA™

1. Italy
2. France, 1998
3. Teofilo Cubillas (Peru)
4. Rob Rensenbrink
5. Argentina & Netherlands
6. Hansi
7. Iran
8. President Juan Peron's signature gesture – a salute to the crowd with both arms extended above his head
9. Hugo Sanchez
10. Uruguay
11. 1,000th goal in FIFA World Cup history
12. Hans Krankl
13. Austria
14. Four goals
15. Gauchito
16. Manchester United
17. False (1982 would be the first)
18. Mario Kempes, Valencia
19. Van de Kerkhof (Willy and Rene)
20. Hungary
21. Paolo Rossi
22. Austria
23. Willie Johnston
24. Peru
25. Dick Nanninga
26. Estadio Monumental, Buenos Aires

27. Mar del Plata
28. Tunisia
29. Marius Tresor
30. Mexico

1982 FIFA WORLD CUP SPAIN™

1. 0-0
2. Honduras
3. Lothar Matthaus
4. Tim
5. Paul Breitner (West Germany)
6. Peter Shilton
7. Cameroon
8. Carlos Alberto Parreira
9. The first FIFA World Cup match to be decided by a penalty shoot-out
10. England
11. France
12. Norman Whiteside
13. True
14. New Zealand
15. Tony Woodcock (Cologne)
16. Karl-Heinz Rummenigge
17. Zbigniew Boniek
18. Italy, West Germany, Poland & France
19. Someone scored a goal (Belgium's Erwin Vandenbergh)
20. Sarria Stadium
21. Three
22. Patrick Battiston
23. Diego Maradona
24. Bryan Robson (England v France)
25. West Germany v Austria
26. Dino Zoff & Giuseppe Bergomi
27. Italy & Northern Ireland
28. Hungary
29. Malaga
30. Northern Ireland

1986 FIFA WORLD CUP MEXICO™

1. The Mexican wave
2. Maracana, Rio de Janeiro, Brazil
3. Iraq
4. Italy, Uruguay, England & West Germany
5. Uruguay
6. Colombia
7. 114,600
8. Preben Elkjaer
9. Morocco
10. Jorge Valdano
11. True (1986, 1990 & 2014)
12. Monterrey
13. Hungary and Northern Ireland
14. Igor Belanov
15. Korea Republic
16. Gyorgy Sarosi (Hungary, 1938), Ferenc Puskas (Hungary, 1954), Nils Liedholm (Sweden, 1958), Carlos Alberto (Brazil, 1970) and Zinedine Zidane (France, 2006)
17. Belgium
18. Josimar
19. Careca
20. Argentina 2 England 1
21. Rome (1934 and 1990), Paris (1938 and 1998) and Rio de Janeiro (1950 and 2014)
22. Morocco
23. 19 (10 in 1970 & 9 in 1986)
24. Manuel Negrete for Mexico v Bulgaria
25. Bryan Robson and Ray Wilkins
26. Sampdoria and Barcelona
27. Socrates and Julio Cesar
28. Pique, a jalapeno pepper
29. Denmark
30. Canada

1990 FIFA WORLD CUP ITALY™

1. Paolo Maldini
2. Tony Meola (USA v Czechoslovakia)
3. Pedro Monzon and Gustavo Dezotti
4. Palermo (Sicily)
5. Argentina
6. Walter Zenga (Italy)

7. Egypt
8. False (1994 was)
9. Rangers
10. Eight
11. Dave Beasant
12. Jurgen Klinsmann
13. True (2.21 goals per game)
14. Giuseppe Bergomi
15. "Nessun Dorma"
16. Andre Kana-Biyik and Benjamin Massing
17. Eight (Italy three, West Germany two, Argentina two and England one)
18. Five
19. Francois Omam-Biyik
20. Republic of Ireland & Netherlands
21. They became the first nation to fail to score in a FIFA World Cup final
22. Rudi Voller (West Germany) and Frank Rijkaard (Netherlands)
23. United Arab Emirates
24. France
25. England
26. Stadio San Nicola (Bari) and Stadio delle Alpi (Turin)
27. David O'Leary
28. Poland
29. Sergio Goycochea (for Argentina v Yugoslavia and Italy)
30. Mark Wright

1991 FIFA WOMEN'S WORLD CUP CHINA™

1. China and Norway
2. Linda Medalen
3. Germany
4. Sun Wen
5. April Heinrichs
6. Chinese Taipei
7. Guangzhou
8. Brazil
9. Nigeria
10. Pia Sundhage
11. Anson Dorrance
12. Lena Videkull
13. Japan and Nigeria
14. Carin Jennings
15. Sweden
16. Italy
17. United States & Sweden
18. Even Pellerud
19. The youngest ever FIFA Women's World Cup-winning team (23 years & 8 months)
20. Heidi Mohr
21. Germany
22. USA 7 Chinese Taipei 0
23. Four
24. 80 minutes
25. Norway, Sweden & Chinese Taipei
26. New Zealand
27. Germany
28. True
29. Japan
30. Bettina Wiegmann

1994 FIFA WORLD CUP UNITED STATES™

1. Norway
2. Hristo Stoichkov (6), Oleg Salenko (6), Romario (5), Roberto Baggio (5), Jurgen Klinsmann (5), Kennet Andersson (5)
3. Roger Milla
4. Romario
5. Cafu
6. 68,991
7. Bora Milutinovic
8. Roberto Baggio
9. Greece
10. Sweden
11. Gabriel Batistuta
12. Oprah Winfrey
13. Roy Hodgson
14. Orlando, Florida
15. Andres Escobar (Colombia)
16. False (32 first played in 1998)

17. 1938
18. Diana Ross
19. All four teams finished with the same points and goal difference
20. Roger Milla & Rigobert Song
21. First FIFA World Cup match to be played indoors
22. Bolivia
23. Norway
24. Romania
25. Bebeto & Branco
26. Jonas Thern
27. Bulgaria
28. Michel Preud'homme
29. Sami Al-Jaber
30. Striker, a dog

1995 FIFA WOMEN'S WORLD CUP SWEDEN™

1. Canada
2. Homare Sawa
3. Brazil
4. Ann Kristin Aarones (Norway)
5. Bulgaria
6. 3-3
7. Briana Scurry
8. Stockholm
9. None
10. True
11. +22 (scored 23, conceded one)
12. Hege Riise
13. Sweden & China
14. England
15. Japan
16. Australia
17. Quarter-finals
18. Sweden – against Germany
19. Brazil
20. First stadium to host a FIFA World Cup final (1958) and a FIFA Women's World Cup final (1995)
21. USA and China (group stage and 3rd place play-off)
22. 99

23. Germany, Japan and USA
24. Birgit Prinz
25. Helsingborg
26. England (v Canada)
27. Australia
28. True
29. Japan and Sweden
30. Kristin Sandberg

1998 FIFA WORLD CUP FRANCE™

1. Gianfranco Zola
2. Craig Burley
3. Morocco
4. 171
5. Portugal
6. The game ended – FIFA were using the 'golden goal' rule
7. Austria, Bulgaria, Norway, Romania & Scotland
8. Italy
9. True
10. Rigobert Song
11. Czech Republic
12. Patrick Kluivert (v Belgium) and Arthur Numan (v Argentina)
13. Footix, a rooster
14. Samuel Eto'o
15. Ricky Martin
16. Two
17. Chile (3 draws)
18. Lilian Thuram
19. Edgar Davids
20. Belgium
21. Spain
22. Gianluigi Buffon
23. Stade Felix-Bollaert, Lens
24. Zinedine Zidane (v Saudi Arabia), Laurent Blanc (v Croatia) and Marcel Desailly (v Brazil)
25. South Africa
26. Stade Velodrome (Marseille), Stade Municipal (Toulouse), Stade Gerland (Lyon), Parc Lescure (Bordeaux), Parc des Princes (Paris)

27. Clarence Seedorf
28. Jim Leighton
29. Iran
30. Barcelona

1999 FIFA WOMEN'S WORLD CUP UNITED STATES™

1. Chicago
2. China
3. Ghana
4. Sun Wen
5. True
6. Sissi
7. Denmark
8. Australia
9. Mexico
10. Nigeria
11. USA 7-1 Nigeria (6-1 at half-time)
12. Brazil, Germany, Italy and Mexico
13. Norway
14. Jennifer Lopez
15. Russia
16. Christie Rampone
17. Germany
18. Pasadena
19. Ghana
20. China
21. Brazil and Norway (3rd place play-off)
22. Russia
23. Five
24. Giants Stadium
25. Russia and Sweden
26. Germany and Brazil
27. Pretinha
28. Nigeria
29. Liu Yong (China)
30. 1984 Olympic Games gold medal match and 1994 FIFA World Cup final

2002 FIFA WORLD CUP JAPAN AND SOUTH KOREA™

1. Ian Harte
2. Michael Ballack
3. China
4. Togo
5. Portugal
6. Miroslav Klose
7. False (it was 1998)
8. Francesco Totti
9. Carlos Ruiz
10. Rafael Marquez (Mexico)
11. Ecuador
12. Three (Senegal v Sweden, Korea Republic v Italy, Turkey v Senegal)
13. Joaquin
14. Brad Friedel
15. Claudio Caniggia
16. Gaizka Mendieta
17. Ato, Kaz & Nik
18. 31-0
19. Cameroon v Germany
20. Papa Bouba Diop
21. Kubilay Turkyilmaz
22. +14
23. Spain
24. Robbie Keane
25. Uruguay
26. Luis Felipe Scolari
27. Sapporo
28. Ronaldinho
29. Win seven matches
30. Denmark

2003 FIFA WOMEN'S WORLD CUP UNITED STATES™

1. Katia
2. Christie Sinclair
3. Germany 7 Russia 1
4. Nigeria
5. Canada and Sweden
6. Australia
7. China

8. Elena Danilova
9. Cat Reddick
10. Japan
11. Foxborough and Portland
12. United States, North Korea and Nigeria
13. Bettina Wiegmann
14. Argentina
15. Korea Republic
16. Abby Wambach
17. 10
18. Birgit Prinz (Germany)
19. Brazil
20. Nia Kunzer
21. Japan
22. April Heinrichs
23. Canada
24. Carson, California
25. Tiffeny Milbrett
26. France
27. Argentina
28. Japan and North Korea
29. Argentina, Nigeria and Korea Republic
30. Pia Wunderlich

2006 FIFA WORLD CUP GERMANY™

1. Italy
2. Ronaldo
3. Fabien Barthez
4. None
5. Leandro Cufre
6. Switzerland
7. Javier Mascherano
8. Germany
9. Cristiano Ronaldo
10. 345
11. Portugal
12. France
13. Jens Lehmann (36 years and 232 days, Germany v Argentina)
14. Angola, Ghana, Ivory Coast and Togo
15. Tomas Rosicky
16. England

17. Oleksandr Shovkovskiy
18. Serbia and Montenegro
19. Asamoah Gyan
20. Australia
21. Portugal & Netherlands
22. First time in FIFA World Cup history that the first and last goals of the tournament were scored by defenders
23. Argentina
24. Trinidad & Tobago
25. Czech Republic and Ukraine
26. Switzerland, Argentina, England, France and Italy
27. Paul Robinson
28. 28
29. Fabio Grosso and Alessandro Del Piero
30. Ricardo (Portugal v England)

2007 FIFA WOMEN'S WORLD CUP CHINA™

1. Ghana
2. Canada
3. Ragnhild Gulbrandsen
4. Lori Chalupny
5. Denmark
6. Lisa De Vanna
7. None
8. Argentina – versus England
9. Brazil
10. Nadine Angerer (Germany)
11. Catalina Perez
12. England
13. Tianjin
14. Christine Sinclair (Canada)
15. Marta
16. None
17. Australia
18. Kelly Smith
19. Shanghai
20. Norway
21. Birgit Prinz
22. Brazil

23. United States
24. Kristine Lilly
25. True
26. Australia
27. Canada
28. Argentina
29. New Zealand
30. Silvia Neid

2010 FIFA WORLD CUP SOUTH AFRICA™

1. Thomas Muller
2. None
3. Netherlands (nine in final)
4. England, Argentina and Uruguay
5. New Zealand (3 draws out of 3)
6. Matthew Upson
7. Eight
8. Slovakia
9. First European nation to win FIFA World Cup outside Europe
10. South Africa 2 France 1
11. David Villa
12. Germany
13. Croatia
14. Honduras
15. Soccer City (FNB) Stadium and Ellis Park Stadium
16. Jerome Boateng (Germany) and Kevin-Prince Boateng (Ghana)
17. Fernando Torres and Pepe Reina
18. South America
19. Otto Rehhagel (Greece)
20. Polokwane
21. Gonzalo Higuain
22. Algeria & Honduras
23. Nigeria
24. Brazil (1966) and France (2002)
25. John Heitinga
26. England
27. Zakumi, a leopard
28. Denis Caniza
29. Vicente del Bosque (59 years and 200 days)
30. North Korea

2011 FIFA WOMEN'S WORLD CUP GERMANY™

1. Brazil and England
2. Equatorial Guinea
3. Sandrine Soubeyrand
4. Azusa Iwashimizu
5. Colombia
6. Three
7. Homare Sawa
8. England
9. Canada and Equatorial Guinea
10. Ayumi Kaihori
11. France
12. 12
13. Brazil
14. Colombia and North Korea
15. 86
16. Augsburg
17. Four
18. Norway
19. Norio Sasaki
20. Josefine Oqvist
21. Abby Wambach
22. True
23. Nigeria
24. Eight
25. United States
26. Australia
27. Mexico
28. Colombia and North Korea
29. Germany
30. Equatorial Guinea

2014 FIFA WORLD CUP BRAZIL™

1. Faryd Mondragon (Colombia)
2. Miroslav Klose
3. Mario Gotze and Mario Kempes
4. Marcelo
5. Abdelmoumene Djabou (Algeria)
6. Argentina
7. Costa Rica
8. Rashed Al Hooti
9. Giorgio Chiellini

10. Germany
11. Iran
12. Bosnia and Herzegovina
13. Mats Hummels
14. Goal-line technology & vanishing spray for free-kicks
15. Toni Kroos
16. Thomas Muller
17. Netherlands
18. Pierre-Emerick Aubameyang
19. Nordic countries
20. Mesut Ozil, Lukas Podolski and Per Mertesacker
21. David Luiz
22. Manaus
23. 32 degrees Celsius
24. Algeria
25. Fuleco, an armadillo
26. Lionel Messi
27. Xherdan Shaqiri (v Honduras)
28. James Rodriguez
29. Karim Benzema
30. Eight

2015 FIFA WOMEN'S WORLD CUP CANADA™

1. Netherlands, Spain & Switzerland
2. 90
3. Christie Rampone
4. Ecuador
5. 1995
6. Silvia Neid (all for Germany)
7. Solveig Gulbrandsen
8. Portsmouth
9. Cameroon and Ivory Coast
10. Germany
11. Switzerland
12. Celia Sasic and Anja Mittag
13. Linda Sembrant
14. Marie-Laure Delie
15. 146
16. Vancouver
17. Brazil & Japan
18. Ecuador

19. Australia, China, England, Korea Republic and Switzerland
20. Sweden
21. Quarter-final
22. Germany
23. Formiga (Brazil)
24. Colombia
25. Hope Solo
26. Nigeria & Sweden
27. Cameroon
28. Six
29. Ecuador
30. Thailand

2018 FIFA WORLD CUP RUSSIA™

1. Iceland
2. Croatia & Russia
3. Belgium
4. Artem Dzyuba (Russia)
5. Rafael Marquez
6. Amrabat (Sofyan came on for Nordin)
7. Manchester City
8. Michael Lang
9. Belgium 5-2 Tunisia, England 6-1 Panama and France 4-3 Argentina
10. Aliou Cisse (Senegal)
11. Netherlands
12. Essam El-Hadary (45 years and 161 days)
13. Sochi
14. Matthias Jorgensen (Denmark)
15. Daniel Arzani (Australia)
16. Russia (v Uruguay and Spain)
17. Christian Benteke
18. England
19. Harry Kane & Cristiano Ronaldo
20. Luka Modric
21. Oscar Tabarez (Uruguay)
22. 'Live It Up'
23. Erokhin became the first player to feature as a fourth substitute in a FIFA World Cup match
24. 29

25. Zabivaka, a wolf
26. Fernando Hierro, Julen Lopetegui (Spain)
27. Antoine Griezmann
28. Valon Behrami
29. Oscar Ramirez (Costa Rica)
30. Egypt & Panama

2019 FIFA WOMEN'S WORLD CUP FRANCE™

1. Oldest ever hat-trick scorer in a FIFA Women's World Cup match
2. Korea Republic, South Africa, Jamaica, New Zealand & Thailand
3. Nothando Vilakazi
4. Cristiana Girelli
5. Norway v Australia in last 16 (Norway won 4-1 on pens)
6. Jill Ellis
7. Ellen White
8. Eight
9. Caroline Graham Hansen
10. Argentina v Japan & China v Spain
11. Seven
12. Jennifer Hermoso
13. Australia, v Brazil
14. Jill Scott (England)
15. Nikita Parris
16. Megan Rapinoe
17. Rosemary Lavelle
18. Germany
19. USA 3 Thailand 0
20. Lyon
21. 26
22. USA, Germany, Netherlands, France and England
23. Germany (2003 and 2007)
24. Formiga
25. Jamaica
26. Janine Beckie
27. 18
28. Argentina, v Scotland
29. Alanna Kennedy
30. 20

MAJOR INTERNATIONAL TEAMS QUIZ ANSWERS

ARGENTINA

1. 1978
2. Nigeria
3. Carlos Roa
4. Jose Luis Brown
5. 1990
6. Five
7. Javier Mascherano
8. Alfio Basile
9. AFA (Argentine Football Association)
10. Colombia
11. Carlos Bilardo
12. Saudi Arabia
13. Chile
14. Antonio Rattin
15. Gabriel Batistuta (10)
16. Milito
17. 1990
18. Sergio Aguero
19. Daniel Passarella
20. Serbia and Montenegro
21. Martin Palermo
22. 1,500th
23. Carlos Tevez
24. Gonzalo Higuain
25. 3-3
26. Germany
27. Diego Simeone
28. Jorge Burruchaga
29. Mario Kempes
30. Greece and Jamaica

AUSTRALIA

1. Tim Cahill

2. Brazil
3. Socceroos
4. Italy
5. Penalties
6. Bert van Marwijk
7. 2015
8. Lisa De Vanna
9. Harry Kewell
10. Mark Schwarzer
11. Mile Jedinak
12. Jamie Maclaren
13. Ray Richards
14. 1974
15. Japan (2006)
16. Sam Kerr
17. Lucas Neill
18. 2014
19. Archie Thompson
20. 2000
21. Serbia
22. 2006
23. Copa America
24. Eddie Thomson
25. Marco Bresciano
26. Matildas
27. East Germany
28. Honduras
29. Brett Holman
30. Terry Venables

AUSTRIA

1. 1990 (v USA)
2. Vienna
3. Marc Janko
4. Hans Krankl
5. West Germany
6. One (Robert Almer, Austria Vienna)
7. Most goals in a FIFA World Cup match (12)
8. Andreas Herzog
9. Marcel Koller
10. Uruguay
11. 1998

12. They were all scored in injury time
13. Aleksandar Dragovic
14. Malta
15. Erich Probst
16. Germany
17. Walter Schachner
18. Toni Polster
19. Hungary
20. David Alaba
21. Latvia
22. Ivica Vastic
23. France
24. Marko Arnautovic
25. Alessandro Schopf
26. 17
27. 1954
28. Ernst Happel
29. True
30. Christian Fuchs

BELGIUM

1. Enzo Scifo (17)
2. 1980 (UEFA European Championship)
3. First UEFA European Championship hosts to be eliminated at the group stage
4. Van der Elst
5. Italy
6. Mark Wilmots
7. Adnan Januzaj
8. Reached No. 1 in the FIFA World Rankings
9. Argentina
10. 1998
11. Manchester United (Red Devils)
12. Jan Ceulemans
13. Mpenza (Emile and Mbo)
14. Tottenham Hotspur
15. France, Romania & Yugoslavia
16. Scotland
17. Paul van Himst
18. 1986
19. Michel Preud'homme
20. 1920

21. Japan
22. Romelu Lukaku
23. Steven Defour
24. Gibraltar
25. Leander Dendoncker, Anderlecht
26. Spain
27. Guy Thys
28. Belgium 4 England 4
29. Denmark
30. 1972

BRAZIL

1. Sweden (1958)
2. Felipe Melo
3. Brazil 6 Poland 5
4. Formiga
5. Roberto Carlos
6. Alisson and Roberto Firmino
7. Barcelona four (Neymar four), PSG three (David Luiz two and Thiago Silva one) & Chelsea two (Oscar two)
8. Little Canary
9. Djalma Santos
10. Peru
11. Roberto Dinamite
12. France (1958 semi-final)
13. Cristiane
14. Gabriel Jesus
15. Germany
16. Philippe Coutinho
17. Rivaldo
18. Luis Fabiano
19. Mario Zagallo
20. 2007 (lost to Germany)
21. Marta
22. Carlos Alberto Parreira
23. Ademir
24. 1970
25. Italy (1970 and 1994)
26. Denilson
27. Dunga
28. Jairzinho
29. Turkey
30. 1950

CAMEROON

1. Five
2. Rigobert Song (137 caps)
3. First African nation to reach the quarter-finals
4. 2000
5. 1982
6. Green
7. Vincent Aboubakar
8. Paul Le Guen
9. The Indomitable Lions
10. Patrick Mboma
11. Francois Omam-Biyik (11)
12. African Nations Championship
13. Samuel Eto'o (56 goals)
14. Eric Maxim Choupo-Moting
15. CMR
16. Alex Song
17. Germany, Chile & Australia
18. Ajara Nchout
19. False. Won 4 – Nigeria won 6
20. Yaounde
21. Pierre Webo
22. Clarence Seedorf
23. Jacques Songo'o
24. Romania
25. Marc-Vivien Foe
26. Coton Sport
27. Soviet Union
28. Gaelle Enganamouit
29. Patrick Suffo
30. France

CROATIA

1. 1998
2. Greece
3. Three
4. Robert Jarni
5. Slaven Bilic
6. San Marino
7. Igor Stimac
8. Goran Vlaovic
9. Davor Suker

10. Stipe Pletikosa (114 caps)
11. Ante Rebic
12. Niko and Robert Kovac
13. Ivica Olic
14. Ivan Perisic
15. Robert Prosinecki
16. Danijel Subasic
17. Italy
18. Turkey
19. Germany
20. Red and white
21. 2010
22. Josip Simunic
23. Bruno Petkovic
24. Netherlands
25. Mario Mandzukic
26. Nottingham (UEFA Euro 96)
27. Niko Kranjcar
28. Eduardo da Silva
29. Darijo Srna
30. England

CZECH REPUBLIC (AND CZECHOSLOVAKIA)

1. Milan Baros
2. Pavel Srnicek (Newcastle United)
3. Greece
4. Zikan
5. Turkey
6. England
7. Jan Koller
8. Patrik Schick
9. 1994
10. Belgrade
11. Two
12. 1970 FIFA World Cup
13. First player to score an own goal in UEFA European Championship history
14. Montenegro
15. Patrik Berger
16. Pavel Nedved
17. 2006
18. Tomas Ujfalusi and Jan Polak

19. Vladimir Smicer
20. Michal Bilek
21. Michal Krmencik
22. Yugoslavia
23. Tomas Skuhravy
24. France
25. Oldrich Nejedly
26. Tomas Rosicky
27. Italy
28. Borussia Dortmund
29. Antonin Panenka
30. Dusan Uhrin

DENMARK

1. John Jensen
2. Scotland
3. Preben Elkjaer
4. 2000
5. Allan Simonsen
6. Yugoslavia
7. Sepp Piontek
8. Jorgensen
9. Quarter-finals (1998)
10. Jon Dahl Tomasson
11. Ebbe Sand
12. Brian Laudrup
13. Simon Kjaer
14. 1995
15. Martin Jorgensen
16. Gibraltar
17. Kim Milton Nielsen
18. Thomas
19. Spain
20. Two
21. Gothenburg
22. Michael Krohn-Dehli
23. Parken Stadium, Copenhagen
24. Michael Laudrup
25. 1986
26. Morten Olsen
27. Dennis Rommedahl
28. Three
29. Republic of Ireland
30. Christian Eriksen

ENGLAND

1. Billy Wright
2. Alan Mullery
3. Barnes
4. Bryan Robson
5. Scotland
6. Peter Taylor
7. Tunisia
8. Viv Anderson
9. Portugal
10. Jamaica
11. San Marino
12. Ellen White
13. Villa Park (v Spain)
14. Brian Talbot
15. Andrew Cole
16. Montenegro
17. Bobby Zamora
18. 2015
19. Chile (1950)
20. Joe Corrigan
21. Sol Campbell
22. Gareth Southgate
23. Hungary
24. David Platt
25. Owen Hargreaves
26. Theo Walcott
27. Jill Scott
28. Laurie Cunningham
29. Ray Clemence (v Spain in 1980)
30. Turin

FRANCE

1. Zinedine Zidane
2. Wendie Renard
3. Henri Delaunay
4. Parc des Princes
5. Three
6. Laurent Blanc
7. Just Fontaine
8. Cockerel
9. 1958
10. Japan
11. Fabien Barthez
12. Italy
13. Denmark
14. Lucien Laurent (1930)
15. David Trezeguet
16. Lilian Thuram
17. Le Tournoi de France
18. France 4 Croatia 2
19. France Football
20. Henri Michel
21. Hugo Lloris
22. FIFA Confederations Cup
23. Kylian Mbappe
24. Saint-Denis
25. United States
26. Antoine Griezmann
27. 1988
28. Thierry Henry
29. Group stage
30. 1938

GERMANY

1 Franz Beckenbauer
2 Birgit Prinz
3 Lothar Matthaus
4 1972
5 Germany 7 Brazil 1
6 Jerome Boateng
7 Sepp Maier
8 Mexico
9 Karl-Heinz Rummenigge
10 Chile
11 1974 FIFA World Cup
12 Mario Gotze
13 Helmut Rahn
14 Lukas Podolski
15 1938
16 Erich Ribbeck
17 Bastian Schweinsteiger
18 2007
19 Oliver Bierhoff
20 United Arab Emirates
21 Saudi Arabia (2002)
22 Stadio Olimpico, Rome

23 Ivory Coast
24 1976
25 Michael Ballack
26 Czechoslovakia
27 Paul Breitner
28 1974
29 Switzerland
30 Andreas Moller

GHANA

1. Asamoah Gyan
2. 2006
3. Andre Ayew
4. Czech Republic (2006) & Serbia (2010)
5. South Africa
6. Black Stars
7. Six
8. John Mensah
9. Thomas Partey
10. United States
11. Yellow
12. 1992
13. True
14. Brazil (2006) & Uruguay (2010)
15. Libya
16. Cameroon (1990) & Senegal (2002)
17. Milovan Rajevac
18. Jordan
19. West African Football Union
20. Sulley Muntari (2006 and 2010)
21. Charles Akonnor
22. Egypt
23. Their own TV network (GFA TV)
24. Michael Essien
25. Nigeria
26. Abedi Ayew
27. 9-8 to Ivory Coast
28. Kevin-Prince Boateng
29. Marcel Desailly
30. Samuel Kuffour

GREECE

1. Giorgos Karagounis (139 caps)

2. Costa Rica
3. 1994
4. Kostas Katsouranis
5. Sweden, Russia & Spain
6. John van't Schip
7. Theodoros Zagorakis
8. Italy
9. Argentina
10. National
11. Romania
12. Angelos Charisteas
13. Theofanis Gekas
14. 2005
15. Fernando Santos
16. Kostas Mitroglou
17. Ukraine
18. Dimitris Salpingidis
19. Dimitris Giannoulis
20. 2004
21. Angelos Basinas
22. Claudio Ranieri
23. Vangelis Pavlidis
24. Croatia
25. Otto Rehhagel
26. 1980
27. Sokratis Papastathopoulos
28. Nigeria & Ivory Coast
29. Nikos Anastopoulos
30. Traianos Dellas

HUNGARY

1. Sandor Kocsis
2. Three (1952, 1964, 1968)
3. Balazs Dzsudzsak
4. Netherlands
5. 1986
6. Denmark
7. 84
8. Hungary 2 West Germany 0
9. Puskas Arena, Budapest
10. Gabor Kiraly
11. Magyars
12. 1938
13. Lajos Tichy

14. West Germany
15. UEFA Euro 72 (v Belgium)
16. Five
17. Korea Republic
18. Adam Szalai
19. First
20. 27
21. Egypt
22. 1972
23. Austria
24. Hungary 8 West Germany 3
25. Laszlo Kiss
26. David Holman
27. Norway
28. Two
29. Ferenc Bene
30. Bernd Storck

ITALY

1. France
2. Luigi Riva (35)
3. Salvatore Schillaci
4. Gino Colaussi and Silvio Piola
5. Roberto
6. Daniele De Rossi
7. Gianluigi Buffon (80)
8. Pasadena
9. Dino Zoff
10. Christian Vieri
11. Enzo Bearzot
12. Andrea Pirlo
13. Netherlands
14. Fabio Grosso
15. United States
16. Paolo Maldini
17. Alessandro Altobelli
18. Gianluca Pagliuca (v Norway)
19. Cesare Maldini
20. Cristiana Girelli
21. Giuseppe Bergomi
22. Alessandro Del Piero
23. France
24. Baggio
25. 2010

26. 1958
27. Fabio Cannavaro
28. Armenia
29. 1936
30. Giuseppe Meazza

JAPAN

1. Keisuke Honda (four)
2. 2011
3. Yasuhito Endo
4. France
5. Takumi Minamino
6. Fair play (they received fewer yellow cards than Senegal)
7. Shinji Kagawa
8. Zico
9. Maya Yoshida
10. Jamaica
11. 1964
12. Crow
13. Takashi Inui
14. 2002
15. Kunishige Kamamoto
16. Liverpool
17. Russia
18. Pikachu
19. Copa America
20. Germany
21. USA
22. Philippe Troussier
23. Korea Republic
24. 1998
25. National Stadium
26. Paraguay
27. Samurai Blue
28. Denmark (2010)
29. Homare Sawa
30. Alberto Zaccheroni

KOREA REPUBLIC

1. Park Ji-Sung
2. Guus Hiddink
3. Red

4. 1954
5. Son Heung-Min
6. Lee Young-Pyo
7. Ki Sung-Yueng
8. Tiger
9. Perugia
10. Argentina (1986)
11. 1960
12. Seoul World Cup Stadium (or Sangam Stadium)
13. Lee Seung-Woo
14. Hong Myung-Bo
15. Togo
16. The Red Devils
17. 2015
18. Lee Woon-Jae
19. Poland
20. Paulo Bento
21. KOR
22. 1982
23. Park Chu-Young
24. Cha Bum-Kun
25. Asian Games
26. Hungary
27. Ha Seok-Ju
28. Anderlecht
29. France
30. Uli Stielike

MEXICO

1. 27
2. Javier Hernandez
3. Rafael Marquez
4. Sven-Goran Eriksson
5. One (Bulgaria, 1986)
6. France
7. 1986
8. Fastest caution (15 seconds)
9. Luis Hernandez
10. Claudio Suarez
11. Cesar Luis Menotti
12. Argentina
13. Bora Milutinovic
14. Guillermo Ochoa

15. None
16. Raul Jimenez
17. First nation to host the FIFA World Cup for a second time
18. Brazil
19. Antonio Carbajal
20. Bolton Wanderers
21. Hosted the most ever FIFA World Cup matches
22. Oribe Peralta
23. Nine
24. Uriel Antuna
25. Round of 16
26. New Zealand
27. 2012
28. United States
29. An eagle
30. Cuauhtemoc Blanco

NETHERLANDS

1. Arjen Robben
2. Munich
3. West Germany and Argentina
4. Hans van Breukelen
5. 2014
6. Wesley Sneijder
7. Soviet Union
8. Belgium
9. Ernst Happel
10. Brazil
11. Jackie Groenen
12. Robin van Persie
13. Blind
14. Porto
15. San Marino
16. Dennis Bergkamp
17. Dirk Kuyt
18. Rob Rensenbrink
19. 2011
20. United States
21. de Jong
22. England
23. Rinus Michels
24. Georginio Wijnaldum

25. Guus Hiddink
26. 1990
27. Vivianne Miedema
28. Frank de Boer
29. Johnny Rep
30. Witschge

NIGERIA

1. True (on six occasions)
2. Burkina Faso
3. 1994
4. Berti Vogts
5. Tahiti
6. Nwankwo Kanu
7. Argentina
8. Super Eagles
9. Bora Milutinovic
10. Germany
11. Italy
12. Sani Kaita
13. False – they've never lost all three group stage matches
14. Vincent Enyeama
15. Victor Obinna
16. Moshood Abiola National Stadium
17. Victor Moses
18. Kalu Uche
19. Shola and Sammy Ameobi
20. Joseph Yobo (10)
21. Taribo West
22. 1996
23. Philippe Troussier
24. Bulgaria (1994 & 1998)
25. Yakubu
26. Celestine Babayaro
27. Morocco
28. Jay-Jay Okocha
29. Daniel Amokachi
30. Ahmed Musa

NORTHERN IRELAND

1. Windsor Park
2. Peter McParland
3. Sammy McIlroy
4. Pat Jennings
5. Ukraine
6. Aaron Hughes
7. Mal Donaghy
8. Gavin Whyte
9. France
10. Billy Bingham
11. Czechoslovakia
12. Billy Cush
13. David Healy
14. The Green and White Army
15. Daniel & Kyle
16. Kyle Lafferty
17. Careca
18. British Home Championship
19. Gerry Armstrong
20. Wilson
21. Will Grigg
22. Gareth McAuley
23. Craig Cathcart and Josh Magennis
24. Czechoslovakia
25. Danny & Jackie
26. Martin O'Neill
27. Switzerland
28. Lawrie McMenemy
29. Colin Clarke
30. 13

POLAND

1. Arkadiusz Milik
2. Four (Argentina, Brazil, Italy & Sweden)
3. Haiti
4. Wojciech Szczesny
5. Ebi Smolarek
6. Andrzej Szarmach
7. Wroclaw
8. 1982
9. Zewlakow
10. Bartosz Bosacki
11. Sampdoria
12. San Marino
13. Kazimierz Deyna

14. Japan
15. Artur Boruc
16. Ukraine
17. Krzysztof Piatek
18. Northern Ireland
19. Wladyslaw Zmuda
20. Brazil
21. England
22. Peru
23. Jakub Blaszczykowski
24. 1986
25. Zbigniew Boniek
26. Radoslaw Sobolewski
27. Gary Lineker (England)
28. Robert Lewandowski
29. Smolarek
30. 1972

PORTUGAL

1. Faro
2. Nine
3. Goncalo Guedes
4. Greece
5. Only players to have scored at four different FIFA World Cups
6. White
7. France
8. Pauleta
9. It was the only game they won in normal time
10. Costa
11. Vitor Damas
12. Sa Pinto and Joao Pinto
13. Ricardo Costa
14. Sergio Conceicao
15. Chile
16. 1966
17. Pepe
18. Most FIFA World Cup penalties scored (four)
19. Helder Postiga
20. Nuno Gomes
21. North Korea
22. Luiz Felipe Scolari
23. Ricardo Carvalho
24. Renato Sanches
25. Hungary
26. Ricardo
27. Luis Figo
28. Porto
29. 1986
30. Carlos Queiroz

REPUBLIC OF IRELAND

1. 2002
2. Three
3. England at UEFA Euro 88
4. Eight
5. Robbie Brady
6. Giovanni Trapattoni
7. Steve Staunton
8. John O'Shea
9. Roy Keane
10. Keith Andrews
11. Aviva Stadium
12. France
13. Pat Bonner
14. Saudi Arabia
15. Nine
16. Without winning a match in normal or extra time
17. Ian Harte
18. Shay Given
19. Sean St Ledger
20. LA Galaxy
21. Bosnia & Herzegovina
22. Reid
23. Barnsley
24. David O'Leary
25. Netherlands
26. Shane Duffy
27. Andy Townsend
28. Niall Quinn
29. Damien Duff
30. Two

RUSSIA (INCORPORATING SOVIET UNION AND CIS)

1. 1992
2. Igor Smolnikov
3. Yugoslavia
4. Denis Cheryshev
5. Lev Yashin
6. 1966
7. Oleg Salenko
8. Spain
9. They lost on the toss of a coin
10. Artem Dzyuba
11. Brussels
12. San Marino
13. Fabio Capello
14. Igor Belanov
15. Sergei Ovchinnikov
16. Aleksandr Kerzhakov
17. Dick Advocaat
18. Portugal
19. Dmitri Kirichenko
20. Uruguay
21. West Germany
22. Alan Dzagoev
23. Anatoly Byshovets
24. Hungary
25. Guus Hiddink
26. Roman Pavlyuchenko
27. Yuri Zhirkov
28. Sergei Ignashevich
29. Berezutski
30. 1986

SCOTLAND

1. 1998
2. Kenny Dalglish
3. Hampden Park
4. England
5. Archie Gemmill
6. Thistle
7. Craig Burley
8. Jim Leighton
9. Most appearances never progressing from the group stage (eight)
10. Ally McCoist
11. South America
12. Miller
13. 1872
14. Gary McAllister
15. Denis Law
16. Sweden
17. Berti Vogts
18. Steven Fletcher
19. Scot
20. Lion
21. Joe Jordan
22. Neil Sullivan
23. Stuart Findlay and Lawrence Shankland
24. Alex Ferguson
25. British Home Championship
26. Craig
27. Blackburn Rovers
28. CIS (Russia) in 1992 and Switzerland in 1996
29. John McGinn
30. The Tartan Army

SPAIN

1. 2010
2. David Villa
3. Bulgaria
4. Switzerland
5. Andoni Zubizarreta
6. Jose Antonio Camacho
7. Emilio Butragueno
8. 5-1
9. Tahiti
10. Valencia
11. Fernando Hierro
12. Iago Aspas
13. Jennifer Hermoso
14. Juan Antonio Pizzi
15. Republic of Ireland (2002)
16. Brazil
17. 1964

18. England (UEFA Euro 96)
19. Andres Iniesta
20. Belgium
21. Sergio Ramos
22. Italy
23. Fernando Torres
24. 2008
25. 35
26. Brazil
27. Michel
28. Vienna
29. United States
30. Soviet Union

SWEDEN

1. Anders Svensson
2. 2004 UEFA European Championship
3. Zlatan Ibrahimovic
4. Senegal
5. Lennart Johansson
6. 1990
7. Romania
8. Tomas Brolin
9. Teddy Lucic
10. Alexander Isak
11. Andreas Granqvist
12. 1948
13. Henrik Larsson (1994, 2002 and 2006)
14. 2003
15. George Raynor
16. Tommy Svensson
17. Argentina
18. Kennet Andersson
19. Germany
20. Nils Liedholm
21. England
22. Cuba
23. Robin Quaison
24. None – their only goal was a Ciaran Clark own goal against Ireland
25. 1992
26. None
27. Thomas Ravelli
28. Henrik Larsson

29. Bjorn Nordqvist
30. Olle Nordin

SWITZERLAND

1. Michael Lang
2. 1954
3. Stephan Lichtsteiner
4. Ricardo Rodriguez
5. Alexander Frei
6. Roy Hodgson
7. Argentina (2014 FIFA World Cup)
8. Johann Vogel & Bernt Haas
9. England
10. Johan Vonlanthen
11. Portugal
12. Eren Derdiyok
13. Haris Seferovic
14. Abegglen
15. Austria
16. Ottmar Hitzfeld
17. Honduras
18. Poland
19. Jakob 'Kobi' Kuhn
20. Sepp Hugi
21. Red Crosses
22. Valon Behrami
23. Karl Rappan
24. Italy
25. Yakin
26. Blaise Nkufo
27. Germany
28. None
29. Josip Drmic
30. Degen

TURKEY

1. Czech Republic
2. Hakan Sukur
3. Korea Republic
4. Ilhan Mansiz
5. 2003
6. Arda Turan
7. UEFA Euro 96

8. Semih Senturk
9. 2002
10. Germany
11. Emre Belozoglu
12. Senol Gunes
13. Cenk Tosun
14. England
15. A crescent moon and a star
16. Guus Hiddink
17. Rustu Recber
18. Financial problems
19. Alpay Ozalan
20. Republic of Ireland
21. Volkan Demirel
22. Japan
23. Portugal
24. Fatih Terim
25. Croatia
26. Arif Erdem
27. Fatih Tekke
28. Score a hat-trick
29. Nihat Kahveci
30. West Germany

UKRAINE

1. Vladislav Vashchuk
2. Anatoliy Tymoshchuk
3. Slovenia
4. Oleksandr Shovkovskiy
5. Donetsk
6. 1992
7. Marko Devic
8. Yevhen Konoplyanka
9. Group B1
10. Andriy Rusol
11. Olympic Stadium, Kiev
12. Greece
13. Valeriy Lobanovskyi
14. FIFA Under-20 World Cup
15. European Under-21 Championship
16. Andriy Voronin
17. Roman Yaremchuk
18. Andriy Pyatov
19. Serhiy Rebrov

20. None
21. Yellow
22. Andriy Shevchenko
23. Romania
24. Oleg Blokhin
25. France
26. Oleg Gusev
27. Oleksandr Zinchenko
28. Spain
29. Oleg Luzhny
30. Andriy Yarmolenko

URUGUAY

1. Diego Forlan
2. The smallest country to have won the FIFA World Cup in terms of population (1.75m in 1930)
3. Atletico Madrid
4. Edinson Cavani
5. Most fourth-placed finishes in FIFA World Cup history (three)
6. Jordan
7. Colombia
8. 56
9. Oscar Tabarez
10. Oscar Miguez
11. World Champions Gold Cup
12. Obdulio Varela
13. (West) Germany
14. Maxi Pereira
15. Alcides Ghiggia
16. They did not concede a goal
17. Daniel Passarella
18. Asia
19. 3-2
20. 2006
21. Diego Godin
22. Fernando Muslera
23. 1920s (1924 and 1928)
24. Estadio Centenario
25. Won all three matches
26. Hungary
27. Senegal
28. Argentina (1986)

29. France
30. The Sky Blue

USA

1. CONCACAF Gold Cup
2. Kristine Lilly
3. Ulysses Llanez
4. Brazil
5. Cobi Jones
6. Pablo Mastroeni and Eddie Pope
7. Rose Bowl, Pasadena
8. Megan Rapinoe
9. Trinidad & Tobago
10. Brian McBride
11. 1930
12. Clint Dempsey
13. Michelle Akers
14. Belgium
15. DaMarcus Beasley
16. Landon Donovan
17. Mexico
18. England
19. Tim Howard
20. Abby Wambach
21. Bruce Arena (2002 and 2006)
22. Ghana & Algeria
23. Portugal (2002)
24. Wembley Stadium, London
25. Canada & Mexico
26. Montevideo, Uruguay
27. Alex Morgan
28. 1990
29. True
30. Jamaica

WALES

1. 1958
2. Gareth McAuley
3. The Dragons
4. China
5. John and Mel
6. England & Scotland
7. Ivor Allchurch

8. Bobby Gould
9. Billy Meredith
10. John Hartson and Simon Davies
11. Ashley & Jonny
12. Yugoslavia
13. Ian Rush
14. British Home Championship
15. Neville Southall
16. Aaron Ramsey
17. Jones
18. Smith & England
19. Hungary
20. Ian Edwards
21. Republic of Ireland
22. Robert Earnshaw
23. Wrexham
24. Hal Robson-Kanu
25. Neil Taylor & Ashley Williams (both for Swansea City)
26. Harry Wilson
27. John Charles (1958 FIFA World Cup)
28. Jimmy Murphy
29. Sam Vokes
30. Terry Medwin

OTHER AFRICAN NATIONS

1. Ghana
2. Alain Giresse
3. Togo
4. Morocco
5. Nigeria (1999)
6. South Africa
7. Liberia (George Weah)
8. Gabon
9. Central African Republic
10. Didier Drogba
11. Ian Porterfield
12. Cameroon
13. Tunisia
14. Stephane Sessegnon
15. 2006
16. Zimbabwe
17. 1957
18. Uganda

19. Cameroon
20. Ivory Coast
21. Sudan
22. Cameroon, Morocco (twice), Tunisia, Ivory Coast, Equatorial Guinea and Kenya
23. *Bafana Bafana*
24. Benni McCarthy
25. Frederic Kanoute
26. Egypt
27. Algeria
28. DR Congo
29. Ivory Coast
30. Algeria and Senegal (Algeria won 1-0)

OTHER ASIAN NATIONS

1. Marc Wilmots
2. Vietnam
3. 2007
4. Lebanon
5. Costa Rica, Brazil and Turkey
6. Pakistan and Nepal
7. True
8. Qatar
9. 1990
10. Korea Republic and Japan – Korea Republic won 2-0
11. Kyrgyzstan
12. Iran
13. North Korea
14. Italy
15. Oman, Iraq, Singapore and Syria
16. Japan
17. Almoez Ali
18. Kuwait
19. Masoud Shojaei
20. Saudi Arabia
21. United Arab Emirates
22. Bryan Robson
23. Jordan
24. China
25. Ahmed Hassan
26. United States
27. Ali Daei

28. Israel
29. Argentina
30. Oman

OTHER EUROPEAN NATIONS

1. Alf-Inge
2. (North) Macedonia
3. Armando Sadiku
4. Portugal
5. Cyprus
6. Israel
7. Teemu Pukki
8. Kosovo
9. Malta
10. Luxembourg
11. 2000
12. Gibraltar
13. San Marino
14. Estonia
15. Aleksandar Mitrovic
16. Nice
17. Moldova
18. 2004
19. Scotland
20. Andorra
21. Slovakia
22. Azerbaijan
23. 1992
24. Liechtenstein
25. Armenia
26. Slovenia
27. Georgia
28. Montenegro
29. Stiliyan Petrov
30. Allan Simonsen

OTHER NORTH AMERICAN NATIONS

1. Panama
2. 2003
3. Robbie Earle
4. Russell Latapy
5. Saint Vincent and the Grenadines
6. Christine Sinclair

7. Belize
8. The Confederation of North, Central American and Caribbean Association Football
9. Suriname
10. Sweden
11. Stern John
12. Honduras
13. Felipe Baloy
14. El Salvador
15. 1998
16. Vancouver
17. Canada
18. Anguilla
19. Trinidad and Tobago
20. United States, Costa Rica and Jamaica
21. Ian Woosnam (golfer)
22. Bronze
23. Haiti
24. Mexico
25. Dwight Yorke
26. Guatemala
27. Costa Rica
28. Jamaica
29. Honduras
30. Cuba

OTHER SOUTH AMERICAN NATIONS

1. Ecuador
2. Venezuela
3. Uruguay
4. Paraguay
5. Teofilo Cubillas
6. Feyenoord
7. Edinson Cavani (Uruguay)
8. Bolivia
9. Jordan
10. Bolivia
11. Ten
12. Jose Pekerman
13. Chile
14. Australia
15. Bolivia
16. James Rodriguez

17. Erwin Sanchez
18. Gent
19. Argentina
20. Venezuela
21. New Zealand
22. Roque Santa Cruz
23. Carlos Valderrama
24. Enner Valencia
25. Brazil
26. Luis Suarez (Uruguay)
27. Chile
28. Yerry Mina
29. England (2006)
30. Colombia

LEGENDARY PLAYERS QUIZ ANSWERS

ALFREDO DI STEFANO

1. Argentina, Colombia and Spain
2. Valencia
3. River Plate
4. Barcelona
5. Billy Wright
6. League, Cup & Cup Winners' Cup
7. Argentina
8. Primera Division
9. UEFA President's Award
10. Sevilla
11. Five
12. Servette
13. Hector Rial
14. Netherlands
15. Diego Maradona
16. South American Championship
17. Cup Winners' Cup (1980 with Valencia)
18. Colombia
19. Penarol
20. FIFA Order of Merit

21. Eintracht Frankfurt
22. Boca Juniors
23. 1962
24. Spanish Super Cup (1990)
25. Francisco Gento and Jose Maria Zarraga
26. Espanyol
27. Five
28. 2010s (2014)
29. Blond Arrow
30. Wiener Sport Club

SIR BOBBY CHARLTON

1. Scotland
2. 1930s (1937)
3. BBC Sports Personality of the Year Lifetime Achievement Award
4. Argentina
5. 249
6. 1-1
7. FA Cup
8. FA Charity Shield
9. 1970
10. Tottenham Hotspur
11. Elder
12. 1966
13. Harry Gregg
14. Preston North End
15. Ryan Giggs
16. Switzerland
17. Borussia Dortmund
18. Northumberland
19. Colombia
20. Australia
21. The weather (she was a forecaster)
22. Waterford
23. Mexico
24. Manchester
25. Wayne Rooney
26. 1973
27. Bobby Moore
28. Walter Winterbottom
29. Wigan Athletic
30. Soviet Union

BOBBY MOORE

1. Poland
2. West Bromwich Albion
3. David Beckham
4. England
5. Fulham
6. Essex
7. 'But I still see that tackle from Moore'
8. 1963
9. His shirt number (6)
10. Harry Redknapp
11. Billy Bonds and Frank Lampard Sr
12. BBC Sports Personality of the Year Award
13. Watford
14. 90
15. Hong Kong
16. Preston North End
17. Herning Fremad
18. 22
19. Capital Gold
20. English Heritage Blue Plaque
21. Southend United
22. First & fourth
23. Franz Beckenbauer
24. Bracelet
25. Terry Brady
26. Peru
27. San Antonio Thunder, Seattle Sounders & Carolina Lightnin'
28. OBE
29. 1993
30. 1860 Munich

CRISTIANO RONALDO

1. Madeira
2. Inter Milan
3. Kazakhstan
4. Valencia
5. 2013-14
6. Karim Benzema
7. Newcastle United
8. 438

9. Nicky Butt
10. Michel Platini (both nine)
11. Iran
12. Millwall
13. 44
14. 9 (club captain Raul was wearing the number 7 shirt)
15. Deportivo
16. Wayne Rooney
17. Northern Ireland
18. Portsmouth
19. Oldest ever hat-trick scorer in a FIFA World Cup match
20. Malmo
21. Moreirense
22. Arsenal
23. Atletico Madrid
24. 61 (2014-15 season)
25. 2007-08
26. Sevilla (27 goals)
27. Greece
28. 10 (Serie A, Premier League, La Liga, Champions League, Copa del Rey, Club World Cup, FIFA World Cup, FIFA World Cup qualifiers, Euro qualifiers, Nations League)
29. Nani
30. 2018 FIFA World Cup

DIEGO MARADONA

1. Marek Hamsik
2. 16
3. Stuttgart
4. 1987-88 (15 goals)
5. Apollon Limassol & Magdeburg
6. Most FIFA World Cup games as captain (16 in total)
7. England (1986 FIFA World Cup)
8. Gimnasia de La Plata
9. Dynamo Brest
10. Guillermo Stabile
11. Austria
12. 1990

13. Hampden Park, Glasgow
14. 1960
15. Mexico
16. Hungary
17. England and Belgium
18. Armando
19. 2010
20. Sevilla
21. Atalanta
22. Real Madrid
23. Cesar Luis Menotti
24. FIFA World Youth Championship
25. The Golden Boy
26. Italy
27. Nigeria
28. Juventus
29. Greece
30. Argentinos Juniors

DINO ZOFF

1. Zaccardo, Zambrotta, Zanetti, Zaza, Zenga, Zola
2. Athletic Bilbao
3. UEFA Euro 68
4. Udinese
5. Three
6. Lazio
7. 332
8. Gianluigi Buffon
9. 1968
10. 1940s (1942)
11. Oldest player (41) & most appearances (570)
12. Enrico Albertosi
13. UEFA Euro 2000
14. Gianpiero Combi (1934)
15. Paolo Maldini
16. Arsenal
17. Ajax and Hamburg
18. 1988
19. 784
20. Sven-Goran Eriksson
21. Johan Cruyff
22. Fiorentina

23. Only Italian to have won both the FIFA World Cup and UEFA European Championship
24. Six
25. 1990
26. Inter-Cities Fairs Cup
27. 41
28. Most ever minutes without conceding a goal in international football (1,142 minutes)
29. Mantova
30. 1983

EUSEBIO

1. Nine
2. Mozambique
3. His waxwork at Madame Tussauds
4. Estadio da Luz (Stadium of Light), Lisbon
5. Academica
6. 1965
7. 473
8. Milan
9. 11
10. Turkey (1965)
11. 1973
12. Pele
13. Jose Augusto Torres
14. European Golden Shoe
15. Portuguese Primeira Liga's top scorer award
16. Eusebio da Silva Ferreira
17. 2010s (2014)
18. BBC Overseas Sports Personality of the Year
19. Boston Minutemen, Toronto Metros-Croatia and Las Vegas Quicksilvers
20. Alfredo Di Stefano
21. Pauleta
22. Real Madrid
23. 1976
24. Black Panther & Black Pearl
25. Beira Mar

26. Goodison Park, Liverpool
27. Olimpija Ljubljana
28. Juventus
29. Four
30. Luxembourg

FERENC PUSKAS

1. Budapest
2. Saudi Arabia
3. Purczeld
4. 1952
5. Austria
6. Panathinaikos
7. 30s (31 years old)
8. Mo Salah
9. Barcelona
10. Feyenoord
11. Hercules, Alaves & Real Murcia
12. Albania
13. Three
14. Balkan Cup
15. Spain
16. Athletic Bilbao
17. 1959 & 1966
18. Seven
19. Copa del Rey (Spanish Cup)
20. Jeunesse Esch
21. Hungary
22. 12
23. England
24. Yugoslavia
25. A fractured ankle
26. Korea Republic
27. Four
28. West Germany
29. Atletico Madrid
30. 50

FRANZ BECKENBAUER

1. New York Cosmos
2. St Etienne
3. Der Kaiser (The Emperor)
4. 1972 & 1976

5. Switzerland
6. Stephan
7. Didier Deschamps (captain 1998, manager 2018)
8. Marseille
9. Netherlands
10. A dislocated shoulder
11. First captain to win the FIFA World Cup, UEFA European Championship and European Cup
12. Cruzeiro
13. Centre forward
14. FIFA Presidential Award and UEFA President's Award
15. 1965
16. UEFA Cup
17. German Cup
18. Panathinaikos
19. Jupp Derwall
20. North American Soccer League
21. Cologne
22. Cup Winners' Cup
23. The modern sweeper, or libero
24. *Bild*
25. Anton
26. Hamburg
27. Liverpool (Goodison Park)
28. Rangers
29. England
30. 1860 Munich

GARY LINEKER

1. Ten
2. Cup Winners' Cup
3. Paraguay
4. Leicester City
5. Terry Venables
6. Mark Crossley
7. Scotland
8. Football League Second Division
9. Winston
10. Arsenal
11. Brazil
12. 1985-86
13. Real Madrid
14. Republic of Ireland
15. Cricket
16. Graham Taylor
17. Mark Hughes
18. Tony Woodcock
19. True
20. None
21. Spain (1987) and Malaysia (1991)
22. 1986
23. Everton (11) Leicester (seven)
24. Real Sociedad
25. PFA Players' Player of the Year and Football Writers' Association Footballer of the Year
26. Gareth Bale
27. Rous Cup
28. Nagoya Grampus Eight
29. *Match of the Day*
30. Sweden

GEORGE BEST

1. First Division top scorer (28 goals)
2. Cyprus
3. 17
4. El Beatle (or The Fifth Beatle)
5. Northampton Town
6. Tommy Docherty
7. Hibernian
8. HJK Helsinki & Benfica
9. Bestie's Beach Club
10. Gordon Banks
11. Rapid Vienna
12. Football Writers' Association Footballer of the Year
13. Bournemouth
14. Hong Kong
15. West Bromwich Albion
16. Glentoran
17. Airports
18. Liverpool
19. Two
20. Los Angeles Aztecs, Fort Lauderdale Strikers & San Jose Earthquakes

21. He was 'too small and light'
22. Djurgaardens
23. 59
24. 1940s (1946)
25. Wolves
26. Intercontinental Cup
27. Manchester United 2 Benfica 1
28. South Africa
29. Slack Alice
30. Real Madrid

GERD MULLER

1. 1974
2. Der Bomber
3. Miroslav Klose
4. European Footballer of the Year (Ballon d'Or)
5. Albania, Cyprus, Soviet Union & Switzerland
6. 1861 Nordlingen
7. Peru
8. Cup Winners' Cup
9. Turkey
10. Lionel Messi
11. Karl-Heinz Rummenigge
12. Schalke
13. 1974 FIFA World Cup final
14. UEFA Euro 72, 1974 FIFA World Cup, 1974 & 1975 European Cup
15. Omonia Nicosia
16. 1968-69
17. Seven
18. Ronaldo
19. None
20. Anderlecht
21. Fort Lauderdale Strikers
22. Inter-Cities Fairs Cup
23. 1972-73
24. Regional League South (Second Division)
25. Standard Liege
26. Cruzeiro
27. 68
28. 365

29. Belgium
30. Morocco

JOHAN CRUYFF

1. 1966-67
2. 1971, 1973 & 1974
3. Argentina
4. League & Cup doubles
5. Feyenoord
6. 17
7. Los Angeles Aztecs and Washington Diplomats
8. Cup Winners' Cup
9. The 'Cruyff Turn'
10. None
11. Jordi
12. First-ever Dutch international to be sent off
13. Hendrik Johannes Cruyff
14. 14 years
15. Pep Guardiola
16. Luxembourg
17. Levante
18. The 'Dream Team'
19. Groningen
20. Werder Bremen
21. Total Football
22. 1969
23. AC Milan
24. Liverpool
25. Copa del Rey (Spanish Cup)
26. Sampdoria
27. Hungary
28. Rinus Michels, Guus Hiddink, Louis van Gaal and Frank Rijkaard
29. 14
30. Inter Milan

LEGENDARY WOMEN

1. Umea
2. Canada
3. Megan Rapinoe
4. Christine Sinclair

5. Mexico
6. United States
7. Guyana
8. Ann Kristin Aarones
9. Copa America
10. Christie Rampone
11. Kristine Lilly
12. 2003
13. Five
14. Australia, Japan and Germany
15. Christine Sinclair
16. Brazil
17. Semi-final
18. 28 (Marta 17, Cristiane 11)
19. Olympic Games (2004)
20. Carli Lloyd
21. Costa Rica
22. Pan American Games
23. 128
24. Gold Cup final
25. 13-0
26. Alex Morgan
27. Japan
28. Mexico
29. 2007
30. England

LIONEL MESSI

1. Espanyol
2. Rome and London
3. Javier Mascherano
4. Panathinaikos
5. Only player to score in his teens, his twenties and his thirties in FIFA World Cup history
6. 15
7. The fastest player to reach 100 UEFA Champions League goals in terms of games played
8. Quarter-final
9. Greece
10. 50
11. Panama
12. Athletic Bilbao
13. Frank Rijkaard
14. Most La Liga hat-tricks in one season (eight)
15. La·Liga, Copa del Rey, UEFA Champions League, Copa America, UEFA Super Cup, Spanish Super Cup and FIFA Club World Cup
16. Neymar
17. Hungary
18. 2011-12
19. Arsenal
20. Albacete
21. FIFA World Under-20 Cup (2005) Known as the FIFA World Cup Youth Championship in 2005
22. Gabriel Batistuta
23. Chile
24. Serbia & Montenegro
25. Estudiantes & River Plate
26. Chile
27. Real Madrid
28. 91
29. 2008-09
30. Nigeria

LOTHAR MATTHAUS

1. Most ever FIFA World Cup appearances (25)
2. FIFA World Player of the Year
3. UEFA Euro 80
4. Morocco
5. Paolo Maldini
6. Borussia Monchengladbach
7. Roma
8. 150
9. Nine
10. Herbert
11. 1996
12. Andreas Brehme
13. Rapid Vienna
14. Netherlands
15. Stuttgart, Eintracht Frankfurt and Magdeburg
16. 1982, 1986, 1990, 1994 and 1998

17. Porto
18. UEFA Cup final
19. Hungary & Bulgaria
20. FIFA Confederations Cup
21. Newcastle United
22. Semi-final
23. Rafael Marquez
24. 1992 and 1996
25. Real Madrid
26. 1985-86 and 1999-2000
27. New York/New Jersey MetroStars (now called the New York Red Bulls)
28. Czechoslovakia
29. Maccabi Netanya
30. UEFA Euro 2000

MARCO VAN BASTEN

1. 28
2. European Golden Boot
3. Iceland
4. NEC Nijmegen
5. Luis Suarez
6. Italy & France
7. Five
8. 2006 FIFA World Cup and UEFA Euro 2008
9. Sweden
10. Hristo Stoichkov
11. Arrigo Sacchi
12. True
13. John van't Schip
14. Lokomotive Leipzig
15. Sampdoria & Parma
16. Malta
17. Heerenveen
18. Klaas-Jan Huntelaar
19. Four
20. West Germany
21. Andriy Shevchenko
22. Danny Blind
23. Stanley
24. Portugal
25. Ruud Gullit
26. AZ Alkmaar

27. Den Haag
28. Belgium
29. First player to score four goals in a UEFA Champions League match (v Gothenburg)
30. 1993 UEFA Champions League final v Marseille

MICHEL PLATINI

1. Aston Villa
2. Argentina
3. Lennart Johansson
4. Olympic Games
5. French Division Two title
6. 1966
7. Nice
8. UEFA Cup
9. Belgium & Yugoslavia
10. Argentinos Juniors
11. Francois
12. Czechoslovakia
13. Alain Giresse, Luis Fernandez and Jean Tigana
14. Kuwait
15. *France Football*
16. 1983, 1984 and 1985
17. Hamburg
18. Jean-Pierre Papin
19. Seven
20. Cup Winners' Cup (1984)
21. Henri Michel
22. True
23. Le Roi (The King)
24. Hvidovre
25. Zinedine Zidane
26. Bordeaux
27. Thierry Henry
28. Portugal
29. 31
30. Kuwait

PELE

1. 1940s (1940)

1. Eight
3. Brazil's 100th FIFA World Cup goal
4. France
5. Giants Stadium (Meadowlands, New Jersey)
6. Czechoslovakia
7. 1962 and 1963
8. Six
9. 12
10. Carlos Alberto
11. Argentina
11. Edson Arantes do Nascimento
13. Soviet Union
14. None
15. None, no one else has more than two
16. Argentina (1959)
17. North American Soccer League (NASL)
18. Ullevi Stadium, Gothenburg, Sweden
19. Five
20. One (1970, they were holders for 1962 and 1966)
21. Fulham
22. Runners-up (to Argentina)
23. 77 goals in 94 appearances
24. New York Cosmos
25. Gordon Banks
26. One
27. Wales (1958)
28. Sao Paulo
29. Seven
30. Diego Maradona

RIVALDO

1. Louis van Gaal
2. Morocco
3. 1999
4. Palmeiras
5. Borussia Dortmund
6. Mexico
7. Two v Denmark (1998)
8. Roma
9. Peru

10. China (2002)
11. Five
12. Aris
13. Uruguay
14. 2003
15. Dida
16. Turkey
17. Sonny Anderson
18. Deportivo La Coruna
19. Umbro Cup
20. Eight
21. AEK Athens
22. Uzbekistan
23. 35 goals in 74 caps
24. Eight
25. Mogi Mirim
26. AC Milan (2000) and Wisla Krakow (2001), both for Barcelona
27. Liverpool
28. 1996
29. Spain, Greece & Uzbekistan
30. Argentina

RONALDINHO

1. Gremio
2. Rapid Vienna
3. 33 goals, 97 caps
4. Alexandre Pato
5. Small
6. Saudi Arabia (1999) and Haiti (2004)
7. 2004 & 2005
8. Stamford Bridge (Chelsea) and Fratton Park (Portsmouth)
9. Matador Puchov
10. China
11. FIFA Under-17 World Championship (now called FIFA Under-17 World Cup)
12. Venezuela
13. Arsenal
14. Olympic Games
15. Seven
16. 2013, v Chile
17. Frank Lampard & Steven Gerrard
18. Mauricio Pochettino

19. Latvia
20. South American Footballer of the Year
21. Real Valladolid (2004) and Getafe (2007)
22. FIFA Confederations Cup
23. False (he scored none)
24. Atletico Mineiro
25. Siena
26. Internacional
27. Argentina
28. As a homage to his mother, born in 1949
29. David Seaman
30. Udinese

RONALDO

1. Lithuania
2. False (Romario won it in 1994)
3. Rotterdam
4. 62 goals, 98 caps
5. Cruzeiro
6. Copa do Brasil
7. Olimpia
8. 15
9. True
10. 1994
11. Bolivia
12. Kaka
13. True
14. Lazio
15. Roberto Carlos
16. Siena
17. Finland
18. 1999
19. Bayer Leverkusen
20. Iceland
21. Ten
22. Chile
23. Juventus
24. Romario
25. Old Trafford, Manchester (for Real Madrid in 2003)
26. Tournoi de France

27. Alaves
28. Kaka & Alexandre Pato
29. Morocco (1998) & Ghana (2006)
30. Adriano

ZICO

1. The 'White Pele'
2. Flamengo
3. Fenerbahce
4. New Zealand
5. FIFA Order of Merit
6. Udinese
7. Japan & Iraq
8. Kashima Antlers
9. Qatar
10. Arthur Antunes Coimbra
11. Minister of Sports
12. False – he played two seasons at Udinese
13. Beach Soccer World Cup
14. 508
15. CFZ de Brasilia
16. Uruguay
17. Michel Platini
18. Peru
19. Four
20. Brazil
21. Liverpool
22. Scotland
23. Yugoslavia
24. France
25. CSKA Moscow
26. Asian Cup
27. God of Football
28. *World Soccer*
29. Bolivia
30. Copa America

ZINEDINE ZIDANE

1. Mario Kempes (Argentina v Netherlands, 1978)
2. Cannes
3. Claude Makelele

4. Amsterdam
5. UEFA Intertoto Cup (1995)
6. Three
7. Borussia Dortmund
8. Glasgow
9. 2006 FIFA World Cup final
10. Six
11. Sevilla
12. Spain (Atletico Madrid), Italy (Juventus) and England (Liverpool)
13. Vava, Pele and Paul Breitner
14. 108 caps, 31 goals
15. England
16. 1972 (23 June)
17. Netherlands & Czech Republic
18. Jean-Pierre Papin (1991)
19. 77.5m euros
20. Saudi Arabia
21. Spanish Super Cup (v Real Zaragoza)
22. Marseille
23. AEK Athens
24. Kashima Antlers & Gremio
25. Deportivo (2004) & Villarreal (2005)
26. Feyenoord
27. Czech Republic
28. David Trezeguet
29. 2-0 in Rome v Roma (UEFA Champions League round of 16, first leg)
30. Portugal

THE GREAT CLUBS QUIZ ANSWERS

AC MILAN

1. Record scorer (221 goals from 1948 to 1956)
2. Arrigo Sacchi
3. Liverpool (2007)
4. Kaka
5. Old Trafford, Manchester
6. Alessandro Costacurta
7. Krzysztof Piatek
8. Benfica
9. Juraj Kucka
10. Andre Silva
11. Leeds United
12. Sampdoria
13. Fabio Capello
14. Magdeburg
15. 1899
16. Daniele Massaro
17. First team to win Serie A without losing a game
18. Andriy Shevchenko
19. Dida
20. Inter Milan
21. Frank Rijkaard
22. England
23. Boca Juniors
24. Gianni Rivera
25. Record scorer in Europe (41 goals)
26. Hernan Crespo
27. Mario Balotelli
28. Nereo Rocco
29. Patrick Cutrone
30. Olimpia

AJAX

1. Ajax the Great
2. Patrick Kluivert
3. Real Zaragoza
4. 1992
5. Dusan Tadic
6. Jari Litmanen
7. Matthijs de Ligt
8. Lokomotiv Leipzig
9. 19
10. Lucky Lynx
11. 14 (Johan Cruyff's number)
12. Sjaak Swart
13. Danny
14. Hakim Ziyech

15. Dennis Bergkamp
16. Ruud Krol
17. Clarence Seedorf
18. Ryan Gravenberch
19. Nicolas Tagliafico
20. Luis Suarez
21. Red Boys Differdange
22. Panathinaikos
23. Rotterdam
24. Ronald and Frank de Boer
25. Feyenoord
26. Davy Klaassen
27. 1971, 1972 & 1973
28. Gregory van der Wiel
29. Rinus Michels
30. Arkadiusz Milik

ARSENAL

1. Preston North End
2. Ray Parlour
3. Copenhagen
4. 2006
5. Sheffield Wednesday
6. Sylvain Wiltord
7. AC Milan
8. Herbert Chapman
9. Nwankwo Kanu
10. Blackburn Rovers
11. Cesc Fabregas
12. Gilberto
13. Kenny Sansom
14. Cliff Bastin
15. Graham Rix
16. Terry Neill
17. Emmanuel Adebayor
18. Emmanuel Petit (France 1998)
19. Norwich City
20. Freddie Ljungberg
21. Alan Sunderland
22. Lauren
23. Andrei Arshavin
24. Stewart Houston
25. David O'Leary
26. Manchester United

27. Robin van Persie
28. Steve Morrow
29. Sparta Prague
30. Anderlecht

ATLETICO MADRID

1. Joao Felix
2. Bayern Munich
3. Bear (it's on their emblem)
4. Fernando Torres
5. Gregorio Manzano
6. Chelsea
7. Antoine Griezmann
8. UEFA Champions League final
9. Jimmy Floyd Hasselbaink
10. Jesus Gil
11. Juanfran
12. Luis Aragones
13. Independiente
14. Vicente Calderon Stadium
15. David De Gea
16. Cup Winners' Cup (1962)
17. The League and Cup double
18. Diego Costa
19. La Liga top scorer
20. Felipe VI (King of Spain)
21. Marseille
22. Koke
23. Juventus
24. Falcao
25. Chelsea
26. Kieran Trippier
27. Christian Vieri
28. Dynamo Kiev
29. Thibaut Courtois
30. Diego Forlan

BARCELONA

1. Xavi
2. Espanyol
3. Most UEFA Cup/UEFA Europa League goals for the club (11)
4. 2009

5. Ruud Hesp, Michael Reiziger, Phillip Cocu, Boudewijn Zenden, Patrick Kluivert, Frank de Boer, Ronald de Boer, Winston Bogarde
6. Claudio Bravo
7. Pedro
8. Romario, Ronaldo, Rivaldo & Ronaldinho
9. Cup Winners' Cup
10. Andres Iniesta
11. Most Cup Winners' Cup goals for the club (nine)
12. 131
13. Six (Copa del Rey, La Liga, UEFA Champions League, Spanish Super Cup, UEFA Super Cup & FIFA Club World Cup)
14. Bayer Leverkusen
15. Juliano Belletti
16. Frank Rijkaard
17. Seven
18. Four
19. Hristo Stoichkov
20. 73
21. Radomir Antic
22. Samuel Umtiti
23. Ronald Koeman
24. London XI (1958) and Birmingham City (1960)
25. 100
26. River Plate
27. Ousmane Dembele
28. Reina
29. Miguel Angel Nadal
30. Samuel Eto'o

BAYERN MUNICH

1. Karl-Heinz Rummenigge
2. Ottmar Hitzfeld
3. 1976, v St Etienne
4. Won all six group stage matches
5. Franck Ribery
6. Hans Bauer

7. 2005
8. Udo Lattek
9. 1860 Munich
10. Giovane Elber
11. Cup Winners' Cup
12. Roy Makaay
13. Luca Toni
14. Paris
15. Niko and Robert Kovac
16. Jurgen Klinsmann
17. Stefan Effenberg
18. Dieter Hoeness
19. Bavaria
20. Sporting Lisbon
21. Mario Gomez
22. Willy Sagnol
23. Bixente Lizarazu
24. Arjen Robben
25. Mehmet Scholl
26. Philipp Lahm
27. Sepp Maier
28. Mario Basler
29. Mario Mandzukic
30. Pierre-Emile Hojbjerg

BENFICA

1. 1961 & 1962
2. Porto
3. Sven-Goran Eriksson
4. Nene
5. Sevilla
6. Oscar Cardozo
7. Borussia Dortmund
8. Lima
9. Sevilla
10. The domestic treble
11. Jose Mourinho
12. Jaime Graca
13. Luisao
14. The Eagles
15. Hungarian
16. Stade Dudelange
17. They went undefeated throughout the whole league season

18. Anderlecht
19. Kostas Mitroglou
20. Jorge Jesus
21. Joao Felix
22. Penarol
23. Axel Witsel
24. Jose Aguas & Mario Coluna
25. Jonas
26. Maritimo
27. Nuno Gomes
28. He missed the decisive penalty in the shoot-out defeat to PSV
29. Mats Magnusson
30. Sporting Lisbon

BORUSSIA DORTMUND

1. 1997
2. Nuri Sahin
3. Roman Weidenfeller
4. 2012
5. The Yellow Wall
6. Jan Koller
7. Emre Can
8. Robert Lewandowski
9. Mats Hummels
10. Liverpool
11. Marcio Amoroso
12. Shinji Kagawa
13. Nevio Scala (won Intercontinental Cup)
14. Thorgan
15. Dede
16. BVB
17. Michael Zorc
18. Marco Reus
19. Karl-Heinz Riedle
20. Legia Warsaw
21. Stephane Chapuisat
22. Achraf Hakimi
23. Bert van Marwijk & Peter Bosz
24. Ilkay Gundogan
25. Lucas Barrios
26. Cruzeiro
27. Lothar Emmerich

28. Henrikh Mkhitaryan
29. Ottmar Hitzfeld
30. Feyenoord

CELTIC

1. Four-leaf clover
2. Inter Milan
3. Gary Hooper
4. Seville
5. John Barnes and Tony Mowbray
6. Mark Burchill
7. Jack Aitchison
8. Karamoko Dembele
9. Parkhead
10. Old Firm
11. 69
12. Their record goalscorer in Europe (35)
13. Aberdeen
14. Jock Stein
15. Liverpool
16. Feyenoord
17. Odsonne Edouard
18. Ronny Deila
19. Dion Dublin
20. Eight
21. Chris Sutton
22. The Lisbon Lions
23. *The Celtic View*
24. John Hartson
25. Scott Brown
26. Racing
27. Gordon Strachan
28. Virgil van Dijk
29. Robbie Keane
30. The Bhoys

CHELSEA

1. Mark Schwarzer
2. Ruud Gullit & Guus Hiddink
3. Stuttgart
4. Ron Harris
5. Tromso
6. Mateja Kezman

7. Gianluca Vialli, Carlo Ancelotti, Roberto Di Matteo, Antonio Conte and Maurizio Sarri
8. Paulo Ferreira & Ricardo Carvalho
9. They became the first English club to win all three major UEFA competitions
10. Leeds United
11. Eidur Gudjohnsen
12. Cup Winners' Cup
13. Lion
14. Glenn Hoddle
15. Branislav Ivanovic
16. Peter Bonetti
17. 1955
18. Jimmy Greaves
19. David Speedie
20. Olivier Giroud
21. Nine
22. Carlo Ancelotti
23. Bobby Tambling
24. Didier Drogba
25. Petr Cech
26. Nicolas Anelka
27. Peter Osgood
28. Derby County & Aston Villa
29. Roberto Di Matteo
30. Michael (Ballack & Essien)

CLUB AMERICA

1. Azteca Stadium
2. Guadalajara
3. CONCACAF Champions League
4. Because they were formed on Columbus Day
5. Arsenal de Sarandi
6. Cristobal Ortega
7. British
8. 1968
9. Zague
10. 6-5
11. Copa Interamericana
12. Real Madrid
13. Ivan Zamorano
14. Hugo Norberto Castillo

15. Cruz Azul
16. Manuel Lapuente
17. Dario Benedetto & Oribe Peralta
18. Santiago Solari
19. Christian Benitez
20. Kleber Pereira
21. Edson Alvarez
22. Juarez
23. LDU Quito
24. Real Madrid
25. Francois Omam-Biyik
26. Salvador Cabanas
27. Club Universidad Nacional
28. Leo Beenhakker
29. Barcelona
30. D.C. United

INDEPENDIENTE

1. Avellaneda
2. Sergio Aguero
3. Nacional & Penarol
4. Recopa Sudamericana (equivalent to UEFA Super Cup)
5. Liverpool
6. Facundo Parra
7. 1972, 1973, 1974 & 1975
8. Gabriel Milito
9. Juventus
10. Racing
11. Arsenio Erico
12. Sao Paulo & Gremio
13. Red
14. Jorge Burruchaga
15. 1905
16. Cerezo Osaka
17. Flamengo
18. Colo-Colo & Union Espanola
19. The Red Devils
20. Estadio Libertadores de America
21. Cesar Luis Menotti
22. Boca Juniors, Racing, River Plate & San Lorenzo de Almagro
23. Nicolas Tagliafico
24. Oscar Ustari

25. Mauricio Pellegrino
26. River Plate
27. Monserrat
28. Diego Forlan
29. Rome
30. Inter Milan

INTER MILAN

1. Lothar Matthaus
2. Diego Milito
3. Record scorer in European competitions (35)
4. Independiente
5. Mauro Icardi
6. Lautaro Martinez
7. Christian Vieri
8. Youri Djorkaeff
9. True
10. Giuseppe Meazza
11. Juventus
12. Maurizio Ganz
13. The Black and Blues
14. Alexis Sanchez
15. TP Mazembe
16. Adriano
17. Milan (their home stadium)
18. Massimo Moratti
19. Lazio
20. France & Central African Republic
21. Giovanni Trapattoni
22. They won the treble of League, Cup and UEFA Champions League
23. Javier Zanetti
24. Real Madrid
25. Roy Hodgson
26. Samuel Eto'o
27. Zlatan Ibrahimovic
28. Dennis Bergkamp
29. Marco Materazzi and Fabio Grosso
30. Walter Zenga

JUVENTUS

1. Gianluca Vialli

2. Stadio delle Alpi
3. UEFA Cup
4. Gonzalo Higuain
5. The Old Lady
6. Giovanni Trapattoni
7. First club to win all three major European trophies
8. Marcello Lippi (76)
9. Torino
10. 2011
11. Darko Kovacevic
12. John Charles
13. Carlos Tevez
14. Edgar Davids
15. Alessandro Del Piero
16. 1998 & 2017
17. Fiorentina
18. Paolo Rossi (1982) & Salvatore Schillaci (1990)
19. Pavel Nedved
20. UEFA Intertoto Cup
21. Dino Baggio
22. Roberto Bettega
23. Porto
24. Giorgio Chiellini
25. Eight
26. Parma
27. Michel Platini
28. Blaise Matuidi
29. Paris St Germain
30. Fabrizio Ravanelli

LIVERPOOL

1. Roger Hunt
2. Roy Hodgson
3. David Fairclough
4. Kevin Keegan
5. Alan Kennedy
6. Steven Gerrard
7. CSKA Moscow
8. Leipzig
9. 'You'll Never Walk Alone'
10. Arsenal
11. 91

12. Ian Callaghan
13. Ray Clemence and Emlyn Hughes
14. Dietmar Hamann
15. Wimbledon
16. 2001
17. Ben Woodburn
18. Sami Hyypia
19. Borussia Monchengladbach
20. Graeme Souness
21. Paris
22. Jerome Sinclair
23. Ian Callaghan and Gerry Byrne
24. Bruce Grobbelaar
25. Sander Westerveld
26. Robbie Fowler
27. Besiktas
28. Phil Neal
29. Roberto Firmino
30. Mark Walters

MANCHESTER CITY

1. Stoke City
2. Antoine Sibierski
3. Fernandinho
4. Eric Brook
5. Joe Mercer
6. Alvaro Negredo
7. United Arab Emirates
8. Athletic Bilbao
9. A ship
10. Sergio Aguero
11. 2003
12. Joe Corrigan
13. Queens Park Rangers
14. Francis Lee
15. Marc-Vivien Foe
16. Chelsea (1970-71 Cup Winners' Cup, Liverpool (2017-18 UEFA Champions League), Tottenham (2018-19 UEFA Champions League)
17. Tony Book
18. Gillingham
19. First-ever domestic treble (League, FA Cup, League Cup)

20. Neil Young
21. West Ham United
22. Bernardo Corradi
23. Maine Road
24. Gornik Zabrze
25. Leroy Sane
26. Dennis Tueart
27. Fenerbahce
28. 116 (Bury 6 Derby 0 in 1903)
29. The Poznan
30. Rolando Bianchi

MANCHESTER UNITED

1. LDU Quito
2. Newcastle United
3. 13
4. Paul Scholes
5. Angel Di Maria
6. Sheffield United
7. Manchester City
8. Wembley Stadium
9. Tommy Docherty
10. George Best
11. Fenerbahce
12. Kevin Moran
13. Roy Keane
14. Peter Schmeichel
15. Henrik Larsson
16. Macedonia
17. Rotor Volgograd
18. Ole Gunnar Solskjaer
19. Neil Sullivan
20. Keane (11), Scholes (9)
21. Mark Hughes
22. Ruud van Nistelrooy
23. Raimond van der Gouw
24. West Ham United
25. Keith Gillespie
26. Palmeiras
27. Anderlecht
28. Robin van Persie (30 in 2012-13)
29. Federico Macheda
30. Newton Heath

PARIS ST GERMAIN

1. Thiago Silva
2. UEFA Intertoto Cup
3. Layvin Kurzawa
4. David Beckham
5. Most appearances for the club (435 games from 1975 to 1989)
6. Edinson Cavani
7. 1970
8. David Ginola
9. Marseille
10. Patrice Loko
11. Rai
12. Nene
13. Barcelona
14. The Eiffel Tower
15. Adrien Rabiot
16. Zlatan Ibrahimovic
17. Gerard Houllier
18. Marquinhos
19. Guillaume Hoarau
20. Pauleta
21. Leroy
22. Bruno N'Gotty
23. First player to score 100 goals for the club
24. Hugo Leal
25. 90
26. Marco Verratti
27. Barcelona
28. Zenit St Petersburg
29. Laurent Blanc
30. Djorkaeff (Jean & Youri)

RANGERS

1. Mark Warburton
2. Manchester
3. Brian Laudrup (Denmark v Portugal at UEFA Euro 96)
4. Dougie Gray
5. Dynamo Moscow
6. Dick Advocaat
7. Lorenzo Amoruso
8. John Greig
9. Gareth McAuley
10. Dave McPherson
11. Wolves
12. Lionel Charbonnier
13. 54
14. First British club to reach a major European final
15. 12
16. Hearts
17. Gary McAllister
18. Kris Boyd
19. David Weir
20. Tottenham
21. Tore-Andre Flo
22. Steven Davis
23. Nacho Novo
24. Fiorentina
25. Stefan Klos (298)
26. Chris Woods (England at UEFA Euro 88)
27. Fernando Ricksen
28. Kenny Miller
29. Eintracht Frankfurt
30. Jorg Albertz

REAL MADRID

1. Reims
2. Santillana
3. Christian Karembeu
4. Monaco
5. Roberto Carlos
6. Jupp Heynckes
7. Alfredo Di Stefano
8. Predrag Mijatovic
9. Sergio Ramos
10. Ruud van Nistelrooy
11. Roberto Carlos, Beckham, Zidane, Figo, Raul, Ronaldo
12. Rodrygo
13. Isco
14. Luka Modric
15. Manuel Sanchis

16. Chendo
17. Kashima Antlers
18. Uli Stielike (308)
19. Florentino Perez
20. Francisco Gento
21. Benfica, 1962
22. Hugo Sanchez
23. Liverpool (1981 European Cup) & Aberdeen (1983 Cup Winners' Cup)
24. Martin Odegaard
25. Francisco Buyo
26. Marco Asensio
27. Ferenc Puskas (4 in 1960 & 3 in 1962)
28. Athletic Bilbao
29. Jorge Valdano
30. Al-Ain

SANTOS

1. Benfica
2. 1956
3. Vila Belmiro
4. Corinthians
5. Jorge Sampaoli
6. Dunga
7. White
8. Penarol
9. False (they did achieve this feat in 1963 though)
10. Wanderley Luxemburgo
11. Alex
12. Robinho
13. Yokohama
14. Vitoria
15. Neymar
16. Porto
17. Fish
18. Renato
19. Os Santasticos
20. 10,000
21. Rosario Central
22. Elano
23. Jesualdo Ferreira
24. Universidad de Chile

25. Nine
26. Gilmar
27. 1,091
28. Four (Paulistao, Brasileiro, Copa Libertadores & Intercontinental Cup)
29. Palmeiras
30. AC Milan

PICTURE QUIZ ANSWERS

Picture Quiz 1 – Famous Goalkeepers

The goalkeepers are Michel Preud'homme, Gianluigi Buffon, Lev Yashin and Manuel Neuer. Each has won the FIFA World Cup Golden Glove award except for Lev Yashin, for whom the award was originally named when it was introduced in 1994.

Picture Quiz 2 – Odd One Out

No. 4, it hosted a semi-final in 1994.

Picture Quiz 3 – Goalscorers

The goalscorers are Andres Iniesta, Jorge Burruchaga, Mario Gotze, Nia Künzer and Zinedine Zidane. Each of them is pictured scoring the World Cup final winner, except for Zidane, whose French team went on to lose on penalties after he was sent off.

Picture Quiz 4 – Champions

The teams are the USA 1999 women's team, the France 1998 men's team, the Argentina 1978 men's team, the West Germany 1974 men's team, the England 1966 men's team, the Italy 1934 men's team, and the Uruguay 1930 men's team. Each of these teams won the FIFA World Cup as host nations.

Picture Quiz 5 – Most Appearances

The correct order is Kristine Lilly (30 appearances), Formiga (27), Abby Wambach (25), Carli Lloyd (25), Lothar Matthaus (25), Miroslav Klose (24) and Paolo Maldini (23).

Picture Quiz 6 – Unwanted Record 1

The teams are Cameroon in 1982, England in 1982, Belgium in 1998 and New Zealand in 2010. They were all knocked out in the group stages without losing a single match. Scotland achieved the same in 1974, so they are the missing team.

Picture Quiz 7 – Unwanted Record 2

The teams are Italy in 1950, Brazil in 1966, France in 2002, Italy in 2010, Spain in 2014 and Germany in 2018. They were all knocked out in the group stage while appearing as defending champions.

Picture Quiz 8 – Super Strikers

The top goalscorer at FIFA World Cups is Brazil's Marta, with 17. Miroslav Klose is a close second on 16, followed by Ronaldo with 15. Gerd Muller, Birgit Prinz and Abby Wambach have all scored 14, and should be placed in that order because they have played 13, 24 and 25 games respectively.

Picture Quiz 9 – Best of the Best

Megan Rapinoe, Marta and Lionel Messi have all won the FIFA World Cup Golden Ball award. Cristiano Ronaldo has not.

Credits